EATING
YOUR
WORDS

EATING
YOUR
WORDS

WILLIAM GRIMES
Editor

OXFORD
UNIVERSITY PRESS
2004

Oxford University Press

Oxford   New York
Auckland   Bangkok   Buenos Aires   Cape Town   Chennai
Dar es Salaam   Delhi   Hong Kong   Istanbul   Karachi   Kolkata
Kuala Lumpur   Madrid   Melbourne   Mexico City   Mumbai
Nairobi   São Paulo   Shanghai   Taipei   Tokyo   Toronto

Published by Oxford University Press, Inc.
198 Madison Avenue, New York, New York, 10016
http://www.oup.com/us

Oxford is a registered trademark of Oxford University Press

Library of Congress Cataloging-in-Publication Data

Eating your words / William Grimes, editor.
   p. cm.
   ISBN 0-19-517406-2
   1. Food—Dictionaries. 2. Cookery—Dictionaries. I. Grimes, William.
   TX349.E33 2004
   641.3'003—dc22

                                    2004013725

This book includes some words that are, or are asserted to be, proprietary
names or trademarks. Their inclusion does not imply that they have acquired
for legal purposes a nonproprietary or general significance, nor is any other
judgment implied concerning their legal status. In cases where the editor has
some evidence that a word is used as a proprietary name or trademark, this is
indicated by the designation trademark, but no judgment concerning the legal
status of such words is made or implied thereby.

Printing number: 9 8 7 6 5 4 3 2 1

Printed in the United States of America
on acid-free paper

Ten Signs of a Bad Restaurant is reprinted by special permission
from REAL SIMPLE Magazine's November 2003 issue (c) 2003 Time Inc.
All rights reserved.

"A Hoagie by Any Other Name" by David Wilton first appeared in
VERBATIM: The Language Quarterly, http://www.verbatimmag.com

"Food Fad Timeline" by David Leite appeared in longer form at Leite's
Culinaria http://www.leitesculinaria.com.

"Mock Foods" and "Food Web Sites" first appeared in *The Oxford Encyclopedia
of Food and Drink in America*, edited by Andrew F. Smith. Copyright 2004 by
Oxford University Press, Inc.

CONTENTS

Editorial Staff vi

Introduction vii

Pronunciation Key xiii

EATING YOUR WORDS 1

    A Hoagie by Any Other Name 24

    Let Us Now Praise Famous Bars 70

    Mock Foods 101

    Ten Signs of a Bad Restaurant 119

    Hot or Dog? That's the Question 163

    Slang with Bite: An Eatimology 208

    Ten Fruits You Haven't Tasted but Should 228

More Food for Thought 239

    Cooking Weights and Measures 240

    Food Fads Timeline 242

    Fad Diets Timeline 249

    Food Web Sites 252

EDITORIAL STAFF

INTRODUCTION

There are a couple of good reasons for knowing the word *huitlacoche*. The first is social. It can be embarrassing trying to say it for the first time in front of a waiter and a tableful of diners. The second reason is pure self-defense. *Huitlacoche* (pronounced Wheat-luh-coach-ay, with a long "a" at the end, like "bay") is, in fact, a fungus that grows on corn. Sometimes translated as "corn smut," it ranks as a delicacy in Mexico, where cooks use it to impart a rich, mushroomy flavor to food.

How often is anyone likely to run across the word? The answer is, often enough. And if it's not *huitlacoche*, it will be *chipotle*, *serrano*, *mojo*, or *epazote*, to name just a few of the more common culinary terms that have found their way onto American menus. And those are just the Mexican ones. Add *nam pla* from Vietnam, *edamame* from Japan, *chorizo* from Spain, *borek* from Turkey and *harissa* from Morocco and you have a fully represented United Nations of dining, all present and accounted for in cookbooks and restaurants across the United States.

The vocabulary of food has exploded in recent years. Foreign travel, the globalization of cuisine, and the missionary work of the Food Network have changed the way we eat, the way we think about eating, and the words we use to talk about eating. There are a lot more of them. Some are French—Americans now know that what they used to call "French bread" is a *baguette*—but France no longer enjoys a monopoly over the language of cooking and dining. A wave of culinary immigration, from Japan, China, Southeast Asia, the Middle East, North

Africa, South America, and Spain, has brought an onslaught of new dishes, new ingredients, and new words.

The change has been profound. Just for a moment, turn the clock back to the day before yesterday—say, 1970. A reasonably sophisticated American diner could wander through the world of international dining with a slim phrasebook. *Teriyaki* and *sukiyaki* would take care of Japan. *Sushi*, if anyone had bothered to explain it, would have seemed like a bad joke. Pieces of raw fish on a block of rice? No way. The rich regional cuisines of Mexico were represented by a mere handful of words: *tortilla, taco, tamale, enchilada, chile*. And *chile*, to most Americans, meant *chili*, a dish that's not even Mexican. Spain, whose *tapas* tradition has seduced American chefs in recent years, barely even registered on the radar screen. It was a flavor or an accent, dragged in to suggest spice and romance in Fifties-style concoctions like *Spanish rice*. Chinese cuisine, amazingly, was reduced to *egg rolls, egg foo yung, chop suey*, and *fried rice*.

Then came the revolution. As a child of the 1950's, I like to think of the changes in American tastes, and the expanding food universe, as a revolt against provincialism, and, even more important, against canned asparagus. The two, in many ways, are one and the same. No one who has never tasted asparagus out of the can can imagine its unspeakable foulness. That slimy texture and skunky, slightly metallic flavor still haunt my taste buds. It went hand in hand with a thousand other atrocities perpetrated in the dark ages of American cuisine, the postwar decades when unimagined prosperity coexisted with culinary poverty. Never in human history have a people enjoyed such material prosperity and eaten so badly.

When Alice Waters opened Chez Panisse, her landmark restaurant, in the early 1970's, the time was more than ripe for sweeping change. The American palate, stifled and confined, yearned for liberation. It came, from this small restaurant in radical Berkeley, along with a slew of names and words that fell strangely on the ear. *Arugula?* What was that, exactly? Suddenly, California-influenced menus sprouted a garden's-worth of exotic terms. *Iceberg lettuce*, the only lettuce that Americans knew, made way on the menu, and on store shelves, for *romaine*, *Boston*, *chicory*, and *radicchio*. France was undergoing its own upheavals, shaken to the core by the fire-breathing apostles of nouvelle cuisine, who insisted on the primacy of fresh ingredients and pure flavors. As a result, the old vocabulary of classic sauces, styles, and techniques gave way to a different kind of language, in which dishes were defined, on menus, by what was in them, a practice that was adopted enthusiastically in the United States. Diners used to the comfortable shorthand of *meuniere*, *Mornay*, or *marchand de vin* now confronted a brave new vocabulary of ingredients that sent them running to the dictionary. An all-purpose word like *mushroom*, which had done yeoman's work on a thousand menus, was finished. The chef wanted his customers to know that the exquisite, earthy flavors in his soup came from *oyster mushrooms*, or *porcinis*, or *shiitakes*. Suddenly, diners found themselves learning a whole new language.

The new words keep coming, as the world grows smaller and smaller. French chefs who for generations trained only in France, found that their services were in demand in hotels and restaurants in Bangkok, Hong Kong, and Tokyo. They traveled. They learned. They brought new dishes and ingredients back with them. Asian chefs, for their part, went to France. And a rising generation of American chefs, turned out by ambitious new culinary schools all over the country, went everywhere. The mingling of flavors and cultures and ingredients found expression in a new global approach to cooking, the international style known as fusion, which, naturally enough, brought in its trail a host of new dining terms, as chefs prepared Louisiana crayfish Spanish-style, *a la plancha*, or Japanese-influenced sea-urchin soufflés. Fast international shipping meant that trend-conscious chef could get their hands on exotic specimens like *picorocos*, foot-high Chilean barnacles that look like a volcano.

The new international outlook operates with two lenses. In wide-focus mode, chefs and diners scan the entire world, which presents itself like a grand buffet table. Zooming in, they can isolate a specific region and turn up a world's worth of culinary riches. Travel has made the world one, but it has also made the world many. Serious diners and the chefs who feed them have discovered that all food, like politics, is local. There is no such thing as French cuisine, or Italian cuisine, or Chinese cuisine or Mexican cuisine. The food of Normandy bears no resemblance to the food of Gascony. The tomato, dominant in Naples, plays a minor role in Bologna. Mole sauce, many diners are discovering, is not one sauce but many. All of them are native to Oaxaca, "land of the seven moles," and chocolate, believe it or not, is not a main ingredient.

Oddly enough, narrowing the focus can expand the horizon. In the far-off days when "ethnic cuisine" meant French or Italian, the food picture could be comically blurry. Italian meant, to Americans circa 1910, "macaroni." A generation century later, "macaroni" had become "spaghetti." Not much progress. Today, diners even casually familiar with Italian food can probably tell you the difference between *linguine*, *penne*, *fusilli*, and *rigatoni*. Amateur home bakers know that a *ficelle* is a skinny baguette (literally, "stick"), and, if they thought about it for a few moments, might make the connection between that long, thin loaf and the technique of cooking beef "a la ficelle," or suspended in cooking liquid by a string, the literal meaning of the word.

I've often thought that the easiest way to learn a language is to eat. Every menu is, after all, a list of words. And there's no better way to remember a new vocabulary word than to eat it, as a friend of mine discovered when he ordered *andouillettes* in France. The word has a lilting sound on the ear. It happens to be a sausage made from pork intestines, with a highly distinctive fragrance. My friend does not speak French, but that's one word that remains part of his permanent vocabulary. If he'd persevered, all of France might be at his disposal today. That, at least, is the approach of one language school, the Institut Parisien de Langue et de Civilisation Francaises, which takes the reasonable view that if you understand food, you understand France and its history. French sauces, for example, are a historical roll call, since many of them were named in honor of aristocratic patrons, or were intended to commemorate military victories. *Albufera sauce*, which Alain Ducasse serves at his restaurant in New York, was created by the great chef Careme to honor Marshal Suchet, who beat the English near Lake Albufera during the Napoleonic War. Dishes in the style of *Quercy* or *Rouergue* or *Perigord* transport the amateur chef back to pre-revolutionary France, when the map was divided by provinces rather than the present-day departments.

France is the extreme example, of course. Ever since the days of Louis XIV, when French cuisine became the fashion for all Europe, the language of cooking has been, by and large, French. But all people in all cultures cook and eat. The growing, procuring and preparation of food loom large in daily life and, for much of the earth's population, take up most of the daylight hours. The vocabulary of food, and the thinking that it reflects, offer a window in a nation's soul. I'm convinced that if I could truly understand *umame*, the Japanese term for a so-called "fifth taste," I would be well on my way to understanding Japan.

Even if I can't understand *umame*, I can at least enjoy saying it. That's the other thing about food language. It pleases the ear and the mind. It poses puzzles and leads the culinary explorer down fascinating, crooked byways. The student who takes a basic cooking course soon discovers, when slicing and dicing vegetables, that all the little shapes and sizes have their own names, from *brunoise* (small dice) to *julienne* (thin slivers). Why julienne? No one knows. Its origin is obscure, like *bistro*. Half the fun of ordering *sushi* is the chance to use names like *hamachi*, *tako*, and *unagi*, words now as familiar to many Americans as *tempura* and *miso*. Starbucks customers, in the same way, get a small thrill ordering their *latte grandes* and *macchiatos*. Without the specialized lingo, your corner Starbucks would be just another coffee shop.

The world of dining and cooking is dominated by the sight,

the smell, and the taste of food. But it's also a world of words that have their own savor and tang. Was it the taste of the *madeleine* that sent Proust's narrator into a reverie, or the name itself? Or were they somehow, for one magic instant, one and the same? Anyone who's ever ordered from a menu, or read a cookbook, knows the answer.

PRONUNCIATION KEY

Pronunciations are provided for dificult and foreign words, using a simple respelling system. The following symbols are used:

a   *as in*   **hat** /hat/, **fashion** /ˈfasHən/, **carry** /ˈkarē/

ā   *as in*   **day** /dā/, **rate** /rāt/, **maid** /mād/, **prey** /prā/

ä   *as in*   **lot** /lät/, **father** /ˈfäTHər/, **barnyard** /ˈbärn‚yärd/

b   *as in*   **big** /big/

CH   *as in*   **church** /CHərCH/, **picture** /ˈpikCHər/

d   *as in*   **dog** /dôg/, **bed** /bed/

e   *as in*   **men** /men/, **bet** /bet/, **ferry** /ˈferē/

ē   *as in*   **feet** /fēt/, **receive** /riˈsēv/

e(ə)r *as in*   **air** /e(ə)r/, **care** /ke(ə)r/

ə   *as in*   **about** /əˈbout/, **soda** /ˈsōdə/, **mother** /ˈməTHər/, **person** /ˈpərsən/

f   *as in*   **free** /frē/, **graph** /graf/, **tough** /təf/

g   *as in*   **get** /get/, **exist** /igˈzist/, **egg** /eg/

h   *as in*   **her** /hər/, **behave** /biˈhāv/

i   *as in*   **guild** /gild/, **women** /ˈwimin/

ī   *as in*   **time** /tīm/, **fight** /fīt/, **guide** /gīd/

i(ə)r *as in*   **ear** /i(ə)r/, **beer** /bi(ə)r/, **pierce** /pi(ə)rs/

j   *as in*   **judge** /jəj/, **carriage** /ˈkarij/

k   *as in*   **kettle** /ˈketl/, **cut** /kət/

l   *as in*   **lap** /lap/, **cellar** /ˈselər/, **cradle** /ˈkrādl/

m   *as in*   **main** /mān/, **dam** /dam/

n   *as in*   **honor** /ˈänər/, **maiden** /ˈmādn/

NG   *as in*   **sing** /siNG/, **anger** /'aNGgər/

ō   *as in*   **go** /gō/, **promote** /prə'mōt/

ô   *as in*   **law** /lô/, **thought** /THôt/, **lore** / lôr/

oi   *as in*   **boy** /boi/, **noisy** /'noizē/

o͞o   *as in*   **wood** /wo͞od/, **football** /'fo͞ot‚bôl/, **sure** /sHo͞or/

o͞o   *as in*   **food** /fo͞od/, **music** /'myo͞ozik/

ou   *as in*   **mouse** /mous/, **coward** /'kouərd/

p   *as in*   **put** /po͞ot/, **cap** /kap/

r   *as in*   **run** /rən/, **fur** /fər/, **spirit** /'spirit/

s   *as in*   **sit** /sit/, **lesson** /'lesən/

SH   *as in*   **shut** /sHət/, **social** /'sōsHəl/, **action** /'aksHən/

t   *as in*   **top** /täp/, **seat** /sēt/, **forty** /'fôrtē/

TH   *as in*   **thin** /THin/, **truth** /tro͞oTH/

T̲H̲   *as in*   **then** /T̲H̲en/, **father** /'fäT̲H̲ər/

v   *as in*   **never** /'nevər/, **very** /'verē/

w   *as in*   **wait** /wāt/, **quick** /kwik/

(h)w   *as in*   **when** /(h)wen/, **which** /(h)wicH/

y   *as in*   **yet** /yet/, **accuse** /ə'kyo͞oz/

z   *as in*   **zipper** /'zipər/, **musician** /myo͞o'zisHən/

ZH   *as in*   **measure** /'mezHər/, **vision** /'vizHən/

Foreign Sounds

KH   *as in*   **Bach** /bäKH/

N   *as in*   **en route** /äN 'ro͞ot/, **Rodin** /rō'daN/

œ   *as in*   **hors d'oeuvre** /ôr 'dœvrə/, **Goethe** /'gœtə/

Y   *as in*   **Lully** /lY'lē/, **Utrecht** /'Y‚treKHt/

Stress Marks

Stress marks are placed before the affected syllable. The primary stress mark is a short, raised vertical line ['] and signifies greater pronunciation emphasis should be placed on that syllable. The secondary stress mark is a short, lowered vertical line [‚] and signifies a weaker pronunciation emphasis.

acorn squash ▸ a winter squash, typically dark green, with a longitudinally ridged rind.

adobo /əˈdōbō/ ▸ (also **adobo sauce**) a paste or marinade made from chili peppers, vinegar, herbs, and spices, used in Mexican cooking. ▪ a spicy Filipino dish of chicken or pork stewed in vinegar, garlic, soy sauce, bay leaves, and peppercorns.

–ORIGIN Spanish, literally 'marinade.'

adzuki bean /adˈzōōkē/ ▸ a small, round, dark red, edible bean used in Asian cooking.

–ORIGIN Japanese *azuki*.

aging (also **ageing**) ▸ the process of change by which cheese, meat, or fermented drinks are allowed to mature under controlled conditions.

agnolotti /ˌanyəˈlätē/ ▸ pasta circles folded and stuffed with meat, cheese, or other fillings.

–ORIGIN Italian, alteration of *anellotto* 'little ring.'

aioli /īˈōlē; ā-/ (also **aïoli**) ▸ mayonnaise seasoned with garlic.

–ORIGIN French, from Provençal *ai* 'garlic' + *oli* 'oil.'

à la /ˈä ˌlä/ ▸ (of a dish) cooked or prepared in a specified style or manner: *fish cooked à la meunière.*

–ORIGIN French, from À LA MODE.

à la carte /ˌä lä ˈkärt/ ▸ (of a menu or restaurant) listing or serving food that can be ordered as separate items, rather than part of a set meal. ▪ (of food) available on such a menu. ▸ as separately priced items from a menu, not as part of a set meal: *wine and good food served à la carte.*

–ORIGIN French, literally 'according to the (menu) card.'

à la mode /ˌä lä ˈmōd/ ▶ served with ice cream: *apple pie à la mode.*
■ (of beef) braised in wine, typically with vegetables.
–ORIGIN French, literally 'in the fashion.'

albondigas /ˌälbônˈdēgäs/ ▶ small meatballs, prepared in the Mexican, Spanish, or South American way.
–ORIGIN Spanish, from Arabic *al-bunduq* 'hazelnut.'

al dente /äl ˈdentā/ ▶ (of food, typically pasta) cooked so as to be still firm when bitten.
–ORIGIN Italian, literally 'to the tooth.'

ale ▶ a type of beer with a bitter flavor and higher alcoholic content.
■ chiefly British beer.
–ORIGIN Old English *alu*, *ealu*, of Germanic origin.

Alfredo ▶ denoting a rich pasta sauce incorporating butter, cream, garlic, and Parmesan cheese: *fettucine Alfredo.*
–ORIGIN named after *Alfredo* di Lelio, the Italian chef and restaurateur who invented the sauce.

allspice ▶ the dried aromatic fruit of a West Indian tree, used whole or ground as a culinary spice.
–ORIGIN from the resemblance of the spice's taste to a mixture of cinnamon, cloves, and nutmeg.

almond ▶ the oval nutlike seed (kernel) of the almond tree, used as food.
▶ made of or flavored with almonds: *almond cookies.*
–ORIGIN Middle English: from Old French *alemande*, from medieval Latin *amandula*, from Greek *amugdalē*.

almond paste ▶ another term for MARZIPAN.

amaretti /ˌaməˈretē/ ▶ Italian almond-flavored cookies.
–ORIGIN Italian, based on *amaro* 'bitter' (with reference to a bitter variety of almond).

American cheese ▶ a type of mild-flavored semisoft processed cheese.

amuse-gueule /ˌamYz ˈgo͞ol/ (also **amuse-bouche** /ˈbo͞osH/) ▶ a small, savory item of food served as an appetizer before a meal.
–ORIGIN French, literally 'amuse mouth.'

anadama bread /ˌanəˈdamə/ ▶ a type of yeast bread typically made with cornmeal and dark molasses.

ancho /'anCHō/ (also **ancho chili**) ▸ a large aromatic chili, used (usually dried) in dishes of Mexican origin or style.
-ORIGIN from Mexican Spanish *(chile) ancho* 'wide (chili).'

anchoïade (also **anchoiade**) /ˌanSHwī'äd; -CHoi'äd/ ▸ a purée of anchovies, crushed garlic, and olive oil that is served with vegetables as a dip or spread on bread.
-ORIGIN Provençal, from French *anchois* 'anchovy.'

anchovy ▸ a small fish that is strongly flavored and usually preserved in salt and oil.
-ORIGIN from Spanish and Portuguese *anchova.*

andouille /an'do͞oē/ ▸ a spicy pork sausage seasoned with garlic, used especially in Cajun cooking.
-ORIGIN French.

andouillette /ˌandwē'yet/ ▸ a very small French sausage similar to andouille.
-ORIGIN French.

angel food cake ▸ a light, pale sponge cake made of flour, egg whites, and no fat, typically baked in a ring shape and covered with soft icing.

angel hair (also **angel's hair**) ▸ pasta consisting of very fine long strands.

angelica /an'jelikə/ ▸ an aromatic plant of the parsley family, used in cooking and herbal medicine.
■ the candied stalk of this plant.
-ORIGIN from medieval Latin *(herba) angelica* 'angelic (herb)' (believed to be efficacious against poisoning and disease).

anise /'anis/ ▸ (also **aniseseed**) the aromatic seed of a Mediterranean plant of the parsley family, used for flavoring food.
■ see STAR ANISE.
-ORIGIN Middle English: via Old French from Latin *anisum,* from Greek *anison.*

antipasto /ˌantē'pästō/ ▸ (in Italian cooking) an appetizer typically consisting of olives, anchovies, cheeses, and meats.
-ORIGIN Italian, from *anti-* 'before' + *pasto* (from Latin *pastus* 'food').

aperitif /ä͵peri'tēf/ ▸ an alcoholic drink taken before a meal to stimulate the appetite.

–ORIGIN from French *apéritif,* from medieval Latin *aperitivus,* based on Latin *aperire* 'to open.'

appetizer ▸ a small dish of food or a drink taken before a meal or the main course of a meal to stimulate one's appetite.

apple ▸ the round fruit of a tree of the rose family, which typically has thin red or green skin and crisp flesh. Many varieties have been developed as dessert or cooking fruit or for making cider.

Varieties of Apples

Ambrosia	Granny Smith	Mutsu
Baldwin	Gravenstein	Northern Spy
Braeburn	Greening	Paula Red
Cameo	Honeycrisp	Pink Lady
Cortland	Ida Red	Pippin
crabapple	Jerseymac	Red Delicious
Crispin	Jonagold	Rome
Criterion	Jonamac	Spartan
Discovery	Jonathan	Stayman
Empire	Lady	Sundowner
Fortune	Liberty	Sunrise
Fuji	Lodi	Tydeman
Gala	Macintosh	Winesap
Ginger Gold	Macoun	Winter Banana
Golden Delicious	may apple	Yellow Transparent
Golden Russet	Monarch	York

apple butter ▸ a paste of spiced stewed apple used as a spread or condiment, usually made with cider.

applesauce ▸ a purée of stewed apples, usually sweetened.

arabica /ə'rabikə/ ▸ coffee from the most widely grown kind of coffee plant. Compare with ROBUSTA.

–ORIGIN from Latin, feminine of *arabicus* 'Arabian.'

arame /'arə͵mä/ ▸ an edible Pacific seaweed with broad brown leaves, used in Japanese cooking.

–ORIGIN Japanese.

Arborio (also **arborio**) /är'bôrē͵ō/ ▸ a round-grained Italian rice used in making risotto.

–ORIGIN Italian.

arepa /äˈräpə/ ▸ a corn pancake, sweetened or unsweetened, eaten in Venezuela and Colombia.
-ORIGIN Cariban.

argan oil /ˈärgan/ ▸ an aromatic culinary oil expressed from the seeds of the argan tree, native to an area of southwestern Morocco.

aromatic ▸ having a pleasant and distinctive smell: *aromatic herbs*.
▸ a substance or plant emitting a pleasant and distinctive smell.
-ORIGIN Middle English: via Old French from late Latin *aromaticus*, from Greek *arōmatikos*, from *arōma* 'spice.'

arrowroot ▸ the fine-grained starch obtained from a West Indian herbaceous plant, used to thicken foods.
-ORIGIN alteration of Arawak *aru-aru* (literally 'meal of meals') by association with *arrow* and *root*, the tubers being used to absorb poison from arrow wounds.

arroz con pollo /äˈrôs kôn ˈpô(l)yô/ ▸ a Spanish and Latin American dish of chicken and rice simmered with tomatoes, stock, and herbs.
-ORIGIN Spanish, 'chicken with rice.'

artichoke ▸ (also **globe artichoke**) the unopened large flowerhead of a European plant, of which the heart and the fleshy bases of the bracts are edible.
■ see **JERUSALEM ARTICHOKE**.
-ORIGIN from northern Italian *articiocco*, from Spanish *alcarchofa*, from Arabic *al-karšūfa*.

arugula /əˈro͞ogələ/ ▸ the pungent leaves of the rocket plant, used in salads.
-ORIGIN from Italian dialect, ultimately a diminutive of Latin *eruca* 'down-stemmed plant.'

asiago /ˌäsēˈägō/ ▸ a strong-flavored cow's milk cheese made in northern Italy.
-ORIGIN named after *Asiago*, the plateau and town in northern Italy where the cheese was first made.

asparagus ▸ the tender young shoots of a tall plant of the lily family, eaten as a vegetable.
-ORIGIN via Latin from Greek *asparagos*.

aspic ▸ a savory jelly, usually or often made with meat stock, used as a garnish, or to contain pieces of food such as meat, seafood, or eggs, set in a mold.

-ORIGIN from French, literally 'asp,' from the colors of the jelly as compared with those of the snake.

aubergine /ˈōbərˌzнēn/ ▶ chiefly British another term for EGGPLANT.

-ORIGIN from French, from Catalan *alberginia*, from Arabic.

au gratin /ˌō ˈgrätn/ ▶ sprinkled with breadcrumbs or grated cheese, or both, and browned: *mushrooms au gratin.*

-ORIGIN French, literally 'by grating.'

avocado ▶ a pear-shaped fruit with a rough leathery skin, smooth oily edible flesh, and a large stone.

-ORIGIN from Spanish, alteration (influenced by *avocado* 'advocate') of *aguacate*, from Nahuatl *ahuacatl.*

B

baba /ˈbäˌbä/ (also **baba au rhum** /ō ˈrəm/) ▸ a small rich sponge cake, typically soaked in rum-flavored syrup.
‑ORIGIN via French from Polish, literally 'married peasant woman.'

baba ghanouj /ˌbäbə gäˈno͞ozh/ (also **baba ganoush** /gäˈno͞osh/) ▸ a thick sauce or spread made from ground eggplant and sesame seeds, olive oil, lemon, and garlic, typical of eastern Mediterranean cuisine.
‑ORIGIN from Egyptian Arabic, from Arabic bābā, literally 'father' + gannuug, perhaps a personal name.

babka /ˈbäbkə/ ▸ a loaf-shaped coffee cake made with sweet yeast dough to which raisins, chocolate, or nuts may be added.
‑ORIGIN from Polish, diminutive of baba (see **BABA**).

bacalao /ˌbäkəˈlou/ ▸ cod, dried and salted, used in Spanish and Latin American cooking.
‑ORIGIN Spanish.

baccalà /ˌbakəˈlä/ ▸ Italian term for **BACALAO**.

bacon ▸ cured meat from the back or sides of a pig.
‑ORIGIN Middle English: from Old French, of Germanic origin.

bagel ▸ a dense ring-shaped bread roll, made by boiling dough and then baking it.
‑ORIGIN from Yiddish beygel.

baguette /baˈget/ ▸ a long, narrow loaf of French bread.
‑ORIGIN from French, from Italian bacchetto, diminutive of bacchio, from Latin baculum 'staff.'

bain-marie /ˌban məˈrē/ ▸ a container holding hot water into which a pan is placed for slow cooking.

-ORIGIN French, translation of medieval Latin *balneum Mariae* 'bath of Maria,' translating Greek *kaminos Marias* 'furnace of Maria,' said to be a Jewish alchemist.

baked Alaska ▶ sponge cake and ice cream in a meringue covering, baked for a very short time.

-ORIGIN named after the state of *Alaska*.

baked beans ▶ short for BOSTON BAKED BEANS.

baking powder ▶ a mixture of sodium bicarbonate and cream of tartar, used as a leavening in baking.

baking soda ▶ sodium bicarbonate used in cooking and baking.

baklava /ˌbäklə'vä/ ▶ a dessert originating in the Middle East made of phyllo pastry filled with chopped nuts and soaked in honey.

-ORIGIN Turkish.

ballottine /'balə,tēn/ ▶ a dish of meat, poultry, or fish that is stuffed and rolled and usually served hot.

-ORIGIN French.

balsamic vinegar /bôl'samik/ ▶ dark, sweet Italian vinegar that has been matured in wooden barrels.

banana split ▶ a dessert made with a split banana, ice cream, sauce, whipped cream, nuts, and a cherry.

bannock /'banək/ ▶ a round, flat loaf, typically unleavened, associated with Scotland and northern England.

-ORIGIN Old English *bannuc*, of Celtic origin.

barbecue ▶ a meal or gathering at which meat, fish, or other food is cooked out of doors on a rack over an open fire or on a portable grill.

■ a portable grill used for the preparation of food at a barbecue, or a brick fireplace containing a grill.

■ food cooked in such a way.

▶ to cook (meat, fish, or other food) on a barbecue.

-ORIGIN from Spanish *barbacoa*, perhaps from Arawak *barbacoa* 'wooden frame on posts.'

USAGE: The common misspelling **barbeque** arises understandably from a confused conflation of the proper spelling *barbecue*, the abbr. *Bar-B-Q*, and sound-spelling. Its frequency (well over one million hits on web sites) does not quite justify it: in no other English word does *que* attain the status of a standalone, terminal syllable.

barbecue sauce ▸ a highly seasoned sauce containing tomatoes, vinegar, sugar, and spices.

bard ▸ a slice of bacon placed on meat or game before roasting.
▸ to cover (meat or game) with slices of bacon.
–ORIGIN from French *barde*, a transferred sense of *barde* 'armor for a warhorse,' based on Arabic *bar̠da'a* 'padded saddle.'

barley ▸ the grain of a cereal plant, used especially in brewing and in soups and stews. See also PEARL BARLEY.
–ORIGIN Old English *bærlic* (adjective), from *bære*, *bere* 'barley' + the suffix *-lic*.

baron of beef ▸ a large cut of beef consisting of two sirloins joined at the backbone.

Bartlett (also **Bartlett pear**) ▸ an eating pear of a juicy, early-ripening variety.

basil ▸ an aromatic annual herb of the mint family, native to tropical Asia.
■ the leaves of this plant used as a culinary herb, especially in Mediterranean dishes.
–ORIGIN Middle English: from Old French *basile*, via medieval Latin from Greek *basilikon*, neuter of *basilikos* 'royal.'

basmati /bäsˈmätē/ (also **basmati rice**) ▸ a kind of long-grain Indian rice of a high quality.
–ORIGIN from Hindi *bāsmatī*, literally 'fragrant.'

baste ▸ to pour fat or juices over (meat) during cooking in order to keep it moist.

batata /bəˈtätə/ ▸ (in the southern West Indies) a sweet potato.
–ORIGIN via Spanish from Taino.

batter /ˈbatər/ ▸ a semiliquid mixture of flour, egg, and milk or water used in cooking, especially for making cakes or for coating food before frying.
□ **battered**: *battered and deep-fried.*
–ORIGIN Middle English: from Old French *bateure* 'beating,' from *batre* 'to beat.'

batterie de cuisine /bat(ə)ˈrē də kwiˈzēn/ ▸ the apparatus or set of utensils for serving or preparing a meal.
–ORIGIN French, literally 'set of kitchen equipment.' The original

meaning was 'collection of artillery equipment (for "beating" the enemy).'

bavarois /ˌbävärˈwä/ (also **bavaroise** /-ˈwäz/) ▶ a dessert of whipped cream stiffened with gelatin and chilled in a mold.

–ORIGIN French, literally 'Bavarian.'

bay leaf ▶ the aromatic, usually dried, leaf of the bay tree, used in cooking.

bean ▶ the edible seed, typically kidney-shaped, or the long pod of certain legumes. See also KIDNEY BEAN, BROAD BEAN, SCARLET RUNNER.

■ the hard seed of coffee, cocoa, and certain other plants.

–ORIGIN Old English *bēan*, of Germanic origin.

Beans and Peas

aduke	flageolet	pulse
adzuki	garbanzo	red
anasazi	garden pea	rice
bambara	green pea	rice bean
black	Great Northern	runner
black turtle	green	scarlet runner
black-eyed pea	haricot	snap
bram	horse	snow pea
broad	hyacinth	soy
butter	jack	split pea
butterfly pea	kidney	string
cajan pea	lablab	stylo
cannellini	lentil	sugar pea
carob	lima	sugar snap pea
castor	lupin	Swedish brown
chickpea	marrow	sword
cluster	moth	tepary
congo	mung	velvet
copper	mungo	vetch
cowpea	navy	wax
cranberry	nothern	white
dal	peanut	winged
English pea	pigeon pea	yam bean
fava	pink	yard-long
field	pinto	yellow pea
field pea	protein pea	yellow-eyed

bean curd ▸ another term for **TOFU**.

bean sprouts ▸ the sprouting seeds of certain beans, especially mung beans or soybeans, used in Asian cooking.

Béarnaise sauce /ˌberˈnāz/ ▸ a rich sauce thickened with egg yolks and flavored with tarragon.
–ORIGIN French *Béarnaise*, feminine of *Béarnais* 'of *Béarn*,' region of southwestern France.

béchamel /ˌbāSHəˈmel/ (also **béchamel sauce**) ▸ a rich white sauce made with milk infused with herbs and other flavorings.
–ORIGIN named after the Marquis Louis de *Béchamel*, steward to Louis XIV of France, said to have invented a similar sauce.

bêche-de-mer /ˌbeSH də ˈme(ə)r/ ▸ a large sea cucumber that is eaten as a delicacy in China and Japan.
–ORIGIN pseudo-French, alteration of Portuguese *bicho do mar*, literally 'sea worm.'

beef /bēf/ ▸ the flesh of a cow, bull, or ox, used as food.
–ORIGIN Middle English: from Old French *boef*, from Latin *bos*, *bov-* 'ox.'

beef bourguignon /ˌbo͞orgēˈnyôn/ ▸ variant spelling of **BOEUF BOURGUIGNON**.

beef Wellington ▸ a dish of beef, typically coated in pâté de foie gras, wrapped in puff pastry, and baked.

beer ▸ an alcoholic drink made from yeast-fermented malt flavored with hops.
■ any of several other fermented drinks: *ginger beer.*
–ORIGIN Old English *bēor*, of West Germanic origin, probably from Latin *bibere* 'to drink.'

beet ▸ a herbaceous plant widely cultivated as a source of food for humans and livestock, and for processing into sugar. Some varieties are grown for their leaves and some for their large nutritious root.
–ORIGIN Old English *bēte*, of West Germanic origin, from Latin *beta*.

beggar's purse ▸ an appetizer consisting of a crepe stuffed with a savory filling, typically caviar and crème fraîche, then gathered and tied to form a bag.

beignet /benˈyā/ ▸ a fritter: *a cheese beignet.*

Beers

abbey	ginger	Oktoberfest
ale	green	old ale
alt	Gueuze	oud bruin
altbier	heavy	pale ale
barley wine	Hefe	pils
Berliner Weisse	Hell	pilsner
Biere de Garde	honey beer	poire
bitter	ice	porter
bock	India Pale Ale	Schwarzbier
brown ale	Irish ale	season
celery	Kölsch	shandy
chili beer	Kriek	special
cream ale	Kristall	Sticke
diat pils	lager	stock ale
doppelbock	lambic	stout
Dortmunder	light	trappist
draught	malt	Vienna
dry	malt liquor	weiss
dunkel	Märzen	wheat
Eisbock	mild	Zwickl
faro	Muncher	
franboise	Munich	

■ a square of fried dough sprinkled with confectioners' sugar.

–ORIGIN French, from archaic *buyne* 'hump, bump.'

Belgian endive ▸ another term for ENDIVE.

Belgian waffle ▸ a waffle made with a special utensil that creates deep indentations in it.

bell pepper ▸ another term for SWEET PEPPER.

belly ▸ a cut of pork from the underside between the legs, usually smoked to make bacon.

–ORIGIN Old English *belig* 'bag,' of Germanic origin.

Bel Paese /ˌbel päˈāzē/ ▸ trademark a rich, white, mild, creamy cheese of a kind originally made in Italy.

–ORIGIN Italian, literally 'fair country.'

beluga /bəˈlo͞ogə/ (also **beluga caviar**) ▸ caviar obtained from a very large sturgeon occurring in the inland seas and associated rivers of central Eurasia.

–ORIGIN from Russian *beluga*, from *belyĭ* 'white.'

Berries

akala	darrowberry	nectarberry
aronia berry	dewberry	olallieberry
barberry	elderberry	passionberry
bearberry	fraise des bois	paw paw
bilberry	golden raspberry	raspberry
black currant	gooseberry	red currant
black raspberry	grapes	salmonberry
blackberry	hackberry	saskatoon berry
blueberry	huckleberry	serviceberry
boysenberry	hurtleberry	silvanberry
buffaloberry	jostaberry	squashberry
candleberry	juneberry	strawberry
cape gooseberry	juniper berry	tayberry
checkerberry	kiwi	thimbleberry
Chinese wolfberry	lingonberry	tummelberry
chokeberry	loganberry	white currant
chokecherry	maidenhair berry	whortleberry
cloudberry	marionberry	wild blueberry
cowberry	marlberry	wild strawberry
cranberry	mayhaw	wineberry
crowberry	mulberry	youngberry

bergamot /ˈbərɡəˌmät/ ▸ an aromatic oil extracted from the rind of an Italian citrus fruit, used to flavor confectionery and Earl Grey tea.

-ORIGIN named after *Bergamo*, city and province in northern Italy.

berry ▸ a small roundish juicy fruit without a stone.

■ any of various kernels or seeds, such as the coffee bean.

■ a fish egg or the roe of a lobster or similar creature.

beurre blanc /ˈbər ˈbläNGk/ ▸ a creamy sauce made with butter, onions or shallots, and vinegar or lemon juice, usually served with seafood dishes.

-ORIGIN French, literally 'white butter.'

beurre noir /ˈbər ˈnwär/ ▸ a sauce made by heating butter until it is dark brown, often flavored with vinegar and herbs.

-ORIGIN French, literally 'black butter.'

beurre noisette /ˈbər nwäˈzet/ ▸ a sauce of butter cooked until golden or brown, usually flavored with capers, herbs, vinegar, etc.

-ORIGIN French, literally 'hazelnut butter.'

bialy /bēˈälē/ ▸ a flat bread roll topped with minced onions.

‒ORIGIN from *Bialystok*, Poland, where the bread originated.

Bing cherry ▸ a large heart-shaped cherry, juicy and sweet in flavor and dark blackish-red in color.

bird's-eye ▸ (also **bird's-eye chile** or **bird's-eye pepper**) a small, very hot chili pepper.

bird's nest soup ▸ a Chinese soup made from the dried gelatinous coating of the nests of swifts and other birds.

biryani (also **biriani**) /ˌbirēˈänē/ ▸ an Indian dish made with highly seasoned rice and meat, fish, or vegetables.

‒ORIGIN Urdu, from Persian *biryāni*, from *biriyān* 'fried, grilled.'

biscotti /biˈskätē/ ▸ small, crisp rectangular cookies typically containing nuts, made originally in Italy. The dough is baked as a loaf, then sliced and baked again.

‒ORIGIN Italian, from medieval Latin *bis coctus* 'twice cooked' (see BISCUIT).

biscuit ▸ a small, typically round cake of bread leavened with baking powder, baking soda, or sometimes yeast.

■ British a cookie or cracker.

‒ORIGIN Middle English: from Old French *bescuit*, based on Latin *bis* 'twice' + *coctus*, past participle of *coquere* 'to cook' (originally biscuits were first baked and then dried out in a slow oven so they would keep).

USAGE: See usage note at MUFFIN.

bisque /bisk/ ▸ a rich, creamy soup typically made with shellfish, especially lobster.

‒ORIGIN French, literally 'crayfish soup.'

bitter ▸ having a sharp, pungent taste or smell; not sweet.

■ (of chocolate) dark and unsweetened.

▸ British ale that is strongly flavored with hops and has a bitter taste.

■ (**bitters**) liquor flavored with the pungent taste of plant extracts, used as an additive in cocktails.

black bean ▸ a small black soybean, used fermented in Asian cooking.

■ a Mexican variety of kidney bean.

black bread ▸ a coarse, dark rye bread.

black-eyed pea ▶ the edible seed of a plant of the pea family native to the Old World tropics.
–ORIGIN from the black marking on one edge of the seed.

Black Forest cake ▶ a chocolate sponge cake with layers of morello cherries or cherry jam and whipped cream.
–ORIGIN a translation of German *Schwarzwald*, forested area in Germany.

black pepper /'blak 'pepər/ ▶ the berries of the pepper vine, which are harvested while still green and unripe, and dried until black. Black pepper is widely used as a spice and condiment and may be used whole (peppercorns) or ground.

black pudding ▶ another term for BLOOD SAUSAGE.

black tea ▶ the most common type of tea, fully fermented before drying. Compare with GREEN TEA.

blade ▶ a shoulder bone in a cut of meat, or the cut of meat itself.

blanch ▶ to prepare (vegetables) for freezing or further cooking by immersing briefly in boiling water.
■ to peel (almonds) by scalding them: *blanched almonds*.
–ORIGIN Middle English: from Old French *blanchir*, from *blanc* 'white,' of Germanic origin.

blancmange /blə'mänj/ ▶ a sweet, opaque, gelatinous dessert made with cornstarch and milk.
–ORIGIN Middle English *blancmanger*, from Old French *blanc mangier*, from *blanc* 'white' + *mangier* 'eat' (used as a noun to mean 'food').

blanquette /bläNG'ket/ ▶ a dish consisting of white meat in a white sauce.
–ORIGIN French, based on *blanc* 'white.'

bleu cheese /'bloō/ ▶ variant spelling of BLUE CHEESE.
–ORIGIN French *bleu* 'blue.'

blini (also **bliny**) /'blinē; 'blēnē/ ▶ pancakes made from buckwheat flour and served with sour cream.
–ORIGIN Russian.

blintz /blints/ (also **blintze**) ▶ a thin rolled pancake filled with cheese or fruit and then fried or baked.

-ORIGIN from Yiddish *blintse*, from Russian *blinets* 'little pancakes'; compare with BLINI.

blood sausage (also **blood pudding**) ▸ a dark sausage containing pork, dried pig's blood, and suet.

BLT ▸ informal a sandwich filled with bacon, lettuce, and tomato.

blue cheese (also **bleu cheese**) ▸ cheese containing veins of blue mold, such as Gorgonzola and Danish Blue.

blue corn ▸ a variety of corn with bluish grains.

bocconcini /ˌbäkənˈCHēnē/ ▸ small balls of mozzarella cheese.
-ORIGIN Italian.

boeuf bourguignon /ˈbœf ˌbo͞orgēˈnyôN/ ▸ a dish consisting of beef stewed in red wine.
-ORIGIN French, literally 'Burgundy beef.'

boil ▸ to cook (food) by immersing in a liquid that is bubbling.
■ to be cooked in a bubbling liquid.
■ (**boil down**) to reduce the volume of (a liquid) by boiling.
▸ the temperature at which a liquid bubbles and turns to vapor.
■ a process of heating a liquid to such a temperature.
■ an outdoor meal at which seafood is boiled.
■ a blend of seasonings added to water to enhance the flavor of boiled seafood.
-ORIGIN Middle English: from Old French *boillir*, from Latin *bullire* 'to bubble.'

bok choy /ˈbäk ˈCHoi/ ▸ Chinese cabbage of a variety with smooth-edged tapering leaves and thick white stalks.
-ORIGIN from Chinese (Cantonese dialect) *paâk ts'oì* 'white vegetable.'

bologna (also **bologna sausage**) ▸ a large smoked, seasoned sausage made of various meats, especially beef and pork.
-ORIGIN named after *Bologna* in Italy.

Bombay duck ▸ the bummalo (fish), especially when dried and eaten as an accompaniment to curry.
-ORIGIN alteration of BUMMALO by association with Bombay, India, from which bummalo were exported.

bombe /bäm(b)/ ▸ a frozen dome-shaped dessert.
■ a dome-shaped mold in which this dessert is made.

-ORIGIN French, literally 'bomb.'

bonbon ▸ a piece of candy, especially one covered with chocolate.
-ORIGIN from French, reduplication of *bon* 'good,' from Latin *bonus*.

boned ▸ (of meat or fish) having had the bones removed before cooking or serving.

boneless ▸ (of a piece of meat or fish) having had the bones removed.

boniato /ˌbänēˈätō/ ▸ a variety of sweet potato with white flesh.
-ORIGIN American Spanish.

bonne femme /ˌbän ˈfam/ ▸ (of fish dishes, stews, and soups) cooked in a simple way.
-ORIGIN French, from *à la bonne femme* 'in the manner of a good housewife.'

bordelaise /ˌbôrdlˈāz/ ▸ served with a sauce of red wine and shallots: *steak bordelaise.*
-ORIGIN French, from *à la bordelaise* 'Bordeaux-style.'

USAGE: See usage note at **PARMIGIANA.**

borek /bôˈrek/ ▸ an envelope of thin pastry filled with cheese, spinach, or ground meat and baked or fried.
-ORIGIN from Turkish, 'pie.'

borscht /bôrSHt/ (also **borsch** /bôrSH/) ▸ a Russian or Polish soup made with beets and usually served with sour cream.
-ORIGIN from Russian *borshch*.

Bosc (also **Bosc pear**) ▸ a medium- to large-sized variety of eatnig pear, golden brown in color.
-ORIGIN named after L. *Bosc* d'Antic (1759–1828), French naturalist.

Boston baked beans ▸ a dish of baked beans made with salt pork and molasses.

Boston lettuce ▸ a butterhead lettuce that has medium- or light-green leaves.

bottarga /bōˈtärgə/ ▸ the dried, pressed roe of the mullet, which is sold in blocks and shaved over Italian dishes.
-ORIGIN from Italian, from Arabic *butarkhah*.

bouchée /bo͞oˈSHā/ ▸ a small pastry with a sweet or savory filling.
-ORIGIN French, literally 'mouthful.'

boudin /bŏŏ'dan/ ▶ a French type of blood sausage.

■ a spicy sausage used especially in Louisiana cuisine.

–ORIGIN French, literally 'blood sausage.'

bouillabaisse /ˌbŏŏ(l)yə'bās/ ▶ a rich, spicy stew or soup made with various kinds of fish, originally from Provence.

–ORIGIN French, from Provençal *bouiabaisso* 'boil down.'

bouillon ▶ a broth made by stewing meat, fish, or vegetables in water.

–ORIGIN French, literally 'liquid in which something has boiled.'

bouillon cube ▶ a small cube of dehydrated stock.

bouquet garni /gär'nē/ ▶ a bunch of herbs, often thyme, bay leaf, parsley, and rosemary, typically encased in a cheesecloth bag, used for flavoring a sauce, stock, stew, or soup.

–ORIGIN French, literally 'garnished bouquet.'

Boursin /bŏŏr'san/ ▶ trademark a kind of soft cheese from France.

–ORIGIN French.

Braeburn /'brābərn/ ▶ an eating apple with crisp flesh, first grown in New Zealand.

braise ▶ to sauté (food) lightly and then stew it slowly in a closed container: *braised veal*.

–ORIGIN from French *braiser*, from *braise* 'live coals' (in which the container was formerly placed).

bran ▶ pieces of grain husk separated from flour after milling.

brandade /brän'däd/ ▶ a Provençal dish consisting of salt cod mixed into a purée with olive oil, garlic, and milk.

–ORIGIN French, from Provençal *brandado*, literally 'something shaken.'

brandy /'brandē/ ▶ a strong alcoholic spirit distilled from wine or fermented fruit juice.

–ORIGIN from Dutch *brandewijn*, from *branden* 'burn, distill' + *wijn* 'wine.'

bratwurst (also **brats**) ▶ a type of fine German pork sausage that is typically fried or grilled.

–ORIGIN German, from *Brat* 'a spit' + *Wurst* 'sausage.'

brazier ▶ a pan or other cooking device for holding coals or charcoal; a barbecue.

–ORIGIN from French *brasier*, from *braise* 'hot coals.'

bread ▶ food made of flour, water, and yeast or another leavening agent, mixed together and baked.

–ORIGIN Old English *brēad*, of Germanic origin.

Bread and Rolls

anadama
bagel
baguette
bannock
bara brith
Barbari
barmbrack
batter bread
beaten biscuit
bialy
biscuit
black bread
Boston brown
breadstick
brioche
brown bread
bun
challah
chapati
ciabatta
cinnamon raisin
cinnamon roll
cob
coburg
coffee cake
concha
corn dodger
corn pone
cornbread
Cornish split
cottage loaf
crepe
crescent roll
crispbread
croissant
crumpet
dosa
English muffin

farmhouse
ficelle
flapjack
flatbread
foccaccia
French
fry bread
gordita
graham
grissini
hoecake
hot cross bun
hotcake
houska
hush puppy
injera
Irish soda
Italian
Jewish rye
johnny cake
Kaiser roll
kulick
landbroed
lavash
matzo
monkey bread
muffin
nan
oatcake
oatmeal
onion roll
pain au chocolat
pain au levain
pan de sal
pancake
pane francese
panettone
pappadum

paratha
Parker House roll
pistolette
pita
poori
popover
Portuguese
potato
pretzel
Pugliese
pull apart
Pullman
pumpernickel
raisin
roll
roti
Russian rye
rye
Sally Lunn
salt rising
salt stick
scone
semolina
seven-grain
sourdough
sticky bun
stollen
taralli
tea bread
tea ring
tortilla
vasilopita
waffle
white
whole wheat
wholemeal
zephyr bun

breadcrumb ▸ a small fragment of bread. Breadcrumbs are used as a topping or coating for various foods. See also CRUMB.

breadfruit ▸ the large, round, starchy fruit of a tropical tree, which is used as a vegetable and sometimes to make a substitute for flour.

bread pudding ▸ a dessert consisting of slices of bread baked together with dried fruit, sugar, spices, eggs, and milk.

breadstick ▸ a long, thin, often crisp piece of baked dough.

breast ▸ a large piece of meat or portion of poultry cut from the chest muscle of an animal.

bresaola /bre'sōlə/ ▸ an Italian dish of raw beef cured by salting and air-drying, served typically in slices with a dressing of olive oil, lemon juice, and black pepper.
–ORIGIN Italian, from *bresada*, past participle of *brasare* 'braise.'

brew ▸ to make (beer) by soaking, boiling, and fermentation.
■ to make (tea or coffee) by mixing it with boiling water.
▸ a kind of beer.
–ORIGIN Old English *brēowan* (verb), of Germanic origin.

Brie /brē/ ▸ a soft, mild, creamy cheese with a firm, white skin.
–ORIGIN named after *Brie* in northern France, where it was originally made.

brine ▸ water saturated or strongly impregnated with salt.
▸ to soak in or saturate with salty water: *brined anchovies.*

brioche /brē'ōsн/ ▸ a light, sweet yeast bread typically in the form of a small, round roll.
–ORIGIN French, from Norman French *brier*, synonym of *broyer*, literally 'split up into very small pieces by pressure.'

brisket ▸ meat cut from the breast of an animal, typically a cow.
–ORIGIN Middle English: perhaps from Old Norse *brjósk* 'cartilage, gristle.'

brittle ▸ a candy made from nuts set in melted sugar: *peanut brittle.*
–ORIGIN Middle English, of Germanic origin and related to Old English *brēotan* 'break up.'

broad bean ▸ a large edible flat green bean that is typically eaten without the pod. Also called FAVA BEAN.

broccoli ▸ a plant of the cabbage family related to the cauliflower, bearing heads of green or purplish flower buds.

■ the flower stalk and head eaten as a vegetable.

-ORIGIN from Italian, plural of *broccolo* 'cabbage sprout,' diminutive of *brocco* 'shoot.'

broccolini /ˌbräkəˈlēnē/ ▸ a vegetable that is a hybrid of broccoli and kale, with small florets on slender stalks. It has a mild, nutty flavor.

broccoli rabe /räb/ ▸ a leafy green vegetable with broccolilike buds and bitter-flavored greens and stalks.

brochette /brōˈsHet/ ▸ a skewer or spit on which chunks of meat or fish are barbecued, grilled, or roasted. Various dishes cooked in this way are described as *en brochette*.

-ORIGIN French, diminutive of *broche* 'spit.'

broil ▸ to cook (meat or fish) by exposure to direct, intense heat: *a broiled sirloin steak.*

-ORIGIN Middle English: from Old French *bruler* 'to burn.'

USAGE: See usage note at **MUFFIN**.

broiler ▸ (also **broiler chicken**) a young chicken suitable for roasting, grilling, or barbecuing.

■ a grill or special part of a stove for cooking meat or fish by exposure to direct heat.

broth ▸ soup consisting of meat or vegetable chunks, and often rice, cooked in stock.

■ meat, fish, or vegetable stock.

-ORIGIN Old English, of Germanic origin; related to **BREW**.

brown ▸ (of bread) made from a dark, unsifted, or unbleached flour.

▸ to make or become brown, typically by cooking: *a skillet in which onions have been browned | bake the pizza until the cheese has browned.*

brown betty ▸ a baked pudding made with apples or other fruit and breadcrumbs.

brownie ▸ a small square of rich cake, typically chocolate cake with nuts.

brown rice ▸ unpolished rice with only the husk of the grain removed.

brown sauce ▸ a savory sauce made with fat and flour cooked to a brown color.

brown sugar ▸ unrefined or partially refined sugar.

Brunswick stew ▸ a stew originally made with squirrel or rabbit, but now consisting of chicken and vegetables including onion and tomatoes.

bruschetta /brŏŏˈsHetə; -ˈsketə/ ▸ toasted Italian bread drenched in olive oil and served typically with garlic or tomatoes.
–ORIGIN Italian.

Brussels sprout (also **brussels sprout**) ▸ a vegetable consisting of the small compact bud of a variety of cabbage.

bucatini /ˌbŏŏkəˈtēnē/ ▸ pasta in the shape of small tubes.
–ORIGIN Italian, literally 'little holes.'

buckwheat ▸ an Asian plant of the dock family, the starchy seeds of which are used whole or milled into flour. See also **KASHA**.
–ORIGIN from Middle Dutch *boecweite* 'beech wheat,' its grains being shaped like beech mast.

buffalo mozzarella ▸ mozzarella cheese made in the traditional way, from the milk of the water buffalo.

Buffalo wings (also **buffalo wings** or **Buffalo chicken wings**) ▸ deep-fried chicken wings coated in a spicy sauce and usually served with blue cheese dressing and celery.
–ORIGIN popularized by a restaurant in *Buffalo*, New York.

bulgar /ˈbəlgər/ (also **bulgur, bulgar wheat**) ▸ a cereal food made from whole wheat partially boiled then dried.
–ORIGIN from Turkish *bulgur* 'bruised grain.'

bulgogi /bŏŏlˈgōgē/ ▸ a Korean dish of thin beef slices marinated and grilled on a barbecue.

bummalo /ˈbəməˌlō/ ▸ a small elongated fish of South Asian coasts that is dried and used as food. Also called **BOMBAY DUCK**.
–ORIGIN perhaps from Marathi *bombīl*.

bun ▸ a bread roll of various shapes and flavorings, sometimes sweetened and containing dried fruit.

Bundt cake /ˈbənt/ ▸ a ring-shaped cake made in a fluted tube pan, called a **Bundt pan**.

burger ▸ short for **HAMBURGER**.
■ a hamburger with substitute ingredients: *a veggie burger.*

burrito /bəˈrētō/ ▸ (in Mexican cooking) a tortilla rolled around a filling, typically of beans or ground or shredded beef.

-ORIGIN Latin American Spanish, diminutive of Spanish *burro*, literally 'donkey.'

butter ▸ a pale yellow edible fatty substance made by churning cream and used as a spread or in cooking.

■ a substance of a similar consistency: *cocoa butter.*

▸ to spread (something) with butter.

buttercream ▸ a soft mixture of butter and sugar used as a filling or topping for a cake (also called **butter icing**).

buttercup squash ▸ a winter squash with dark green skin and orange flesh.

butterfly ▸ to split (a piece of meat, fish, or shrimp) almost in two and spread it out flat: *butterflied shrimp.*

butterhead lettuce ▸ a class of lettuce varieties having soft leaves that grow in a loose head.

buttermilk ▸ the slightly sour liquid left after butter has been churned, used in baking or consumed as a drink.

■ a cultured sour milk made from cow's milk.

butterscotch ▸ a flavor created by combining melted butter with brown sugar.

■ a candy with this flavor.

button mushroom ▸ a young unopened mushroom.

A HOAGIE
BY ANY OTHER NAME

A *hoagie*, a *grinder*, a *sub*, and a *hero* are one and the same thing. They are simply regional names for a sandwich served on a large Italian roll and filled with Italian meat, cheese, lettuce, tomato, onion, and sprinkled with olive oil and spices. Variations on the basic recipe are made by filling the sandwich with other things, such as tuna fish, roast beef, ham and cheese, meatballs, and all manner of other ingredients. Subs can be served either hot or cold.

In addition to these names, there are plenty of others: *poor boy, torpedo, Italian sandwich, rocket, zeppelin* or *zep, blimpie, garibaldi, bomber, wedge, muffuletta, Cuban sandwich*, and *spuckie*. Most of these names are associated with a particular region of the United States. The names also fall into several distinct patterns of origin, from the shape (sub, torpedo, rocket, zeppelin, blimpie, and bomber), from the size (hero, hoagie), from ethnic association (Italian sandwich, Cuban sandwich), from the type of bread used (muffuletta, spuckie), or from the fact that the sandwich is a cheap meal (poor boy).

Sub, or *submarine sandwich*, is the general name for the sandwich, found throughout the United States and not associated with any particular region. The name dates to 1941, although there is at least one claim (made in 1967) that the word existed as early as 1928.

It is often asserted that the name *submarine sandwich* began in

New London, Connecticut, after the naval submarine base there, but there is no evidence to support this contention. *Sub*, the sandwich, is not associated with Connecticut in particular. (Although the Subway® chain of sandwich shops got its start in 1965 as Pete's Super Submarine Shop in Bridgeport, about 70 miles from New London.) And if the 1928 claim were true, it would seem unlikely, as that citation is from Philadelphia.

Related to the name *sub* is *torpedo*. Like *sub*, this term is found throughout the U.S. It is often used to refer to a small or half-sized sub, a *torpedo roll* being a smaller piece of bread than that used in a full-sized sub.

Hoagie is the name given to the sandwich in Philadelphia. *Hoagie* is common throughout Pennsylvania and much of southern New Jersey. Linguists Edwin Eames and Howard Robboy ("The Submarine Sandwich: Lexical Variations in a Cultural Context," *American Speech*, Dec 1967) point to uses of both *hoagie* and *hoggy* in a 1945 Philadelphia telephone directory. Indefatigable word sleuth Barry Popik has done thorough and meticulous research into early citations and origins of American culinary terms. He has found *hoggie* in an October 1944 Philadelphia phone directory, *hogie* from September 1943, and *hoogie* from January 1941.

How it got its name is an often-debated topic. The most commonly touted explanation is that it comes from the name of Hog Island, Philadelphia. In the early part of the 20th century there was a shipyard on Hog Island (now the site of the Philadelphia airport). According to this tale, during the First World War, Italian-American shipyard workers, or *hoggies* as they are known in the legend, would bring large sandwiches to work with them. The early spelling of *hoggie* makes this hypothesis attractive, but there is a gap between the shipyard's years of operation and the earliest attestation of the sandwich name in 1941. The shipyard operated full-bore from 1917-20, after which production rapidly declined before it closed completely in 1925. That leaves only a handful of years for the name to catch on in the city's consciousness and a gap of some fifteen years before the name is found in print. If the name can be antedated further, the Hog Island hypothesis will seem more likely, but for now this explanation seems doubtful.

A variant on the above is that it comes from *Hogan*, a nickname for Irish workers at the shipyard. This has the same problem of dating, plus it seems unlikely that an Irish name would be associated with the Italian sandwich.

A second and more likely explanation is that an enterprising restaurateur coined it. Al De Palma, the self-proclaimed "King of the Hoagies," claims to have coined *hoggie*. In 1928 while working as a jazz musician, De Palma saw some fellow musicians eating a submarine. Impressed with the size of the sandwich, De Palma remarked that, "you had to be hog to eat one." When the depression hit, De Palma couldn't find work as a musician and in 1936 opened up a sandwich shop in Philadelphia. Recalling the sandwich and his remark from eight years before, he made and sold *hoggies* in the shop. He was quite successful, eventually opening a chain of hoagie shops and earning himself his sobriquet. He opened his sandwich shop in 1936 and the term (*hoggie*) appears in advertising copy by 1941.

Hero is attested to as early as the February 19, 1947 issue of *The New York Naval Shipyard Shipworker* and is distinctly a New York name for the sandwich. The most common etymological explanation is that it is so called because of its large size. It is often claimed that New York *Herald Tribune* food columnist Clementine Paddleford coined the name in the 1930s, claiming the sandwich was so large "you had to be a hero to eat it." Alas, no one can find any record of this in any of Paddleford's columns, or any use of the term before 1947. But it does seem likely that the name comes from the size of the sandwich.

An alternative explanation is that it is a folk etymology of *gyro* (pronounced yee-roh; phonetics experts and those fluent in Greek may feel free to pick at my representation of the proper pronunciation). Non-Greek New Yorkers took the unfamiliar word and made it into the familiar *hero*. This is a plausible explanation from a phonological standpoint, but not from a cultural one. The *hero* is a distinctly Italian sandwich, not a Greek one. And there is no way that someone could mistake cold cuts on an Italian roll for a *gyro*, which is lamb and tzatziki sauce in a pita. Besides, *gyro* isn't attested to in English until 1968 and appears to be a later addition to the American bill of fare.

Blimpie® is a registered trademark of the eponymous chain of sub shops. The chain was founded in Hoboken, New Jersey in 1964 and is still in existence, second only to Subway in number of franchises. According to the chain's website, the name was chosen by the chain's founders, a combination of *blimp*, from the shape of the sandwich, and the *–ie* ending from *hoagie*. *Blimpie* is etymologically unrelated to *zeppelin* or *zep* (1960), another name for the sandwich, common in eastern Pennsylvania.

Grinder is the term of art throughout most of New England, with the notable exception of Boston where it is less common. The name probably comes from the chewing or grinding your teeth do when consuming the sandwich and dates to at least 1946. Many people make a distinction between grinders and other subs in that they use *grinder* to mean a hot sub, but this is not the original sense. The original grinders were the familiar coldcut subs we know and love. Hot sandwiches are often known as *oven grinders*. And you occasionally see the alliterative *guinea grinder* that associates the sandwich with its Italian-American heritage, however derogatorily.

Boston has its own local name for the sandwich, *spuckie* (also *spukie, spooky,* and *spucky*). The name comes from *spucadella,* a type of Italian sandwich roll. This local Hub name appears to be dying, being replaced by the generic *sub*.

The *poor boy* got its start in New Orleans and spread out across the South from there. It is attested to as early as 1931. The name most likely comes from the fact that subs are cheap, but filling meals for "poor boys." But like *sub* and *hoagie*, the origin of *poor boy* is somewhat uncertain.

The best-substantiated claim for the coinage of *poor boy* is that of Clovis and Benjamin Martin, brothers who opened a sandwich shop on the New Orleans waterfront in 1921. They claim to have invented the sandwich and its name, which were quickly copied by their competitors. Their justification for the name is that it is a hearty sandwich for the workingman who doesn't make much money.

In Puerto Rico there is a similar sandwich, known as the *niño pobre*. Whether the sandwich and its name emigrated from New Orleans or whether it came to that city from the Caribbean is not known. The same sandwich is available elsewhere in Latin America under the name *obrero* (laborer). The Martin brothers profess to have been unaware of these Spanish variants.

Because the poor boy comes from New Orleans, some insist that the *poor boy* has a French origin. Two theories contend. One is that it is from *pour le bois*, a meal taken into the woods by lumberjacks. The second is that it is from *pourbois*, a tip or gratuity. Supposedly, street urchins would knock at convent doors seeking a *pourbois*, and the nuns would give them a sandwich.

There are two Southern variants of the *poor boy* that are not subs in the strictest sense. The first is another New Orleans creation, the *muffuletta*. The *muffuletta* takes its name from the bread, a Sicilian dialectical name. Unlike the long, tubular shape of a sub, the *muffuletta* is round. The second Southern variation is the *Cuban Sandwich*. While it has the familiar tubular shape of a sub, it is Cuban rather than Italian in origin and, properly made, contains a different combination of meats and is flattened in a sandwich press. Found mainly in Miami and southern Florida (no surprise), the sandwich has been part of the local cuisine since 1901.

In a few places, subs are called *rockets*. In Madison, Wisconsin they have been known as *garibaldis*. And there are undoubtedly other local names for the venerable sandwich. The name *bomber* is common in Buffalo and in other places scattered throughout the U.S. The term in Westchester County and the Hudson Valley is *wedge*.

Why so much lexical diversity in a sandwich? Probably because no single person can lay claim to inventing it. Slicing an Italian roll and filling it with meat, cheese, lettuce, and tomatoes hardly requires culinary expertise or inventiveness. It was undoubtedly created *de novo* many times across the United States and given a different name each time. Many of the more regional names appear to be going by the wayside as American culture becomes more and more homogenized, but *hoagie, hero, grinder,* and *poor boy* remain strong and so far are resisting being overtaken by *sub,* even as *garibaldi, wedge, bomber, zeppelin, rocket,* and *spuckie* fade from the American lexicon.

Dave Wilton is the author of the forthcoming *Word Myths* from Oxford University Press. His monthly newsletter, *A Way With Words,* is available at his website, *www.wordorigins.org.*

C

cabbage ▸ a cultivated plant eaten as a vegetable, having thick green or purple leaves surrounding a spherical heart or head of young leaves.

-ORIGIN Middle English: from Old French (Picard dialect) *caboche* 'head.'

Cabrales /kä'brälās/ ▸ a pungent blue cheese from Spain.

-ORIGIN Spanish, from *cabra* 'goat.'

cacao /kə'kou/ ▸ beanlike seeds of a tropical American evergreen tree, from which cocoa, cocoa butter, and chocolate are made.

-ORIGIN via Spanish from Nahuatl *cacaua*.

cacciatore /ˌkäCHə'tôrē/ (also **cacciatora** /-ˌtôrə/) ▸ prepared in a spicy tomato sauce with mushrooms and herbs: *chicken cacciatore.*

-ORIGIN Italian, literally 'hunter' (because of ingredients a hunter might have on hand).

Caerphilly /kär'filē/ ▸ a mild white cheese, originally made in Caerphilly in Wales.

Caesar salad ▸ a salad consisting of romaine lettuce and croutons served with a dressing of olive oil, lemon juice, raw egg, anchovy paste, Worcestershire sauce, and seasonings.

-ORIGIN named after *Caesar* Cardini, Mexican restaurateur who invented it in 1924.

café au lait /'kafā ō 'lā/ ▸ coffee with milk.

-ORIGIN from French.

café noir /'kafā 'nwär/ ▸ black coffee.

-ORIGIN French.

caffè latte /ˌkafā 'lätā/ ▸ a drink made by adding a shot of espresso to a glass or cup of frothy steamed milk.

-ORIGIN Italian, literally 'milk coffee.'

Cajun /'kājən/ ▸ in the style of cooking of the Louisiana Cajuns, characterized by the use of pungent peppers and spices and a dark roux.
–ORIGIN alteration of *Acadian.*

cake ▸ an item of soft, sweet food made from a mixture of flour, shortening, eggs, sugar, and other ingredients, baked and often decorated.
▪ an item of savory food formed into a flat, round shape, and typically baked or fried: *crab cakes.*
–ORIGIN Middle English (in the sense 'flat bread roll'): of Scandinavian origin.

calamari /ˌkälə'märē/ ▸ squid served as food.
–ORIGIN Italian, plural of *calamaro,* from medieval Latin *calamarium* 'pen case,' from Greek *kalamos* 'pen,' with reference to the squid's long tapering internal shell and its ink.

callaloo (also **callalou**) /ˌkalə'lо̄о̄/ ▸ the spinachlike leaves of a tropical American plant, widely used in Caribbean cooking.
▪ a soup or stew made with such leaves.
–ORIGIN from American Spanish *calalú.*

calzone /kal'zо̄n(ā)/ ▸ a type of pizza that is folded in half before cooking to contain a filling.
–ORIGIN Italian dialect, probably a special use of *calzone* 'trouser leg,' with reference to the shape of the pizza.

cambozola (also **cambazola**) /ˌkambə'zо̄lə/ ▸ a German blue soft cheese with a rind like Camembert, produced using Gorgonzola blue mold.
–ORIGIN an invented name, blend of CAMEMBERT and GORGONZOLA, with the insertion of *-bo-.*

Camembert /'kaməmˌbe(ə)r/ ▸ a rich, soft, creamy cheese with a whitish rind, originally made near Camembert in Normandy.

camomile ▸ a variant spelling of CHAMOMILE.

canapé ▸ a small piece of bread or pastry with a savory topping, often served with drinks at a reception or formal party.
–ORIGIN French, a figurative extension of the sense 'sofa' (as a "couch" on which to place toppings).

Cakes, Puddings, and Desserts

ambrosia
angel food cake
apple pandowdy
baba au rhum
babka
Baked Alaska
banana pudding
banana split
bananas Foster
Banbury tart
Battenburg cake
Bavarian cream
bavarois
Black Forest cake
blancmange
blueberry buckle
bombe
Boston cream pie
bread pudding
brown Betty
buche de Noel
Bundt cake
carrot cake
cassata
Charlotte Russe
cheesecake
cherries in the snow
cherries jubilee
chocolate pudding
chocolate fondue
clafoutis
cobbler
coffee cake
compote
coupe
crème brûlée
crème caramel
crepes Suzette
crisp
croquembouche
crumb cake
crumble
cupcake

custard
dacquoise
devil's food cake
Dobos torte
duff
dulce de leche
Dundee cake
financier
flan
floating island
flummery
fool
fruitcake
galette des rois
gateau
genoise
German chocolate cake
gingerbread
granita
honey cake
hummingbird cake
ice cream
Indian pudding
Italian ice
jelly roll
kuchen
Kugelhopf
kulfi
lemon chiffon cake
Lord Baltimore cake
Madeira cake
madeleine
marquise
Mississippi mud
mooncake
mousse
mousseline
nougatine
panettone
panforte
panna cotta
parfait
pashka

pavlova
peach Melba
persimmon pudding
plum pudding
poached pear
poires belle-Hélène
pot de crème
pound cake
red velvet cake
rice pudding
roulade
sabayon
Sachertorte
savarin
semifreddo
sherbet
simnel cake
snow pudding
sorbet
souffle
spice cake
sponge cake
stollen
strawberry shortcake
streusel
syllabub
tapioca pudding
tarte Tatin
tea cake
timbale
tiramisù
toffee pudding
torte
tortoni
tres leches
trifle
upside down cake
vacherin
vanilla pudding
wedding cake
whoopie pie
zabaglione
zuppa inglese

candy ▶ a sweet food made with sugar or syrup combined with fruit, chocolate, or nuts.

■ sugar crystallized by repeated boiling and slow evaporation.

▶ to preserve (fruit) by coating and impregnating it with a sugar syrup: *candied citrus fruit.*

-ORIGIN Middle English *sugar-candy*, from French *sucre candi* 'crystallized sugar,' from Arabic *sukkar* 'sugar' + *kandī* 'candied.'

Candy and Other Sweets

angel's hair	friandise	mint
barfi	fruit paste	mostarda di frutta
bark	fruit slice	nonpareil
boiled sweet	fudge	nougat
bonbon	ganache	nougatine
brittle	gianduia	Nutella
bubble gum	glyko (spoon sweet)	opera cream
buckeye	gobstopper	pastille
bullseye	gulab jamun	pâte de fruits
burnt peanut	gum ball	peanut butter cup
buttermint	gumdrop	pecan log
butterscotch	gummy candy	penuche
candied fruit	halvah	peppermint patty
candied nut	haystack	praline
candied peel	heavenly hash	pulled candy
candied violet	horehound	ratafia
candy apple	jawbreaker	red hot
candy buttons	Jordan almond	rock candy
candy cane	kiss	rum ball
caramel	lemon drop	s'more
caramel apple	licorice	saltwater taffy
caramel corn	Life Saver	sesame brittle
chewing gum	lollipop	stroopballetje
chocolate	lozenge	Swedish fish
chocolate covered	macaroon	taffy
cherry	malted milk ball	toffee
comfit	maple sugar	torrone
cotton candy	marchpane	truffle
divinity	marron glacé	Turkish delight
dragée	marshmallow	turtle
fondant	marzipan	
frangipane	meringue	

candy apple ▶ an apple coated with a thin layer of cooked sugar or caramel and fixed on a stick.

cane sugar ▶ sugar obtained from sugar cane.

cannellini bean /ˌkanl'ēnē/ ▶ a kidney-shaped bean of a medium-sized, creamy-white variety.
–ORIGIN Italian *cannellini*, literally 'small tubes.'

cannelloni /ˌkanl'ōnē/ ▶ long pasta rolls stuffed with a meat, cheese, or vegetable mixture.

■ an Italian dish consisting of such pasta cooked in a tomato or cheese sauce.
–ORIGIN Italian, literally 'large tubes,' from *cannello* 'tube.'

cannoli /kə'nōlē/ ▶ Italian pastries in the form of hard tubular shells filled with sweetened ricotta cheese and often containing nuts, citron, or chocolate bits.
–ORIGIN Italian, plural of *cannolo*, from *canna* 'reed,' from Greek *kanna*, of Semitic origin.

cantal /kan'täl/ ▶ a hard, strong cheese made chiefly in the Auvergne.
–ORIGIN named after *Cantal*, department of Auvergne, France.

cantaloupe ▶ a small, round melon of a variety with orange flesh and netted rind.
–ORIGIN from French *cantaloup*, from *Cantaluppi* near Rome, where it was first grown in Europe after being introduced from Armenia.

caper ▶ (usually **capers**) the cooked and pickled flower buds of a bramblelike southern European shrub, used to flavor food.
–ORIGIN Middle English: from Latin *capparis*, from Greek *kapparis*; later interpreted as plural, hence the loss of the final -*s*.

capon /'kā,pän/ ▶ a castrated domestic cock fattened for eating.

caponata /ˌkäpə'nätə/ ▶ a dish of eggplant, olives, and onions seasoned with herbs, typically served as an appetizer.
–ORIGIN Italian.

cappelletti /ˌkapə'letē/ ▶ small pieces of pasta folded and stuffed with meat or cheese.
–ORIGIN Italian, literally 'little hats.'

cappuccino /ˌkäpə'CHēnō/ ▶ coffee made with milk that has been frothed up with pressurized steam.

-ORIGIN from Italian, literally 'Capuchin,' because its color resembles that of a Capuchin's habit.

capsicum /ˈkapsikəm/ ▸ the edible fruit of any of various tropical American pepper plants of the nightshade family. The fruits vary in size, color and pungency.
-ORIGIN modern Latin.

carambola /ˌkarəmˈbōlə/ ▸ the golden-yellow juicy fruit of a tropical tree, having a star-shaped cross section (also called **star fruit**).
-ORIGIN from Portuguese, probably from Marathi *karambal.*

caramel ▸ sugar or syrup heated until it turns brown, used as a flavoring or coloring for food or drink.
■ a soft candy made with sugar and butter that have been melted and cooked together.
-ORIGIN from French, from Spanish *caramelo.*

caramelize ▸ (of sugar or syrup) to be converted into caramel.
■ to cook (food) with sugar so that it becomes coated with caramel.

caraway ▸ (also **caraway seed**) the seeds of a plant of the parsley family, used for flavoring and as a source of oil.
-ORIGIN Middle English: from medieval Latin *carui*, from Arabic *alkarāwiyā*, probably from Greek *karon* 'cumin.'

carbonara /ˌkärbəˈnärə/ ▸ denoting a pasta sauce made with bacon or ham, egg, and cream: *spaghetti carbonara.*
-ORIGIN Italian, literally 'charcoal kiln.'

carbonate ▸ to dissolve carbon dioxide in (a liquid) to make it effervescent: *a carbonated soft drink.*

carbonnade /ˌkärbəˈnäd/ ▸ a rich beef stew made with onions and beer.
-ORIGIN from French, from Latin *carbo* 'charcoal.'

cardamom /ˈkärdəməm/ ▸ the aromatic seeds of an Asian plant of the ginger family, used as a spice.
-ORIGIN Middle English: from Latin *cardamomum*, from Greek *kardamomon.*

carob ▸ the long edible pod of an Arabian evergreen tree (also called **locust bean**).
■ a brown floury powder extracted from the carob bean, used as a substitute for chocolate.

-ORIGIN Middle English: from Old French *carobe*, from medieval Latin *carrubia*, from Arabic *ḵarrūba*.

carpaccio /kär'päcH(ē)ō/ ▸ an Italian hors d'oeuvre consisting of thin slices of raw beef or fish served with a sauce.

-ORIGIN Italian, named after Vittore *Carpaccio*, Italian painter (from his use of red pigments, resembling raw meat).

casaba (also **cassaba**) /kə'säbə/ ▸ a winter melon with a wrinkled yellow rind and sweet flesh.

-ORIGIN named after *Kasaba* (now Turgutlu) in Turkey, from which the melons were first exported.

cascabel /'kaskə,bel/ ▸ a small red chili pepper of a mild-flavored variety.

-ORIGIN from Spanish, from Catalan *cascavel*, from medieval Latin *cascabellus* 'little bell.'

cashew (also **cashew nut**) ▸ an edible kidney-shaped nut of a tropical American tree, rich in oil and protein.

-ORIGIN from Portuguese, from Tupi *acajú*, *cajú*.

cassareep /'kasə,rēp/ ▸ a condiment made from cassava.

cassata /kə'sätə/ ▸ a Neapolitan ice cream containing candied fruit and nuts.

-ORIGIN from Italian, literally 'little case.'

cassava /kə'sävə/ ▸ the starchy tuberous root of a tropical tree, used as food in tropical countries but requiring careful preparation to remove traces of cyanide from the flesh (also called **manioc**).

■ a starch or flour obtained from such a root.

-ORIGIN from Taino *casávi*, *cazábbi*, influenced by French *cassave*.

casserole ▸ a stew that is cooked slowly in an oven: *a chicken casserole*. See word bank at **STEW**.

■ a large covered dish, typically of earthenware or glass, used for cooking such stews.

▸ to cook (food) slowly in such a dish: *casseroled chicken*.

-ORIGIN from French, diminutive of *casse* 'spoonlike container,' from Old Provençal *cassa*, from late Latin *cattia* 'ladle, pan' from Greek *kuathion*, diminutive of *kuathos* 'cup.'

cassoulet /ˌkaso͞o'lā/ ▸ a stew made with various meats and white beans.

-ORIGIN French, diminutive of dialect *cassolo* 'stewpan,' from Old Provençal *cassa* 'pan'; related to CASSEROLE.

catsup ▶ variant spelling of KETCHUP.

cauliflower ▶ a plant of the cabbage family that bears a large immature flower head of small creamy-white flower buds.
■ the flower head of this plant eaten as a vegetable.
-ORIGIN alteration (influenced by *flower*) of obsolete French *chou fleuri* 'flowered cabbage,' probably from Italian *cavolfiore* or modern Latin *cauliflora.*

caviar ▶ the pickled roe of sturgeon or other large fish, eaten as a delicacy.
-ORIGIN from obsolete Italian *caviaro*) or French *caviar*, probably from medieval Greek *khaviari.*

cayenne (also **cayenne pepper**) ▶ a pungent hot-tasting red powder prepared from ground dried chili peppers.
-ORIGIN from Tupi *kyynha*, *quiynha*, later associated with *Cayenne* in French Guiana.

celeriac /sə'lerē,ak/ ▶ a variety of celery that forms a large swollen turniplike root that can be eaten cooked or raw (also called **celery root**).
-ORIGIN from *celery* + an arbitrary use of the suffix *-ac.*

celery ▶ a cultivated plant of the parsley family, with closely packed succulent leafstalks that are eaten raw or cooked.
-ORIGIN from French *céleri*, from Italian dialect *selleri*, based on Greek *selinon* 'parsley.'

celery salt ▶ a mixture of salt and ground celery seed used for seasoning.

celery seed ▶ the seed of a plant related to the celery plant, with a celery-like flavor and aroma.

cèpe (also **cep**) /sep/ ▶ an edible mushroom with a smooth brown cap, found growing under evergreen trees and prized for its flavor.
-ORIGIN from French, from Gascon *cep* 'tree trunk, mushroom', from Latin *cippus* 'stake.'

cereal ▶ a grain used for food, such as wheat, oats, or corn.
■ a breakfast food made from roasted grain, typically eaten with milk.

Cereal Grains

amaranth	hominy	rice
barley	kamut	rye
bran	kasha	semolina
buckwheat	maize	sorghum
bulgur	malt	spelt
corn	masa	tapioca
couscous	millet	teff
farina	oat bran	triticale
flaxseed	oats	wheat
grits	polenta	wheat germ
groats	quinoa	wild rice

-ORIGIN from Latin *cerealis*, from *Ceres*, the Roman goddess of agriculture.

ceviche (also **seviche**) /sə'vēCHā/ ▶ a South American dish of marinated raw fish or seafood, typically garnished and served as an appetizer.

-ORIGIN South American Spanish.

chafing dish ▶ a metal pan with an outer pan of hot water, used for keeping food warm.

■ a metal pan, typically one containing an alcohol lamp, used for cooking at the table.

-ORIGIN from the obsolete sense of *chafe* 'become warm, warm up.'

chai /CHī/ ▶ tea, especially when made by boiling the tea leaves with milk, sugar, and cardamom.

-ORIGIN a term in various Indian languages.

challah /'hälə; 'KHälə/ ▶ a loaf of rich white bread, typically plaited in form, traditionally baked to celebrate the Jewish Sabbath.

-ORIGIN from Hebrew *ḥallah*.

chalupa /chə'lo͞opə/ ▶ a fried tortilla in the shape of a boat, with a spicy filling.

-ORIGIN Spanish, ultimately related to Dutch *sloep* 'sloop.'

chamomile (also **camomile**) ▶ an infusion of dried flowers of an aromatic perennial plant, used to make tea.

chanterelle /ˌSHantə'rel/ ▶ an edible woodland mushroom with a yellow funnel-shaped cap and a faint smell of apricots.

-ORIGIN French, from modern Latin *cantharellus*, from Latin *cantharus*, from Greek *kantharos* 'drinking container.'

chapati (also **chapatti**) /chə'pätē/ ▸ (in Indian cooking) a thin pancake of unleavened whole-grain bread cooked on a griddle.
-ORIGIN from Hindi *capātī*, from *capānā* 'flatten, roll out.'

charbroil ▸ to grill (food, especially meat) on a rack over charcoal: *charbroiled steak.*
-ORIGIN blend of *charcoal* and *broil.*

charcuterie /shär‚koōtə'rē/ ▸ cold cooked meats collectively.
■ a store selling such meats.
-ORIGIN French, from obsolete *char* 'flesh' + *cuite* 'cooked.'

chard ▸ (also **Swiss chard**) a variety of beet with broad fleshy white stalks and green leaves, eaten as a vegetable.
-ORIGIN from French *carde*, perhaps influenced by *chardon* 'thistle.'

charlotte ▸ a dessert made of stewed fruit or mousse with a casing or covering of bread, sponge cake, ladyfingers, or breadcrumbs.
-ORIGIN French, from the female name *Charlotte.*

charlotte russe /'roōs/ ▸ a dessert consisting of custard enclosed in sponge cake or a casing of ladyfingers.
-ORIGIN French, literally 'Russian charlotte.'

chateaubriand /sha‚tōbrē'än/ ▸ a thick tenderloin of beef, typically served with Béarnaise sauce.
-ORIGIN named after François-René, Vicomte de *Chateaubriand*, French writer and diplomat, whose chef is said to have created the dish.

chayote /chī'ōtē/ ▸ a green pear-shaped tropical fruit that resembles cucumber in flavor.
■ the tropical American vine that yields this fruit, also producing an edible yamlike tuberous root.
-ORIGIN from Spanish, from Nahuatl *chayotli.*

cheddar ▸ a kind of firm smooth cheese, originally made in Cheddar in southern England.

cheese ▸ a food made from the pressed curds of milk.
■ a molded mass of such food with its rind, often in a round flat shape: *a 50-pound, muslin-wrapped cheese.*
-ORIGIN Old English *cēse, cȳse*, of West Germanic origin, from Latin *caseus.*

Cheeses

American	Cantadou	Edam
anthotyros	Cantal	Edelpilzkäse
Appenzell	Capitoul baskeriu	Elbo
Aragon	Caprice des Dieux	Emmental
asiago	carré	Époisses
Aveyronnais	Castellano	Esrom
Bagnes	Castello	Estribeiro
Banon	Cebrero	Etorki
Beaufort	cendré	Explorateur
Bel paese	Chabichou du Poitou	farmer cheese
Bellamonte	Chamois d'Or	Feliciano
Bergader	Chaource	feta
bleu/blue	Charolais	Fiore Sardo
blue vinney	Chaumes	florette
Bonbel	cheddar	Fol Epi
Bonifaz	Cheshire	Fontina
boule	chèvre	Fougeru
Bourdin	Chevret	fourme
Boursin	chevrotin	Friesian
Bouyssou	Cîmes	fromage blanc
Brebicet	clabber	Fromager d'Affinois
Brebiou	clochette	Fynbo
Brebis	coeur à la crème	galotyri
Brébol	colby	Gammelost
Bresse bleu	Colwick	Gaperon
brick	Comté	Géramont
Brie	Corsu Vecchiu	gervais
Brillat-Savarin	Cotherstone	Gjetost
brique	cottage cheese	Gloucester
Brocciu	Coulommiers	goat cheese
Bruder	cream cheese	Gorgonzola
brynza	crema Danica	Gouda
Burgos	Cremoulin	Goutou
Burrini	Crescenza	Graddost
Cabrales	crottin	Grana Bagozzo
Cabreiro	crowdie	Grana Lodigiano
Cacetti	Curworthy	Grana Padano
caciotta	Danablu	Grana Piacentino
Caciovallo	Danbo	graviera
Caerphilly	Danish blue	Groviera
Cambozola	Derby	Gruyère
Camembert	Devon	halloumi
Campo de Montalban	Dolcelatte	hand cheese
Cana de Cabra	Doppelrhamstufe	Harleca
Cancoillotte	Dorset	Havarti
Canestrato	Dunlop	Henri

hoop cheese	Montrachet	Roncal
Idiazabal	mozzarella	Roquefort
Istara	muenster	Saanen
jack cheese	Murolait	Saint Agur
Jarlsberg	Mycella	Saint Albray
Jurassic	myzithra	Saint André
Kalathaki	Neufchâtel	Sainte-Maure
kashkaval	Normantal	Saint-Marcellin
kasseri	Nostrale/Nostrano	Saint-Nectaire
kefalotiri	Oka	Saint-Paulin
Kernhem	P'tit Basque	Salers
Kiri	panela	Samsoe
Klosterkaese	panir	sapsago
kopanisti	Pannerone	Sbrinz
Kumminost	Parmesan	Scamorza
La Peillouté	Parmigiano Reggiano	Schabziger
La Roche	Passendale	Selles-sur-Cher
labneh	Pecorino	Shropshire
ladotyri	Pecos	Steppe
Laguiole	Pélardon	Stilton
Lancashire	perilla	Stracchino
Langres	Peyrigoux	string cheese
Le Brin	Picandou	Suprême
Le Roulé	Picodon	Swaledale
Le Tartare	Pont L'Évêque	Swiss
Leiden	Port-Salut	Taleggio
Liederkranz	pot cheese	Teleme
Limburger	Président	Telemea
Liptauer	Prince-Jean	Tête de Moine
Livarot	provolone	Tetilla
long horn	Quargel	Tillamook
Mâçonnais	quark	Tilsit
Madrigal	Queijo Evora	Tilsiter
Mahon	queso blanco	Tintern
manouri	raclette	Tipperary
manteche	Rambol	tomme
Margotin	reblochon	Toscanello
Maribo	red Windsor	Tourrée d'Aubier
Maroilles	Ribafria	trappist cheese
mascarpone	ricotta	tvorog
metsovone	ricotta salata	Tybo
Mimolette	Ridder	Vacherin
Mirableu	robiola	Valençay
Molbo	Rocamadour	Vare
Mont d'Or	Rochebaron	Weichkaese
Montasio	Rocketou	Wensleydale
Montegrappa	Romadur	York
Monterey jack	Romano	

cheesecake ▸ a kind of rich dessert cake made with cream and soft cheese on a sweet crust, often topped with a fruit sauce.

cheesecloth ▸ thin, loosely woven cloth of cotton, used originally for making and wrapping cheese and now used especially for straining thick liquids.

cheese steak (also **Philadelphia cheese steak** or **Philly cheese steak**) ▸ a hot sandwich consisting of a large roll filled with thin slices of beef, American or provolone cheese, and sautéed onions.

cheese straw ▸ a thin strip of pastry, flavored with cheese and eaten as a snack.

chef ▸ a professional cook, typically the chief cook in a restaurant or hotel.
   -ORIGIN French, literally 'head.'

cherimoya /ˌCHerəˈmoiə/ ▸ a tropical American fruit with a flavor like pineapple and scaly green skin.
   -ORIGIN from Spanish, from Quechua, from *chiri* 'cold or refreshing' + *muya* 'circle.'

chervil ▸ the delicate fernlike leaves of a plant of the parsley family, used as a culinary herb.
   -ORIGIN Old English, from Latin *chaerephylla*, from Greek *khairephullon*.

Cheshire /ˈCHesHər/ ▸ a kind of firm crumbly cheese, originally made in Cheshire, England.

chess pie ▸ a type of pie filled with a mixture of eggs, butter, and sugar, to which nuts and fruits may be added.

chestnut ▸ a glossy brown nut of a large European tree, which is roasted before it can be eaten.
   -ORIGIN from Old English *chesten* (from Old French *chastaine*, via Latin from Greek *kastanea*) + NUT.

chèvre /ˈsHev(rə)/ ▸ cheese made with goat's milk.
   -ORIGIN French, literally 'goat, she-goat,' from Latin *capra*.

chicharron /ˌCHēCHəˈrōn/ ▸ (in Mexican cooking) a piece of fried pork crackling.
   -ORIGIN from American Spanish *chicharrón*.

chicken ▸ a domestic fowl kept for its eggs or meat, especially a young one.
   ▪ meat from such a bird: *roast chicken.*

chicken à la king ▶ diced chicken in a cream sauce with mushrooms and peppers.
−ORIGIN said to be named after E. Clark *King*, proprietor of a New York hotel.

chicken-fried steak ▶ a thin piece of beef that is lightly battered and fried until crisp, typically served with a milk gravy.
−ORIGIN perhaps because the beef is prepared like southern-fried chicken.

chickpea ▶ a round yellowish seed of an Old World legume, used widely as food (also called **garbanzo**).
−ORIGIN Middle English *chiche* (from Old French, from Latin *cicer* 'chickpea') + *pease* (see **PEA**).

chicory ▶ a blue-flowered Mediterranean plant of the daisy family, cultivated for its edible salad leaves and carrot-shaped root.
■ the root of this plant, which is roasted and ground for use as an additive to or substitute for coffee.
■ another term for **ENDIVE**.
−ORIGIN Middle English: from obsolete French *cicorée* 'endive,' via Latin from Greek *kikhorion*.
USAGE: See usage note at **ENDIVE**.

chiffon ▶ (of a dessert) made with beaten egg whites or gelatin to give a light consistency: *lemon chiffon pie*.
−ORIGIN from French, 'sheer fabric,'from *chiffe* 'rag.'

chiffonade /ˌsʜifəˈnäd/ ▶ a preparation of shredded or finely cut leaf vegetables, used as a garnish for soup.
−ORIGIN French, from *chiffonner* 'to crumple.'

chilaquiles /ˌcʜēläˈkēläs/ ▶ (in Mexican cooking) a dish of fried tortilla strips typically topped with a spicy tomato sauce and cheese.
−ORIGIN from Nahuatl.

chile relleno /ˈcʜilē rə(l)ˈyänō/ ▶ (in Mexican cooking) a chili pepper stuffed with cheese, typically battered and deep-fried.
−ORIGIN Spanish, literally 'stuffed chili.'

chili (also **chili pepper** or **chile**) ▶ a small hot-tasting pod of a variety of capsicum, often dried, and used chopped in sauces, relishes, and spice powders. There are various forms with pods of differing size, color, and strength of flavor, such as **CASCABELS** and **JALAPEÑOS**.

■ short for CHILI POWDER.

■ short for CHILI CON CARNE.

■ a meatless version of chili con carne.

–ORIGIN from Spanish *chile*, from Nahuatl *chilli*.

chili con carne ▶ a spicy stew of beef and red chilies or chili powder, often with beans and tomatoes.

–ORIGIN from Spanish *chile con carne*, literally 'chili pepper with meat.'

chili dog ▶ a hot dog garnished with chili con carne.

chili powder ▶ a hot-tasting mixture of ground dried red chilies and other spices.

chili sauce ▶ a hot sauce made with tomatoes, chilies, and spices.

chimichanga /ˌCHimēˈCHäNGgə/ ▶ (in Mexican cooking) a tortilla wrapped around a filling, typically of meat, and deep-fried.

–ORIGIN Mexican Spanish, literally 'trinket.'

China tea ▶ tea made from a small-leaved type of tea plant grown in China, typically flavored by smoke curing or the addition of flower petals.

Chinese cabbage ▶ an Asian cabbage that does not form a firm heart. Two generally available varieties are BOK CHOY and PE-TSAI.

chip ▶ a thin slice of food made crisp by being fried, baked, or dried and typically eaten as a snack: *tortilla chips | banana chips.*

■ a small chunk of candy added to baked goods, desserts, or sweet snacks, especially of chocolate.

■ (**chips**) chiefly British French fries.

–ORIGIN Middle English: related to Old English *forcippian* 'cut off.'

chipotle /CHiˈpōtlā/ ▶ a smoked hot chili pepper used especially in Mexican cooking.

–ORIGIN Mexican Spanish, from Nahuatl.

chives ▶ the long tubular leaves of a small Eurasian plant related to the onion, used as a culinary herb.

–ORIGIN Middle English: from Old French dialect *cive*, from Latin *cepa* 'onion.'

chocolate ▶ a food preparation in the form of a paste or solid block made from roasted and ground cacao seeds, typically sweetened.

■ a candy made of or covered with this.

■ a drink made by mixing milk with chocolate: *a cup of hot chocolate.*

-ORIGIN from French *chocolat* or Spanish *chocolate*, from Nahuatl *chocolatl* 'food made from cacao seeds.'

USAGE: The confection known as **white chocolate** is not really chocolate, but a mixture of cocoa butter, milk solids, sugar, and flavorings. It is often molded in various shapes and tinted in pastel colors.

chocolate chip ▶ a small piece of chocolate used in making cookies and other sweet foods.

choice ▶ of very good quality: *some choice early plums.*

■ (of beef) of the grade below prime.

choke ▶ the inedible mass of silky fibers at the center of a globe artichoke.

cholent /ˈCHôlənt/ ▶ a Jewish Sabbath dish of slowly baked meat and vegetables, prepared on a Friday and cooked overnight.

-ORIGIN from Yiddish *tsholnt.*

chop ▶ to cut (something) into small pieces: *finely chop the parsley.*

▶ a thick slice of meat, especially pork or lamb, adjacent to, and typically including, a rib.

chop suey ▶ a Chinese-style dish of meat stir fried with bean sprouts, bamboo shoots, and onions, and often served with noodles.

-ORIGIN from Chinese (Cantonese dialect) *tsaâp suì* 'mixed bits.'

USAGE: Generally thought to be an American invention and a parody of Chinese food, **chop suey** is actually a local Cantonese dish usually made with leftover vegetables.

chorizo /CHəˈrēzō/ ▶ a spicy Spanish pork sausage.

-ORIGIN Spanish.

choucroute /SHo͞oˈkro͞ot/ ▶ pickled cabbage; sauerkraut.

-ORIGIN French, alteration (influenced by *chou* 'cabbage') of German dialect *Surkrut* 'sauerkraut.'

choucroute garni /SHo͞oˈkro͞ot gärˈnē/ ▶ a French dish consisting of sauerkraut flavored with juniper and served with assorted meats.

-ORIGIN French, literally 'garnished sauerkraut.'

choux pastry /ˈSHo͞o/ ▶ a light dough which, when cooked, makes a container for sweet fillings, typically used for éclairs and profiteroles.

-ORIGIN from French *choux*, plural of *chou* 'cabbage, rosette' + PASTRY.

chow chow (also **chow-chow**) ▶ a Chinese preserve of ginger, orange peel, and other ingredients, in syrup.
■ a mixed vegetable pickle.
-ORIGIN pidgin English.

chowder ▶ a rich soup typically containing fish, clams, or corn with potatoes and onions: *clam chowder*.
-ORIGIN perhaps from French *chaudière* 'stew pot.'

chow mein ▶ a Chinese-style dish of fried noodles with shredded meat or seafood and vegetables.
-ORIGIN from Chinese *chǎo miàn* 'fried noodles.'

chuck ▶ a cut of beef that extends from the neck to the ribs, typically used for stewing.

churro /'CHŌŌrō/ ▶ in Mexico and Latin America, a deep-fried fluted dough stick or spiral, often dusted with cinnamon and sugar.
-ORIGIN Spanish.

chutney ▶ a spicy condiment made of fruits or vegetables with vinegar, spices, and sugar, originating in India.
-ORIGIN from Hindi *caṭnī*.

ciabatta /CHə'bätə/ ▶ a flattish, open-textured Italian bread with a crisp, floury crust, made with olive oil.
-ORIGIN Italian, literally 'slipper,' from its shape.

cider ▶ a drink made by crushing fruit, typically apples.
-ORIGIN Middle English: from Old French, via ecclesiastical Latin from ecclesiastical Greek *sikera*, from Hebrew *šēkār* 'strong drink.'

cilantro /si'län,trō/ ▶ another term for CORIANDER (especially the leaves).
-ORIGIN from Spanish, from Latin *coliandrum*.

cinnamon ▶ an aromatic spice made from the peeled, dried, and rolled bark of a Southeast Asian tree.
-ORIGIN Middle English: from Old French *cinnamome* (from Greek *kinnamōmon*), and Latin *cinnamon*, both from a Semitic language.

citron ▶ the large fruit of a shrubby Asian tree. The fruit is similar to a lemon, but with flesh that is less acid and peel that is thicker and more fragrant.
-ORIGIN from French, from Latin *citrus* 'citron tree.'

citrus ▸ (also **citrus fruit**) a juicy edible fruit from a tree of a genus that includes citron, lemon, lime, orange, and grapefruit.
-ORIGIN Latin, 'citron tree.'

clafoutis /klaˈfōōtē/ ▸ a tart made of fruit, typically cherries, baked in a sweet batter.
-ORIGIN French, from dialect *clafir* 'to stuff.'

clam ▸ a marine bivalve mollusk with shells of equal size, eaten raw or cooked. See SOFT-SHELL CLAM.
-ORIGIN from obsolete *clam* 'a clamp,' from Old English *clam*, *clamm* 'a bond or bondage,' of Germanic origin.

clambake ▸ an outdoor social gathering at which clams and other seafood (and often chicken, potatoes, and corn) are baked or steamed, traditionally in a pit, over heated stones and under a bed of seaweed.

clarify ▸ to melt (butter) in order to separate out the impurities.

clementine ▸ a tangerine of a deep orange-red North African variety that is grown around the Mediterranean and in South Africa.
-ORIGIN from French *clémentine*, from the male name *Clément*.

clotted cream ▸ chiefly British thick cream obtained by heating milk slowly and then allowing it to cool while the cream content rises to the top in coagulated lumps.

clove [1] ▸ the dried flower bud of a tropical tree, used as a pungent aromatic spice.
-ORIGIN Middle English: from Old French *clou de girofle*, literally 'nail of gillyflower' (from its shape), *gillyflower* being the original name of the spice.

clove[2] ▸ any of the small bulbs making up a compound bulb of garlic, shallot, etc.
-ORIGIN Old English *clufu*, of Germanic origin.

club sandwich ▸ a sandwich of meat (usually chicken and bacon), tomato, lettuce, and mayonnaise, with two layers of filling between three slices of toast or bread.

club soda ▸ another term for SODA (sense 1).

club steak ▸ another term for DELMONICO STEAK.

cobbler ▸ a fruit pie with a rich, thick, cakelike crust.

cock-a-leekie ▸ a Scottish soup traditionally made with chicken and leeks.
-ORIGIN from *cock* and LEEK.

cocktail ▸ an alcoholic drink consisting of a spirit or several spirits mixed with other ingredients, such as fruit juice, lemonade, or cream.

■ a dish consisting of small pieces of food, typically served cold at the beginning of a meal as an hors d'oeuvre: *a shrimp cocktail.*

-ORIGIN The original use was in describing a horse with a docked tail (like that of a cock); hence, a racehorse that was not a thoroughbred. The alcoholic drink sense is perhaps from the idea of an adulterated spirit.

cocoa ▸ a powder made from roasted and ground cacao seeds.

■ a hot drink made from such a powder mixed with sugar and milk or water.

-ORIGIN alteration of *cacao.*

cocoa bean ▸ a cacao seed.

Cocktails and Mixed Drinks

Alabama Slammer	Highball	Pisco Sour
Amaretto Sour	Hot Buttered Rum	Planter's Punch
American Beauty	Hot Toddy	Red Lion
Apple Jack	Irish Coffee	Rob Roy
Bellini	Jack Rose	Rum Runner
Black Russian	Kamikaze	Rusty Nail
Bloody Mary	Kir Royale	Sangria
Brandy Alexander	Lemon Drop	Screwdriver
Bronx Cocktail	Long Island Iced Tea	Sea Breeze
Caipirinha	Mai Tai	Shandy
Cape Codder	Manhattan	Sidecar
Champagne Cocktail	Margarita	Singapore Sling
Cosmopolitan	Martini	Sloe Gin Fizz
Cuba Libre	Merry Widow	Spritzer
Daiquiri	Mimosa	Stinger
Dirty Martini	Mint Julep	Tequila Sunrise
Fuzzy Navel	Mojito	Toasted Almond
Gibson	Mudslide	Tom & Jerry
Gimlet	Negroni	Tom Collins
Gin and Tonic	New York Sour	Vodka Tonic
Gin Rickey	Old Fashioned	Whiskey Sour
Grasshopper	Pimm's Cup	White Russian
Greyhound	Piña Colada	Yellow Bird
Harvey Wallbanger	Pink Lady	Zombie

cocoa butter ▸ a fatty substance obtained from cocoa beans and used in the manufacture of confectionery.

coconut (also **cocoanut**) ▸ the large, oval, brown seed of a tropical palm, consisting of a hard shell lined with edible white flesh and containing a clear liquid. It grows inside a woody husk, surrounded by fiber.

coconut milk ▸ liquid extracted from the grated flesh of mature coconuts and sold in cans.

cocotte /kô'kôt/ ▸ a heatproof small casserole in which individual portions of food can be both cooked and served. The casserole is used for various dishes that are described as *en cocotte*.
-ORIGIN from French *cocasse*, from Latin *cucuma* 'cooking container.'

cod (also **codfish**) ▸ a marine fish, eaten fresh or salted and dried.
-ORIGIN Middle English: perhaps the same as Old English *cod(d)* 'bag,' because of the fish's appearance.

coddle ▸ to cook (an egg) in water below the boiling point.

coffee ▸ a drink made from the roasted and ground beanlike seeds of a tropical shrub, served hot or iced.
■ these seeds raw, roasted and ground, or processed into a powder that dissolves in hot water: *a jar of instant coffee*. See word bank at SOFT DRINK. See also ARABICA and ROBUSTA.
-ORIGIN from Turkish *kahveh*, from Arabic *ḳahwa*, probably via Dutch *koffie*.

coffee bean ▸ a beanlike seed of the coffee shrub.

coffee cake ▸ a cake or sweet bread typically flavored with cinnamon or topped or filled with cinnamon sugar, eaten usually with coffee.

cola ▸ a brown carbonated drink that is flavored with an extract of cola nuts, or with a similar flavoring.
-ORIGIN from Temne *k'ola* 'cola nut.'

colander ▸ a perforated bowl used to strain off liquid from food, especially after cooking.
-ORIGIN Middle English: based on Latin *colare* 'to strain.'

cola nut ▸ the seed of the cola tree, which contains caffeine and is chewed or made into a drink.

Coffees

Altura	Ethiopia	Mocha/Moka
Amatitlan	Ethiopia Harrar	Moloka'i
Angola	French roast	Mysore
Antiqua	Greek	Narino
Arabica	Guatemala	Nicaragua
Baba Budans	Haiti	Oahu
Barahona	Holualoa	Oaxaca
Blawan	Honduras	Panama
Blue Java	India	Papua New Guinea
Blue Mountain	Italian roast	Peaberry
Bourbon de Coatepec	Ituri	Puerto Rico
Bourbon Santos	Ivory Coast	Reunion
Brazil	Jamaica	Robusta
Bukoba	Jampit	Rwanda
Buqisu	Java	Santo Domingo
Burundi	Kalossi	Santos
Cameroon	Kauai	Sulawesi
Casa Misael	Kenya	Sumatra
Celebes	Kilimanjaro	Tachiras
Chamba	Kivu	Tanzania
Chaqqa	Kona	Tarrazu
chicory	Kopi Luwak	Timor
China	La Lucie	Turkish
cinnamon roast	Liberica	Uganda
city roast	Los Volcanos	Venezuela
Colombia	Malabar	Viennese roast
Costa Rica	Malawi	Vietnam
Cuba	Malaysia	Yemen
Cucutas	Mandelhing	Yirgacheffe
Djimmah	Maui Kaanapali	Yunnan
Ecuador	Medellin Excelso	Zambia
El Salvador	Mexico	Zimbabwe
espresso	Mocca	

cold cuts ▸ slices of cold cooked or processed meats. See **LUNCHMEAT**.

coleslaw ▸ shredded or chopped raw cabbage and other vegetables dressed with mayonnaise or oil, vinegar, and seasonings, eaten as a salad.

–ORIGIN from Dutch *koolsla*, from *kool* 'cabbage' + *sla* (see **SLAW**).

collard ▸ a variety of cabbage, related to kale, that does not develop a heart.

■ (**collards** or **collard greens**) the leaves of the collard, used as a vegetable.

-ORIGIN reduced form of *colewort*, from *cole* 'cabbage' + *wort* 'plant, herb.'

Comice /kə'mēs/ ▸ a large yellow eating pear.

-ORIGIN from French, literally 'association, cooperative,' referring to the *Comice Horticole* of Angers, France, where this variety was developed.

commis /kə'mē/ (also **commis chef**) ▸ a junior chef.

-ORIGIN from French, 'deputy, clerk,' past participle of *commettre* 'entrust,' from Latin *committere*.

compote ▸ fruit preserved or cooked in syrup.

■ a dish consisting of fruit salad or stewed fruit, often in or with syrup.

■ a bowl-shaped dessert dish with a stem.

-ORIGIN from French, from Old French *composte* 'mixture.'

concentrated ▸ (of a substance or solution) present in a high proportion relative to other substances; having had water or other diluting agent removed or reduced: *concentrated fruit juice.*

condensed milk ▸ milk that has been thickened by evaporation and sweetened, sold in cans.

condiment ▸ a substance such as salt or ketchup that is used to add flavor to food.

-ORIGIN Middle English: from Latin *condimentum*, from *condire* 'to pickle.'

confection ▸ a dish or delicacy made with sweet ingredients: *a whipped chocolate and cream confection.*

-ORIGIN Middle English: via Old French from Latin *confectio(n-)*, from *conficere* 'put together.'

confectioner ▸ a person whose occupation is making or selling candy and other sweets.

confectioners' sugar (also **confectioner's sugar**) ▸ finely powdered sugar with cornstarch added, used for making icings and candy.

confectionery ▸ candy and other sweets considered collectively.

■ a shop that sells such items.

confit /kôN'fē/ ▸ duck or other meat cooked slowly in its own fat.

■ a jamlike preparation made from cooked fruit or vegetables.
-ORIGIN French, 'conserved,' from *confire* 'prepare.'

confiture /'känfi‚CHŏŏr/ ▶ a preparation of preserved fruit.

■ a confection.
-ORIGIN from French, from Old French, from *confit* 'confection.'

congee /'känjē/ ▶ (in Chinese cooking) broth or porridge made from rice.
-ORIGIN from Tamil *kañci.*

conserve ▶ to preserve (food, typically fruit) with sugar.

▶ a sweet food made by preserving fruit with sugar; jam.
-ORIGIN Middle English: from Old French *conserver*, from Latin *conservare* 'to preserve.'

consommé ▶ a clear soup made with concentrated stock.
-ORIGIN French, past participle of *consommer* 'consume, consummate,' from Latin *consummare* 'make complete.'

continental breakfast ▶ a light breakfast, typically consisting of coffee and rolls with butter and jam.

convection oven ▶ a cooking device that heats food by the circulation of hot air.

converted rice ▶ white rice prepared from brown rice that has been soaked, steamed under pressure, and then dried and milled.

cook ▶ to prepare (food, a dish, or a meal) by combining and heating the ingredients in various ways.

■ (of food) to be heated so that the condition required for eating is reached.

■ (**cook down**) to heat (food) and cause it to thicken and reduce in volume: *cooking down the chutney can take up to 45 minutes.*

▶ a person who prepares and cooks food, especially as a job or in a specified way: *a short order cook | a good cook.*
-ORIGIN Old English *cōc* (noun), from popular Latin *cocus*, from Latin *coquus.*

cookie ▶ a small sweet cake, typically round, flat, and crisp.
-ORIGIN from Dutch *koekje* 'little cake,' diminutive of *koek.*

cookie sheet ▶ a flat metal tray on which cookies may be baked.

cookware ▶ pots, pans, or dishes in which food can be cooked: *cast-iron cookware.*

Cooking Methods

bake
barbecue
bard
baste
batter
beat
blacken
blanch
blend
boil
boil down
bone
braise
bread
broil
brown
bruise
butterfly
can
candy
caramelize
carbonado
casserole
char broil
chop
clarify
clean
coat
coddle
concentrate
cream
crisp
crust
crystallize
cube
curdle
cure
cut in
deein
deep fry
deglaze
degrease
dehydrate
desiccate
devil
dice
draw
dredge

dress
drizzle
dry
dry-roast
dunk
dust
eviscerate
fillet
flake
flambé
float
flute
foam
fold
force
form
freeze-dry
frizzle
froth
fry
garnish
glaze
grate
grill
grind
hard-boil
hash
hull
julienne
knead
lard
macerate
marinate
mash
melt
mince
mix
mold
nap
pack
pan-broil
pan-fry
parboil
pare
pickle
pipe
plump
poach

pot
pound
preserve
pressure-cook
pureé
raise
reconstitute
reduce
refresh
render
rice
ripen
roast
roll
salt
sauté
scald
scallop
score
scramble
sear
shirr
shock
shred
sift
simmer
slice
smoke
smother
soak
soft-boil
souse
steam
steep
stew
stir
stir-fry
stuff
sweat
temper
thread
toast
toss
whip
whisk
zest

Cookies

amaretti	hermit	ratafia
animal cracker	icebox	rugelach
anisette	jumble	rusk
arrowroot	kiss	sable
bannock	kolacky	sand tart
bar	koulourakia	sandwich
Benne	kringle	shortbread
biscotti	krumkake	slice and bake
biscuit	lace	snickerdoodle
black & white	langue de chat	speculoo
blondie	lebkuchen	spice
brandy snap	lemon bar	springerle
brownie	lady finger	spritz
butter	macaroon	sugar
chew	madeleine	tassie
chocolate chip	mandelbrot	tea cake
crescent	meltaway	thumbprint
crinkle	meringue	tuile
crisp	Mexican wedding	vanilla wafer
digestive	mincemeat	wafer
fig bar	molasses	whoopie pie
florentine	mostaccioli	
fortune	oatmeal raisin	**Trademarks**
garibaldi	palm leaf	
ginger	peanut butter	*Fig Newton*
gingersnap	pecan sandie	*Lorna Doone*
Girl Scout	pepparkakor	*Mallomar*
graham cracker	petit beurre	*Oreo*
hamantashen	pfeffernüsse	*Rice Krispie Treat*
haystack	pinwheel	*Toll House*

coq au vin /ˌkōk ō ˈvan/ ▸ a casserole of chicken pieces cooked in red wine.

–ORIGIN French, literally 'cock in wine.'

coral ▸ the unfertilized roe of a lobster or scallop, which is used as food and becomes reddish when cooked.

cordial ▸ another term for LIQUEUR. See word bank at SPIRIT.

cordon bleu /ˌkôrdôN ˈblo͞o/ ▸ of the highest class: *a cordon bleu chef.*

■ denoting a dish consisting of an escalope of veal or chicken rolled, filled with cheese and ham, and then fried in breadcrumbs: *chicken cordon bleu.*

▸ a cook of the highest class.

–ORIGIN French, literally 'blue ribbon,' which once signified the highest order of chivalry in the reign of the Bourbon kings.

coriander ▸ the leaves and seeds of an aromatic Mediterranean plant of the parsley family, which are used as culinary herbs.

–ORIGIN Middle English: from Old French *coriandre*, from Latin *coriandrum*, from Greek *koriannon*.

corn ▸ a North American cereal plant that yields large grains, or kernels, set in rows on a cob. Its many varieties yield numerous products for human and livestock consumption.

■ British the chief cereal crop of a district, especially (in England) wheat or (in Scotland) oats.

–ORIGIN Old English, of Germanic origin.

USAGE: See usage note at MUFFIN.

cornbread (also **corn bread**) ▸ a type of bread made from cornmeal and typically leavened without yeast.

corn dog ▸ a hot dog covered in cornmeal batter, fried, and served on a stick.

corned beef (also **corn beef**) ▸ beef brisket cured in brine and boiled, served hot typically with cabbage, or cold, sliced for sandwiches.

–ORIGIN *corned*, in the sense 'preserved in salt water.'

cornflakes ▸ a breakfast cereal consisting of toasted flakes made from corn.

corn flour ▸ flour made from corn.

cornmeal ▸ meal made from corn.

corn oil ▸ an oil obtained from the germ of corn, used in cooking and salad dressings.

corn pone ▸ unleavened cornbread in the form of flat oval cakes or loaves.

–ORIGIN *corn + pone* Algonquian 'bread.'

cornstarch ▸ finely ground corn flour, used as a thickener in cooking.

corn syrup ▸ syrup made from cornstarch, consisting of dextrose, maltose, and dextrins.

cos /käs/ (also **cos lettuce**) ▸ another term for ROMAINE.

–ORIGIN named after the Aegean island of *Cos*, where it originated.

cottage cheese ▸ soft, lumpy white cheese made from the curds of skimmed milk.

coulibiac /kōō'lēbyäk/ ▸ a Russian fish pie typically made with salmon or sturgeon, hard-boiled eggs, mushrooms, and herbs, in a puff pastry shell.
–ORIGIN from Russian *kulebyaka*.

coulis /'kōōlē/ ▸ a thin fruit or vegetable purée, used as a sauce.
–ORIGIN French, from *couler* 'to flow.'

courgette /kŏŏr'zHet/ ▸ British a zucchini.
–ORIGIN from French, diminutive of *courge* 'gourd,' from Latin *cucurbita*.

court bouillon ▸ a stock made from wine and vegetables, typically used in fish dishes.
–ORIGIN French, from *court* 'short' and BOUILLON.

couscous /'kōōs,kōōs/ ▸ a type of North African semolina in granules made from crushed durum wheat.
■ a spicy dish made by steaming or soaking such granules and adding meat, vegetables, or fruit.
–ORIGIN from French, from Arabic *kuskus*, from *kaskasa* 'to pound.'

couverture /,kōōver't(y)ŏŏr/ ▸ chocolate made with extra cocoa butter to give a high gloss, used for covering sweets and cakes.
–ORIGIN French, literally 'covering.'

crab ▸ a crustacean with a broad upper shell and five pairs of legs, the first pair of which are modified as pincers, many varieties of which are used as food. See SOFT-SHELL CRAB.

cracked wheat ▸ grains of wheat that have been crushed into small pieces.

cracker ▸ a thin, crisp wafer often eaten with cheese or other savory toppings.

crackling ▸ the crisp, fatty skin of roast pork.

cranberry ▸ a small, red, tart berry used in cooking.
–ORIGIN from German *Kranbeere* or Low German *kranebeere* 'crane-berry.'

cranberry sauce ▸ a jellied sauce made from cranberries, a traditional accompaniment to turkey.

crayfish ▸ a freshwater crustacean that resembles a small lobster and inhabits streams and rivers.

■ another term for SPINY LOBSTER.

–ORIGIN Middle English: from Old French *crevice*, of Germanic origin. The second syllable was altered by association with *fish*.

cream ▸ the thick white or pale yellow fatty liquid that rises to the top when milk is left to stand and that can be eaten as an accompaniment to desserts or used as a cooking ingredient.

■ a sauce, soup, dessert, or similar food containing cream or milk or having the consistency of cream: *cream of mushroom soup.*

■ a candy of a specified flavor that is creamy in texture, typically covered with chocolate: *a peppermint cream.*

▸ to work (butter, typically with sugar) to form a smooth soft paste.

■ to mash (a cooked vegetable) and mix with milk or cream: *creamed turnips.*

–ORIGIN Middle English: from Old French *cresme*, from a blend of late Latin *cramum* and ecclesiastical Latin *chrisma* 'anointing.'

cream cheese ▸ soft, rich cheese made from unskimmed milk and cream.

cream of tartar ▸ a white, crystalline, acidic compound obtained as a by-product of wine fermentation and used chiefly in baking powder.

cream puff ▸ a small cake made of choux pastry filled with cream.

cream soda ▸ a carbonated, vanilla-flavored soft drink.

crème anglaise /'krem äNG'glez/ ▸ a rich egg custard.

–ORIGIN French, literally 'English cream.'

crème brûlée /'krem brōō'lā/ ▸ a dessert of custard topped with caramelized sugar.

–ORIGIN French, literally 'burned cream.'

crème caramel /'krem ˌkarə'mel/ ▸ a custard dessert made with whipped cream and eggs and topped with caramel.

–ORIGIN French, literally 'caramel custard.'

crème fraiche /'krem 'fresH/ ▸ a type of thick cream made from heavy cream with the addition of buttermilk, sour cream, or yogurt.

–ORIGIN from French *crème fraîche*, literally 'fresh cream.'

Creole (also **creole**) /ˈkrēōl/ ▸ in the style of Louisiana cooking that blends French, Spanish, and Afro-Caribbean ingredients and flavors. See also CAJUN.

crepe (also **crêpe**) ▸ a thin pancake, often filled and rolled up.
-ORIGIN French, from Old French *crespe* 'curled, frizzed,' from Latin *crispus*.

crêpe suzette ▸ a thin dessert pancake flamed and served in alcohol.

crépinette /ˌkrāpəˈnet/ ▸ a flat sausage consisting of minced meat and savory stuffing wrapped in pieces of pork caul.
-ORIGIN French, diminutive of *crêpine* 'caul.'

crimp ▸ to compress (the edge of pastry dough) into small folds or ridges.

crinkle-cut ▸ (esp. of French fries) cut with wavy edges.

crisp ▸ (of baked goods or other foods) firm, dry, and brittle in a way considered desirable: *crisp bacon.*

■ (of a fruit or vegetable) firm, indicating freshness: *crisp lettuce.*

▸ a dessert of fruit baked with a crunchy topping of brown sugar, butter, and flour: *rhubarb crisp.*

■ (also **potato crisp**) British term for POTATO CHIP.

▸ to give (food) a crisp surface by placing it in an oven or grill.

■ (of food) to acquire a crisp surface in this way.

crisper ▸ a compartment at the bottom of a refrigerator for storing fruit and vegetables.

croissant /k(r)wäˈsänt/ ▸ a French crescent-shaped roll made of sweet flaky pastry, often eaten for breakfast.
-ORIGIN French, literally 'crescent.'

crookneck (also **crookneck squash**) ▸ a squash of a club-shaped variety with a curved neck and bumpy skin.

croquembouche /ˌkrōkəmˈbo͞oSH/ ▸ a decorative dessert consisting of cream puff pastry and crystallized fruit or other confectionery items arranged in a cone and held together by a caramel sauce.
-ORIGIN French, literally 'crunch in the mouth.'

croquette ▸ a small roll of chopped vegetables, meat, or fish, fried in breadcrumbs: *a potato croquette.*
-ORIGIN French, from *croquer* 'to crunch.'

crostini /krôˈstēnē/ ▸ small pieces of toasted or fried bread served with a topping as an appetizer or canapé.

-ORIGIN Italian, plural of *crostino* 'little crust.'

croustade /krŏo'städ/ ▸ a crisp piece of bread or pastry hollowed to receive a savory filling.
-ORIGIN French, from Old French *crouste* or Italian *crostata* 'tart' (from *crosta* 'crust').

croute /krŏot/ ▸ a piece of toasted bread on which savory snacks can be served. See also EN CROUTE.
-ORIGIN French *croûte* (see CRUST).

crouton ▸ a small piece of fried or toasted bread served with soup or used as a garnish.
-ORIGIN from French *croûton*, from *croûte* (see CRUST).

crown roast ▸ a roast of rib pieces of pork or lamb arranged like a crown in a circle with the bones pointing upward.

crudités /ˌkrŏodə'tā/ ▸ assorted raw vegetables served as an hors d'oeuvre, typically with a sauce into which they may be dipped.
-ORIGIN plural of French *crudité* 'rawness, crudity,' from Latin *crudus* 'raw, rough.'

cruet ▸ a small container for salt, pepper, oil, or vinegar for use at a dining table.
-ORIGIN Middle English: from Anglo-Norman French, diminutive of Old French *crue* 'pot,' from Old Saxon *krūka*; related to *crock*.

cruller ▸ a small cake made of rich dough twisted or curled and fried in deep fat.
-ORIGIN from Dutch *kruller*, from *krullen* 'to curl.'

crumb ▸ a small fragment of bread, cake, or cracker.
■ the soft inner part of a bread.
■ a dessert topping made of brown sugar, butter, flour, and spices and crumbled over a pie or cake.
-ORIGIN Old English *cruma*, of Germanic origin. The final *-b* was added perhaps from *crumble*.

crumble ▸ to cause (food) to break apart into small fragments: *to crumble blue cheese.*
▸ British a mixture of flour and butter that is rubbed to the texture of breadcrumbs and cooked as a topping for fruit.
■ a dessert made with such a topping and a particular fruit: *rhubarb crumble.*
□ **crumbly**: *mix the flour and fat till crumbly.*

crumpet ▸ a thick, flat, savory cake with a soft, porous texture, made from a yeast mixture cooked on a griddle and eaten toasted and buttered.

crush ▸ a drink made from the juice of pressed fruit: *lemon crush.*

crust ▸ the tough outer part of a bread.
- a slice of bread from the end of the loaf.
- a layer of pastry covering a pie.
-ORIGIN Middle English: from Old French *crouste*, from Latin *crusta* 'rind, shell, crust.'

crystallize ▸ to coat and impregnate (fruit or petals) with sugar as a means of preserving them: *a box of crystallized fruits.*

Cuban sandwich ▸ a type of submarine sandwich, typically grilled, especially with ham, roast pork, Swiss cheese, mustard, and pickles.

cube ▸ to cut (food) into small cubes.
- to tenderize (meat) by scoring a pattern of small squares into its surface: *cubed steaks.*

cucumber ▸ a long, green-skinned fruit of a climbing vine of the gourd family. The fruit has watery flesh and is usually eaten raw in salads or pickled.
-ORIGIN Middle English: from Old French *cocombre*, *coucombre*, from Latin *cucumis*, *cucumer-*.

cuisine ▸ a style or method of cooking, especially as characteristic of a particular country, region, or establishment: *Venetian cuisine.*
- food cooked in a certain way: *sampling the local cuisine.*
-ORIGIN French, literally 'kitchen.'

culinary ▸ of or for cooking.
-ORIGIN from Latin *culinarius*, from *culina* 'kitchen.'

Cumberland sauce ▸ a piquant sauce served as a relish with game and cold meats. It is typically made from red currant jelly flavored with orange, mustard, and port.

cumin /'kəmin; 'k(y)o͞o-/ ▸ the aromatic seeds of a plant of the parsley family, used as a spice, especially ground and used in curry powder.
-ORIGIN Middle English from Old French, from Latin *cuminum*, from Greek *kuminon*, probably of Semitic origin.

cup ▸ a small, bowl-shaped container for drinking from, typically having a handle and used with a matching saucer for hot drinks.

■ a measure of capacity used in cooking, equal to half a pint (0.237 liter).

-ORIGIN Old English: from popular Latin *cuppa*, probably from Latin *cupa* 'tub.'

cupcake ▸ a small cake baked in a cup-shaped container and typically iced.

curd ▸ (also **curds**) a soft, white substance formed when milk coagulates, used as the basis for cheese.

curdle ▸ to separate or cause to separate into curds or lumps: *making cheese by curdling milk.*

-ORIGIN frequentative of obsolete *curd* 'congeal.'

cure ▸ to preserve (meat, fish, etc.) by various methods such as salting, drying, or smoking: *farmers who cure their own bacon | home-cured ham.*

curly endive ▸ see ENDIVE.

curly kale ▸ kale of a variety with dark green, tightly curled leaves.

currant ▸ a small dried fruit made from a seedless variety of grape originally grown in the eastern Mediterranean region, now widely produced in California, and much used in baking.

■ a small edible black, red, or white berry from a Eurasian shrub.

-ORIGIN Middle English *raisons of Corauntz*, translating Anglo-Norman French *raisins de Corauntz* 'grapes of *Corinth*' (the original source).

curry ▸ a dish of meat, vegetables, etc., cooked in an Indian-style sauce of strong spices and turmeric and typically served with rice.

■ curry powder.

▸ to prepare or flavor with a sauce of hot-tasting spices: *curried chicken.*

-ORIGIN from Tamil *kari.*

curry powder ▸ a mixture of finely ground spices, such as turmeric, ginger, and coriander, used for making curry.

custard ▸ a dessert or sauce made by heating milk, eggs, and usually sugar, and cooking below the boiling point.

-ORIGIN Middle English *crustarde*, *custarde* (an open pie containing meat or fruit), from Old French *crouste* (see CRUST).

cut ▶ a piece of meat cut from a carcass: *a good lean cut of beef.*

cutlet ▶ a portion of sliced meat breaded and served either grilled or fried.

■ a flat croquette of minced meat, nuts, or beans, typically covered in breadcrumbs and shaped like a veal chop.

–ORIGIN from French *côtelette*, earlier *costelette*, diminutive of *coste* 'rib,' from Latin *costa*.

Cuts of Meat

American leg	chuck blade roast	heel of round
arm roast	club steak	hindshank
arm steak	cold cut	hock
baby back rib	corned beef	joint
back fat	country style rib	jowl
back rib	cross rib roast	Kansas city strip
bacon	crosscut shank	kidney
baron	crown roast	knuckles
belly	cube steak	lard
blade	culotte steak	liver
blade Boston	cushion shoulder	loin
blade chop	cutlet	lung
blade loin	Delmonico	marrow
Boston shoulder	drumstick	medallion
braciola	eye of round	mountain oyster
brains	fatback	neck
breast	filet	neck slice
brisket	filet mignon	New York sirloin
burger	fillet	noisette
butt	flank	numbles
butterfly	flanken	offal
butterfly chop	flitch	oxtail
Canadian bacon	foie gras	paillard
cap steak	fore shank	pastrami
caul	frenched leg	picnic
center loin	gammon	pig tail
center rib	gizzards	pig's foot
charcuterie	ground chuck	pin bone sirloin
charqui	ground round	plate
Chateaubriand	ground sirloin	porterhouse
chitterlings	ham	pot roast
chop	hamburger	prairie oyster
chuck	heart	prosciutto

rack	short loin	strip steak
rib	short rib	suet
rib chop	shortplate	sweetbread
rib eye	shoulder	Swiss steak
rib roast	sirloin	T-bone
rib tip	sirloin chop	tenderloin
riblet	sirloin tip	testicle
roast	skirt steak	thigh
rolled leg	slab bacon	tongue
rolled roast	sparerib	top loin
round bone sirloin	Spencer steak	top sirloin
rump	spleen	tournedo
saddle	square shoulder	triangle steak
Salisbury steak	St. Louis style rib	tripe
salt pork	standing rib roast	tri-tip
sandwich steak	steak	umbles
shank	steamboat round	veal
shell steak	stew meat	wedge bone sirloin
shin	stomach	wing

D

daikon /ˈdīkän/ ▸ a radish with a large slender white root that is eaten raw or cooked, especially in Asian cuisine.

-ORIGIN Japanese, from *dai* 'large' + *kon* 'root.'

dal ▸ variant spelling of DHAL.

dandelion greens ▸ fresh dandelion leaves eaten raw in salads or cooked as a vegetable.

Danish (also **Danish pastry**) ▸ a pastry made of sweetened yeast dough with toppings or fillings such as fruit, nuts, or cheese.

Danish blue ▸ a soft, salty, strong-flavored white cheese with blue veins.

dariole /ˈdarē͵ōl/ ▸ (in French cooking) a small, round metal mold in which an individual sweet or savory dish is cooked and served.

-ORIGIN Middle English: from Old French.

Darjeeling /därˈjēliNG/ ▸ a high-quality tea grown in the mountainous regions of northern India.

dark chocolate ▸ slightly bitter chocolate, of a deep brown color, without added milk.

date ▸ a sweet, dark brown, oval fruit containing a hard stone, usually eaten dried.

-ORIGIN Middle English: from Old French, via Latin from Greek *daktulos* 'finger,' because of the fingerlike shape of its leaves.

daube /dōb/ ▸ a stew of meat, typically beef, braised slowly in wine. Meat cooked in this way is described as *en daube*.

-ORIGIN French; compare with Italian *addobbo* 'seasoning.'

dauphinois /͵dôfinˈwä/ (also **dauphinoise** /-ˈwäz/) ▸ (of potatoes or other vegetables) sliced and cooked in milk, typically with a topping of cheese.

-ORIGIN French, 'from the province of Dauphiné.'

decaf ▶ decaffeinated coffee.

decaffeinate ▶ to remove most or all of the caffeine from (coffee or tea): *decaffeinated coffee.*

deep-dish ▶ (of a pie) baked in a deep dish to allow for a large filling.

■ (of a pizza) baked in a deep dish and having a thick dough base, as opposed to thin-crust pizza.

deep-fry ▶ to fry (food) in an amount of fat or oil sufficient to cover it completely: *deep-fried onion rings.*

deglaze ▶ to dilute meat sediments in (a pan) in order to make a gravy or sauce, typically using wine.

-ORIGIN from French *déglacer.*

delicatessen ▶ a store or a section of a supermarket selling cold cuts, cheeses, and salads, as well as a selection of unusual or foreign prepared foods.

■ foods of this type collectively.

-ORIGIN from German *Delikatessen* or Dutch *delicatessen*, from French *délicatesse* 'delicateness,' from *délicat.*

Delicious ▶ a red or yellow variety of eating apple with a sweet flavor and a slightly elongated shape.

Delmonico steak /delˈmäniˌkō/ ▶ a small steak cut from the front section of the short loin of beef (also called **club steak**).

-ORIGIN named for Lorenzo *Delmonico*, Swiss-born U.S. restaurateur.

demerara /ˌdeməˈre(ə)rə/ (also **demerara sugar**) ▶ light brown cane sugar coming originally and chiefly from Guyana.

-ORIGIN named after the region of *Demerara.*

demi-glace /ˈdemē ˌglas/ (also **demi-glaze** /ˌglāz/) ▶ a rich, glossy brown sauce from which the liquid has been partly evaporated, typically flavored with wine and served with meat.

-ORIGIN French, literally 'half glaze.'

demitasse /ˈdemiˌtas/ ▶ a small coffee cup.

-ORIGIN from French, literally 'half-cup.'

Derby ▸ a hard pressed cheese made from skimmed milk, chiefly in the county of Derbyshire in England.

derma ▸ beef or chicken intestine, stuffed and cooked in dishes such as kishke.

-ORIGIN from Yiddish *derme*, plural of *darm* 'intestine.'

dessert ▸ the sweet course eaten at the end of a meal. See word bank at CAKE.

-ORIGIN from French, past participle of *desservir* 'clear the table.'

dessert wine ▸ a sweet wine drunk with or following dessert.

devein ▸ to remove the main central vein from (a shrimp or prawn).

deviled ▸ (of food) cooked or prepared with hot seasoning: *deviled eggs*.

devil's food cake ▸ a rich chocolate cake.

Devonshire cream ▸ clotted cream.

dhal (also **dal**) /däl/ ▸ split lentils or other legumes, a common foodstuff in India.

▪ a dish made with these.

-ORIGIN from Hindi *dāl*.

dhansak /'dən,säk/ ▸ an Indian dish of meat or vegetables cooked with lentils and coriander: *chicken dhansak*.

-ORIGIN Gujarati.

dice ▸ small cubes of food.

▸ to cut (food or other matter) into small cubes.

digestif /,dējes'tēf/ ▸ a drink or portion of food drunk or eaten in order to aid the digestion.

-ORIGIN French, literally 'digestive.'

dill (also **dillweed**) ▸ the fine blue-green leaves or seeds of an aromatic herb of the parsley family, used fresh or dried to flavor food.

dill pickle ▸ a pickled cucumber flavored with dill.

dim sum /'dim 'səm/ ▸ a Chinese dish of small steamed or fried savory dumplings containing various fillings, served as a snack or main course.

-ORIGIN from Chinese (Cantonese dialect) *tim sam*, from *tim* 'dot' and *sam* 'heart.'

dip ▸ a thick sauce in which pieces of food are dunked before eating.

■ a quantity that has been scooped up from a mass: *ice cream sold by the dip.*

distill /dis'til/ ▸ to purify (a liquid) by vaporizing it, then condensing it by cooling the vapor, and collecting the resulting liquid: *distilled water.*

■ to make (especially liquor or an essence) in this way: *whiskey is distilled from a mash of grains* | *the distilling industry.*

divinity ▸ a fluffy, creamy candy made with stiffly beaten egg whites.

Dobos Torte /'dôbəsH 'tôrtə/ ▸ a rich cake made of alternate layers of sponge and chocolate or mocha cream, with a crisp caramel topping.
–ORIGIN from German *Dobostorte*, named after József C. *Dobos*, Hungarian pastry cook.

dolma /'dôlmə/ ▸ a Greek and Turkish delicacy in which ingredients such as rice, meat, and spices are wrapped in vine or cabbage leaves.
–ORIGIN from modern Greek *ntolmas* or its source, Turkish *dolma*, from *dolmak* 'fill, be filled.'

double boiler ▸ a saucepan with a detachable upper compartment heated by boiling water in the lower one.

double cream ▸ British term for HEAVY CREAM.

dough ▸ a thick, malleable mixture of flour and liquid, used for baking into bread or pastry.
–ORIGIN Old English *dāg*, of Germanic origin.

doughnut (also **donut**) ▸ a small fried cake of sweetened dough, typically in the shape of a ball or ring.

drawn butter ▸ melted butter.

dressing ▸ (also **salad dressing**) a sauce for salads, typically one consisting of oil and vinegar mixed together with herbs or other flavorings.

■ stuffing for poultry.

drippings ▸ the melted fat and juices that have dripped from roasting meat, used in gravies.

drizzle ▸ a thin stream of a liquid ingredient trickled over something.
▸ to cause a thin stream of (a liquid ingredient) to trickle over food: *drizzle the melted butter over the top.*

■ to cause a liquid ingredient to trickle over (food) in this way.

Doughnuts and Deep-fried Sweets

aebleskiver	dango	malassadas
awwamath	doughnut	maple bar
bear claw	elephant ear	nien koh
beignet	farsangi fank	oliebollen
Berliner	fastnacht	paczki
bimuelo	fillozes	pampushky
bismark	French cruller	piskota fank
bitsu-bitsu	fried ice cream	pizzelle
buñuelo	fritter	poffertges
cala	funnel cake	puff
cascaron	hojuela	sata andagi
cenci	jalebi	sfenji
chiacchiere	jelly doughnut	shisky
chrusciki	kooksistas	sopaipilla
churro	laddu	sufganiyot
cruller	longjohn	viccitelli
csoroge	loukoumades	zeppole

drop scone ▸ a small thick pancake made by dropping spoonfuls of batter onto a frying pan or other heated surface.

drumstick ▸ the lower joint of the leg of a cooked chicken, turkey, or other fowl.

dry ▸ (of bread or toast) without butter or other spreads.

▸ to preserve by allowing or encouraging evaporation of moisture: *dried fruit.*

dry-salt ▸ to cure (meat or fish) with salt rather than in liquid.

duchesse potatoes /d(y)o͞o'sHes/ ▸ mashed potatoes mixed with egg yolk, formed into small shapes and baked.

duck ▸ a waterbird with webbed feet, used as food.

duckling ▸ the flesh of a young duck as food.

dulce /'dəlsä/ ▸ a sweet food or drink, especially a candy or jam. -ORIGIN Spanish.

dum ▸ (in Indian cuisine) cooked with steam: *dum aloo.* -ORIGIN from Hindi *dam.*

dumpling ▸ a small savory ball of dough that may be boiled, fried, or baked in a casserole.

■ a pudding consisting of apples or other fruit enclosed in a sweet dough and baked.

-ORIGIN apparently from the rare adjective *dump* 'of the consistency of dough.'

Dundee marmalade ▸ a type of orange marmalade, originally made
in Dundee, Scotland.

dust ▸ to cover lightly with a powdered substance: *roll out the dough
on a surface dusted with flour.*

■ sprinkle (a powdered substance) onto something.

Dutch oven ▸ a large, heavy cooking pot with a lid.

duxelles /do͞ok'sel/ ▸ a preparation of mushrooms sautéed with
onions, shallots, garlic, and parsley and used to make stuffing or
sauce.

-ORIGIN named after the Marquis *d'Uxelles*, 17th-cent. French nobleman.

LET US NOW PRAISE
FAMOUS BARS

A brief and embarrassingly subjective listing of the Top 10 candy bars on planet Earth:

10. *Heath Bar*
The only thing better than butter toffee is butter toffee enrobed in milk chocolate.

9. *Big Hunk*
A comely slab of chewy vanilla nougat, shot through with fried peanuts. If you love the flavor of cake batter, the Hunk is your dreamboat.

8. *Snickers*
Quit laughing. America's top selling candy bar also happens to be one of its best. The key is its exquisite nougat, which has a hint of cinnamon flavor.

7. *Twin Bing*
Narrowly beats out the Idaho Spud as the strangest candy bar still in production. A cherry cream surrounded by a lump (and we do mean *lump*) of chocolate and ground peanuts.

6. *Five Star Bar Hazelnut*
This gourmet bar combines crushed hazelnuts, Belgian chocolate, and feuilletine, a crushed pastry that lends the bar its addictive texture.

5. *Hershey's Cookies N Mint*
Hershey committed a crime against mint lovers when they discontinued this sublime bar.

4. *Raisinettes*
Finally, a raisin d'etre for the common raisin.

3. *Sifer's Valomilk*
A rich vanilla syrup in a creamy chocolate cup, this confection is built to spill. Your tongue (and your dry cleaner) will thank you.

2. *Kit Kat Dark*
The bittersweet coating tastes like a fine chocolate pudding, with hints of French Roast. Devotees have been known to drive across state lines in pursuit of this limited edition.

1. *Caravelle*
Ladies and gentlemen, the greatest candy bar you've never tasted. The Caravelle, sadly extinct, boasted the same ingredients as the *100 Grand*—caramel, crisped rice, milk chocolate—but was approximately 100 times better. To be mathematically precise, then, a *10 Million Dollar Bar*.

Steve Almond is a radio commentator and the author of *Candyfreak: A Journey Through the Chocolate Underbelly of America*.

E

Earl Grey ▶ a kind of China tea flavored with bergamot.

-ORIGIN probably named after the 2nd *Earl Grey* (1764–1845), said to have been given the recipe by a Chinese mandarin.

éclair (also **eclair**) ▶ a small, log-shaped choux pastry filled with cream and typically topped with chocolate icing.

-ORIGIN from French, literally 'lightning.'

Edam ▶ a round Dutch cheese, typically pale yellow with a red wax coating.

-ORIGIN named after the Dutch town of *Edam*.

eddo /ˈedō/ ▶ a taro corm or plant, especially of a West Indian variety with many edible cormlets.

-ORIGIN from a West African language.

effervescent ▶ (of a liquid) giving off bubbles; fizzy.

-ORIGIN from Latin *effervescent*- 'boiling up,' from the verb *effervescere*.

egg ▶ an oval or round object laid by a female bird, reptile, fish, or invertebrate.

■ an infertile egg, typically of the domestic hen, used for food.

■ a thing resembling a bird's egg in shape: *chocolate eggs*.

-ORIGIN Middle English (superseding earlier *ey*, from Old English *ǣg*): from Old Norse.

egg cream ▶ a drink consisting of soda water and milk, flavored with syrup.

USAGE: The **egg cream**, a popular soda fountain treat, contains neither egg nor cream. The name comes from the foamy head that forms when milk is added to the flavored soda water, that resembles beaten egg whites.

egg foo yung ▸ see FOO YUNG.

eggnog ▸ a drink made from a mixture of eggs, cream, and flavorings, often with alcohol.

eggplant ▸ the large egg-shaped fruit of a tropical Old World plant, eaten as a vegetable. Its skin is typically dark purple, but the skin of certain cultivated varieties is white or yellow.

egg roll ▸ a Chinese-style snack consisting of diced meat or shrimp and shredded vegetables wrapped in a dough made with egg and deep-fried.

eggs Benedict ▸ a dish consisting of poached eggs and sliced ham on toasted English muffins, covered with hollandaise sauce.

Emmental (also **Emmenthal**) /ˈemənˌtäl/ ▸ a kind of hard Swiss cheese with many holes in it, similar to Gruyère.
-ORIGIN from German *Emmentaler*, from *Emmental*, valley in Switzerland where the cheese was originally made.

empanada /ˌempəˈnädə/ ▸ a Spanish or Latin American pastry turnover filled with a variety of savory ingredients and baked or fried.
-ORIGIN Spanish, feminine past participle (used as a noun) of *empanar* 'roll in pastry,' based on Latin *panis* 'bread.'

Empire ▸ a variety of apple that is a hybrid of the Red Delicious and McIntosh.
-ORIGIN named after the *Empire State*, nickname of New York.

emulsion ▸ a fine dispersion of minute droplets of one liquid in another in which it is not soluble, for example, oil in vinegar.

enchilada /ˌenCHəˈlädə/ ▸ (in Mexican cooking) a rolled tortilla with a filling typically of meat, served with a chili sauce.
-ORIGIN Latin American Spanish, feminine past participle of *enchilar* 'season with chili.'

en croute /än ˈkro͞ot/ ▸ in a pastry crust: *salmon en croute* | *goat's cheese baked en croute.* See also CROUTE.
-ORIGIN French *en croûte*.

endive ▸ an edible Mediterranean plant whose bitter leaves may be blanched and used in salads. The plant has curly-leaved and smooth-leaved varieties.
 ■ (also **Belgian endive**) a young, typically blanched chicory plant, eaten as a cooked vegetable or in salads.

-ORIGIN Middle English: via Old French from medieval Latin *endivia*, based on Greek *entubon*.

USAGE: Although **chicory** and **endive** are botanically related and share a slightly bitter taste, these terms are usually not interchangeable. **Chicory** has a lettucelike bunch of ragged-edged leaves. The **endive**, or **Belgian endive**, has whitish elongated leaves. **Curly endive** and **radicchio** are varieties of chicory, and **escarole** is a variety of endive. To add to the confusion, chicory is called endive in Britain.

English muffin ▶ a flat circular spongy bread roll made from yeast dough and eaten split, toasted, and buttered.

enoki /i'nōkē/ ▶ an edible Japanese mushroom, growing in clusters, with slender stems and small caps.

-ORIGIN from Japanese *enoki-take*, from *enoki* 'nettle-tree' + *take* 'mushroom.'

en papillote /än ˌpapē'yōt/ ▶ (of food) cooked and served in a paper wrapper: *fish en papillote*.

-ORIGIN French.

entrecôte /'äntrəˌkōt/ ▶ a boned steak cut off of the sirloin.

-ORIGIN French, from *entre* 'between' + *côte* 'rib.'

entrée (also **entree**) ▶ the main course of a meal.

■ a dish served before the main course or between the fish and meat courses at a formal dinner.

-ORIGIN French, feminine past participle of *entrer* 'enter.'

entremets /ˌäntrə'mā/ ▶ a light dish served between two courses of a formal meal.

-ORIGIN French, from *entre* 'between' + *mets* 'dish.'

escabeche /ˌeskä'becHä/ ▶ a Spanish dish consisting of fried fish that is marinated and served cold.

-ORIGIN Spanish.

escallop /i'skäləp/ ▶ another term for SCALLOP.

-ORIGIN from Old French *escalope* 'shell.'

escalope /ˌeskə'lōp/ ▶ a thin slice of meat without any bone, typically a special cut of veal from the leg, that is coated, fried, and served in a sauce (also called **scallop**).

-ORIGIN French; compare with ESCALLOP and SCALLOP.

escargot /ˌeskärˈgō/ ▸ a snail, especially as an item on a menu.
–ORIGIN French, from Old French *escargol*, from Provençal *escaragol*.

escarole ▸ an endive with broad undivided leaves and a slightly bitter flavor, used in salads.
–ORIGIN from French, from Italian *scar(i)ola*, based on Latin *esca* 'food.'
USAGE: See usage note at ENDIVE.

espresso /isˈpresō/ ▸ strong black coffee made by forcing steam through ground coffee beans.
–ORIGIN from Italian *(caffè) espresso*, literally 'pressed out (coffee).'
USAGE: The often-occurring variant spelling **expresso**—and its pronunciation /ikˈspresō/—is incorrect and was probably formed by analogy with **express**.

étouffée /ˌāˌtōōˈfā/ ▸ a spicy Cajun stew made with vegetables and seafood.
–ORIGIN Louisiana French, from French *(a l') étouffée* 'stewed.'

evaporated milk ▸ thick milk that has had some of the liquid removed by evaporation.

extract ▸ a preparation containing the active ingredient of a substance in concentrated form: *vanilla extract.*

extra-virgin ▸ denoting a particularly fine grade of olive oil made from the first pressing of the olives and containing a maximum of one percent oleic acid.

eye ▸ a center cut of meat: *eye of round.*

F

----

fajita /fä'hētä/ (often **fajitas**) ▸ a dish of Mexican origin consisting of strips of spiced beef or chicken, chopped vegetables, and grated cheese, wrapped in a soft tortilla and often served with sour cream.

-ORIGIN Mexican Spanish, literally 'little strip or belt.'

falafel (also **felafel**) /fə'läfəl/ ▸ a Middle Eastern dish of spiced mashed chickpeas or other legumes formed into balls or fritters and deep-fried, usually eaten with or in pita bread.

-ORIGIN from colloquial Egyptian Arabic *falāfil*, plural of Arabic *fulful, filfil* 'pepper.'

farfalle /fär'fälä/ ▸ small pieces of pasta shaped like bows or butterflies' wings.

-ORIGIN Italian, plural of *farfalla* 'butterfly.'

farina ▸ flour or meal made of cereal grains, nuts, or starchy roots.

-ORIGIN Middle English: from Latin, from *far* 'grain.'

farmer cheese ▸ a fresh (unaged) cheese similar to cottage cheese, but smoother.

fat ▸ a natural oily or greasy substance occurring in animal bodies, especially when deposited as a layer under the skin or around certain organs.

■ a substance of this type, or a similar one made from plant products, used in cooking.

▸ (of an animal bred for food) made plump for slaughter.

■ containing much fat: *fat bacon.*

▢ **fatty**: *fatty salmon steaks.*

fatback ▸ fat from the upper part of a side of pork, especially when dried and salted in strips.

fat-free ▸ (of a food) not containing animal or vegetable fats.

fava bean /'fävə/ ▸ another term for BROAD BEAN.
-ORIGIN Italian *fava*, from Latin *faba* 'bean.'
feijoada /ˌfāzHoo'ädə/ ▸ a Brazilian or Portuguese stew of black beans with pork or other meat and vegetables, served with rice.
-ORIGIN Portuguese, from *feijão*, from Latin *phaseolus* 'bean.'
felafel /fə'läfəl/ ▸ variant spelling of FALAFEL.
fennel ▸ an aromatic European plant of the parsley family. One variety has feathery leaves and seeds that are used as a culinary herb, and another variety has swollen leaf bases that are eaten as a vegetable.
-ORIGIN Old English *finule, fenol*, from Latin *faeniculum*, diminutive of *faenum* 'hay.'
fenugreek ▸ a herbaceous plant of the pea family, with aromatic seeds that are used for flavoring, especially ground and used in curry powder.
-ORIGIN Old English *fenogrecum* (superseded in Middle English by forms from Old French *fenugrec*), from Latin *faenugraecum*, from *faenum graecum* 'Greek hay' (the Romans used the dried plant as fodder).
fermentation ▸ the chemical breakdown of a substance by bacteria, yeasts, or other microorganisms, typically involving effervescence and the giving off of heat.
■ the process of this kind involved in the making of beer, wine, and liquor, in which sugars are converted to ethyl alcohol.
▢ **ferment**: *fermenting wine to make vinegar.*
-ORIGIN Middle English: from late Latin *fermentatio(n-)*, from Latin *fermentare* 'to ferment', from *fervere* 'to boil.'
feta (also **feta cheese**) ▸ a white salty Greek cheese made from the milk of ewes or goats.
-ORIGIN from modern Greek *pheta.*
fettuccine (also **fettuccini**) /ˌfetə'CHēnē/ ▸ pasta made in ribbons.
-ORIGIN from Italian, plural of *fettucina*, diminutive of *fetta* 'slice, ribbon.'
fiddlehead (also **fiddlehead fern**) ▸ the young, curled, frond of certain ferns eaten as a vegetable.
-ORIGIN from the resemblance to the head of a violin.

fig ▸ a soft pear-shaped fruit with sweet dark flesh and many small seeds, eaten fresh or dried.

-ORIGIN Middle English: from Old French *figue*, from Provençal *fig(u)a*, based on Latin *ficus*.

filé /fi'lā/ ▸ pounded or powdered sassafras leaves used to flavor and thicken soup, especially gumbo.

-ORIGIN from French, past participle of *filer* 'to twist.'

filet /fi'lā/ ▸ French spelling of FILLET, used especially in the names of French or French-sounding dishes: *filet de boeuf*.

filet mignon /fi'lā min'yän/ ▸ a small tender piece of beef from the end of the tenderloin.

-ORIGIN French, literally 'dainty fillet.'

fillet /fi'lā/ ▸ a fleshy boneless piece of meat from near the loins or the ribs of an animal: *a chicken breast fillet*.

■ (also **fillet steak**) a beef steak cut from the lower part of a sirloin.

■ a boned side of a fish.

▸ to remove the bones from (a fish).

■ to cut (fish or meat) into boneless pieces.

-ORIGIN Middle English: from Old French *filet* 'thread,' based on Latin *filum*.

filling ▸ an edible substance placed between the layers of a sandwich, cake, or other foodstuff: *a jelly roll with a chocolate filling*.

filo /'fēlō/ ▸ variant spelling of PHYLLO.

financier /ˌfēnan'si(ə)r/ ▸ a small cake made with almond dough and egg whites, often sold in French pastry shops in small rectangles or ovals.

-ORIGIN French, literally 'financier (expert in finance),' from the supposed resemblance of the cake to a gold bar.

fines herbes /ˌfēn(z) 'erb/ ▸ mixed herbs used in cooking, especially fresh herbs chopped as a flavoring for omelets.

-ORIGIN French, literally 'fine herbs.'

finger food ▸ food served in such a form and style that it can conveniently be eaten with the fingers.

fingerling ▸ a thin, elongated potato, about the length of a finger, with a yellow, waxy interior.

finnan /'finən/ (also **finnan haddie** /'hadē/) ▸ haddock cured with the smoke of green wood, turf, or peat.

-ORIGIN alteration of *Findon*, a fishing village near Aberdeen in Scotland.

finocchio /fə'nōkē,ō/ ▸ another term for FENNEL (the vegetable).

-ORIGIN from Italian, from a popular Latin variant of Latin *faeniculum* (see FENNEL).

fish ▸ a cold-blooded vertebrate animal with gills and fins and living wholly in water.

■ the flesh of such animals as food: *hot crab appetizers stuffed with fish.* See word bank at SEAFOOD.

USAGE: Most food fish have a common name and one or more regional names. But the accepted market name is often the more palatable one. **Bowfin** is commonly called **mudfish** or **dogfish**, and dogfish and **mako** are market names for **shark**. **Ratfish** and **rabbitfish** are sold under the name **chimaera**. The **dolphin** appears on menus as **mahimahi**.

fish and chips ▸ a British dish of fried fish fillets served with French fries.

fish cake ▸ a patty of shredded fish and mashed potato, typically coated in batter or breadcrumbs and fried.

fish sauce ▸ a Thai and Vietnamese sauce used as a flavoring or condiment, prepared from fermented anchovies and salt.

fish stick ▸ a small, oblong piece of fish fillet, usually breaded and fried.

five-spice (also **five-spice powder**) ▸ a blend of five powdered spices, typically fennel seeds, cinnamon, cloves, star anise, and peppercorns, used in Chinese cuisine.

flageolet /ˌflajə'lā/ ▸ a French kidney bean of a small variety used in cooking.

-ORIGIN from French, based on Latin *phaseolus* 'bean.'

flaky ▸ breaking or separating easily into small thin pieces or layers.

flaky pastry ▸ pastry consisting of thin light layers when baked.

flambé /fläm'bā/ ▸ (of food) covered with liquor and set alight briefly: *crepes flambé.*

▸ to cover (food) with liquor and set it alight briefly.

-ORIGIN French, literally 'singed,' past participle of *flamber*, from *flambe* 'a flame.'

flan ▸ a baked dish consisting of an open-topped pastry case with a savory or sweet filling.

■ a sponge cake base with a sweet topping.

■ a Spanish dessert consisting of an egg custard topped with caramel. See also CRÈME CARAMEL.

–ORIGIN from French, from Old French *flaon*, from medieval Latin *flado, fladon-* 'flat cake,' of West Germanic origin.

USAGE: A culinary term may have two or more meanings depending on the particular ethnic cuisine. A French **flan** is an open-topped pastry, but a Spanish **flan** is a caramel custard. In Mexican cooking a **tortilla** is a thin pancake, but in Spanish cooking it is a thick omelet. To Americans, **sherbet** refers to a frozen dessert, but in Arab countries it refers to a cooling drink.

flank ▸ a cut of meat from the side of an animal between the ribs and the hip.

flapjack ▸ informal a pancake.

–ORIGIN from *flap* (in the dialect sense 'toss a pancake') + *jack*.

flatbread ▸ flat, thin, often unleavened bread.

flavoring ▸ a substance used to give a different, stronger, or more agreeable taste to food or drink: *vanilla flavoring* | *mustard has been used as a flavoring for thousands of years.*

fleur de sel /'floor də 'sel/ ▸ French sea salt.

fleuron /'floorän/ ▸ a flower-shaped ornament, used on pastry.

■ a small pastry puff used for garnishing.

–ORIGIN Middle English: from Old French *floron*, from *flour* 'flower.'

float ▸ a soft drink with a scoop of ice cream floating in it: *a root beer float.*

florentine ▸ (of food) served or prepared on a bed of spinach: *eggs florentine.*

–ORIGIN Middle English: from Latin *Florentinus*, from *Florentia* 'Florence, Italy.'

floret ▸ one of the flowering stems making up a head of cauliflower or broccoli.

–ORIGIN from Latin *flos, flor-* 'flower' + the suffix *-et.*

flounder ▸ a small flatfish that typically occurs in shallow coastal water, used widely for food.

–ORIGIN Middle English: from Old French *flondre*, probably of Scandinavian origin.

flour ▸ a powder obtained by grinding grain, typically wheat, and used to make bread, cakes, and pastry.

■ fine soft powder obtained by grinding the seeds or roots of starchy vegetables.

▸ to sprinkle (something, especially a work surface or cooking utensil) with a thin layer of flour.

–ORIGIN Middle English: a specific use of *flower* in the sense 'the best part,' used originally to mean 'the finest quality of ground wheat.' The spelling *flower* remained in use alongside *flour* until the early 19th century.

flute ▸ a tall, narrow wine glass: *a flute of champagne.*

▸ to make decorative grooves in the edge of a pastry crust: *a fluted crust.*

focaccia /fō'käCH(ē)ə/ ▸ a type of flat Italian bread made with yeast and olive oil and flavored with herbs.

–ORIGIN Italian.

foie gras /'fwä 'grä/ ▸ short for PÂTÉ DE FOIE GRAS.

fold ▸ to mix (an ingredient) gently with another ingredient, especially by lifting a mixture with a spatula so as to enclose it without stirring or beating: *fold the egg whites into the chocolate mixture.*

fondant ▸ a thick paste made of sugar and water and often flavored or colored, used in the making of candy and the icing and decoration of cakes.

■ a candy made of such a paste.

–ORIGIN from French, literally 'melting,' present participle of *fondre* 'to melt.'

fondant potatoes ▸ potatoes trimmed in the shape of eggs, fried in butter and then baked.

fondue ▸ a dish in which small pieces of food are dipped into a hot sauce or a hot cooking medium such as oil or broth: *a Swiss cheese fondue* | *chocolate fondue.*

–ORIGIN French, feminine past participle of *fondre* 'to melt.'

fontina /fän'tēnə/ ▸ a pale yellow Italian cheese.

–ORIGIN Italian.

food processor ▸ an electric kitchen appliance used for chopping, slicing, mixing, or puréeing foods.

food supplement ▸ see SUPPLEMENT.

fool ▸ chiefly British a cold dessert made of puréed fruit mixed or served with cream or custard: *raspberry fool with vanilla cream.*

foo yong ▸ a Chinese dish or sauce made with egg as a main ingredient.

–ORIGIN from Chinese (Cantonese dialect) *foō yung*, literally 'hibiscus.'

forcemeat ▸ a mixture of meat or vegetables chopped and seasoned for use as a stuffing or garnish.

–ORIGIN from obsolete *force* 'to stuff,' alteration (influenced by the verb *force*) of *farce*, from French *farcir.*

fowl ▸ a gallinaceous bird kept chiefly for its eggs and flesh; a domestic cock or hen.

■ any other domesticated bird kept for its eggs or flesh, for example, the turkey, duck, and goose.

fraise /frāz/ ▸ (in cooking) a strawberry.

–ORIGIN French, from Latin *fraga* 'wild strawberries.'

framboise /fräN'bwäz; fram-/ ▸ (in cooking) a raspberry.

–ORIGIN French, from a conflation of Latin *fraga ambrosia* 'ambrosial strawberry.'

frangipane /'franjə,pān/ ▸ an almond-flavored cream or paste.

■ a pastry filled with this.

–ORIGIN from French, named after the Marquis Muzio *Frangipani.* The term originally denoted the frangipani shrub or tree, the perfume of which is said to have been used to flavor the almond cream.

frankfurter ▸ a seasoned smoked sausage usually made of beef and pork.

–ORIGIN from German *Frankfurter Wurst* 'Frankfurt sausage.'

frappé /fra'pā/ ▸ (of a drink) iced or chilled.

▸ a drink served with ice or frozen to a slushy consistency.

■ (**frappe** /frap/) (chiefly in New England) a milk shake, especially one made with ice cream.

–ORIGIN French, literally 'iced.'

French bread ▸ white bread in a long loaf with a crisp crust.

French dressing ▸ a salad dressing of vinegar, oil, and seasonings. ■ a sweet, creamy salad dressing commercially prepared from oil, tomato purée, and spices.

French fries (also **French fried potatoes**) ▸ potatoes cut into strips and deep-fried.

French roll ▸ a crisp roll of French bread.

French toast ▸ bread soaked in egg and milk and fried.

fricassee /ˈfrikəˌsē/ ▸ a dish of stewed or fried pieces of meat served in a thick white sauce.
▸ to make a fricassee of (something).
–ORIGIN from French *fricassée*, feminine past participle of *fricasser* 'cut up and cook in sauce.'

frijoles /frēˈhōlās/ ▸ (in Mexican cooking) beans.
–ORIGIN Spanish, plural of *frijol*.

frijoles refritos /frēˈhōlās rāˈfrētōs/ ▸ Spanish term for REFRIED BEANS.

frisée /frēˈzā/ ▸ the curly endive (see ENDIVE sense 1).
–ORIGIN French, from *chicorée frisée* 'curly endive.'

frites /frēt(s)/ ▸ short for POMMES FRITES.

frittata /frēˈtätə/ ▸ an Italian dish made with fried beaten eggs, resembling a Spanish omelet.
–ORIGIN Italian, from *fritto*, past participle of *friggere* 'to fry.' Compare with FRITTER.

fritter ▸ a piece of fruit, vegetable, or meat that is coated in batter and deep-fried.
–ORIGIN Middle English: from Old French *friture*, based on Latin *frigere* (see FRY¹). Compare with FRITTATA.

fritto misto /ˈfrētō ˈmēstō/ ▸ a dish of various foods, typically seafood, deep-fried in batter.
–ORIGIN Italian, 'mixed fry.'

fromage blanc /frōˈmäzH ˈbläNGk/ ▸ a soft French cheese made from cow's milk and having a creamy sour taste.
–ORIGIN French, literally 'white cheese.'

frost ▸ to cover (a cake, cupcake, or other baked item) with icing.

frosting ▸ icing.

fruit ▸ the sweet and fleshy product of a tree or other plant that contains seed and can be eaten as food.

-ORIGIN Middle English: from Old French, from Latin *fructus* 'enjoyment of produce, harvest,' from *frui* 'enjoy.'

fruitcake ▸ a cake containing candied and dried fruit and nuts.

fruit cocktail ▸ a chopped fruit salad, often commercially produced in cans.

fruit cup ▸ a salad made of chopped fruit and served in a glass dish as an appetizer or dessert.

fruit salad ▸ a mixture of different types of chopped fruit served in syrup or juice.

fry ▸ to cook (food) in hot fat or oil, typically in a shallow pan.
■ (of food) to be cooked in such a way.
▸ a meal of meat or other food cooked in such a way.
■ a social gathering where fried food is served: *a fish fry.*
■ (**fries**) short for FRENCH FRIES.
-ORIGIN Middle English: from Old French *frire*, from Latin *frigere.*

frying pan (also **frypan**) ▸ a shallow pan with a long handle, used for cooking food in hot fat or oil.

fudge ▸ a soft candy made from sugar, butter, and milk or cream.
■ rich chocolate, used especially as a filling for cakes or a sauce on ice cream: *chocolate cake topped with hot fudge.*
-ORIGIN probably an alteration of obsolete *fadge* 'to fit.' Its early use as a verb in the sense 'turn out as expected,' also 'merge together' probably gave rise to its use in confectionery.

fugu /ˈf(y)o͞ogo͞o/ ▸ a puffer fish that is eaten as a Japanese delicacy, after some highly poisonous parts have been removed.
-ORIGIN Japanese.

fumet /fyo͞oˈmā/ ▸ a concentrated stock, especially of game or fish, used as flavoring.
-ORIGIN from French, 'smell of game, game flavor,' from *fumer* 'to smoke.'

funnel ▸ a tube or pipe that is wide at the top and narrow at the bottom, used for guiding liquid or powder into a small opening.

Fruits

abiu
achocha
akebia
akee
ambarella
ananas
apple
apricot
atemoya
avocado
azarole
bael
banana
banana flower
baobab
Barbados cherry
barberry
beach plum
bearberry
bergamot
berry
bignay
bilberry
bilimbi
biriba
blackberry
blackberry jam fruit
blood orange
blueberry
Brazilian cherry
breadfruit
buffaloberry
cabelluda
calamansi
cantaloupe
carambola
casaba
chayote
cherimoya
cherry
Chinese wolfberry
chokecherry
chrry plum
citron
clementine
cloudberry
coconut
corossolier
crabapple
cranberry
Crenshaw melon

crowberry
currant
custard apple
damson
date
dewberry
durian
eggfruit
elderberry
feijoa
fig
gamboge
golden apple
gooseberry
grape
grapefruit
greengage
ground cherry
guava
hackberry
honeydew
huckleberry
ilama
jaboticaba
jackfruit
jujube
kaki
kiwi fruit
kumquat
langsat
lemon
lime
longan
loquat
lychee
mamey
mameyito
mandarin
mango
mangosteen
medlar
melon
monstera
mountain apple
moya
mulberry
muskmelon
mysore raspberry
naranjilla
nectarine
noni

olive
orange
papaw
papaya
passion fruit
pawpaw
peach
peanut butter fruit
pear
pepino
persimmon
pineapple
pitahaya
plantain
plum
pomegranate
pomelo
prickly pear
prune
pummelo
quince
rambutan
raspberry
rhubarb
rollinia
rose apple
salak
salmonberry
santol
sapodilla
sapote
satsuma
serviceberry
soursop
spanspek
squashberry
star fruit
starapple
strawberry
Surinam cherry
sweetsop
tamarillo
tamarind
ugli fruit
wampee
water apple
watermelon
wax jambu
whortleberry
winter melon
yuzu

funnel cake ▸ a cake made of batter that is poured through a funnel into hot fat or oil, deep-fried until crisp, and served sprinkled with sugar.

fusilli /fyo͞o'silē/ ▸ pasta pieces in the form of short spirals.

–ORIGIN Italian, literally 'little spindles,' diminutive of *fuso*.

G

gage ▶ another term for GREENGAGE.

galangal /gəˈlaNGgəl/ (also **galanga**) ▶ the pungent aromatic rhizome of an Asian plant of the ginger family, which is widely used in cooking and herbal medicine.

‒ORIGIN Middle English *galingale*, via Old French from Arabic *ḵalanjān*.

galantine /ˈgalənˌtēn/ ▶ a dish of white meat or fish that is boned, cooked, pressed, and served cold in aspic.

galette /gəˈlet/ ▶ a flat round cake.
■ a pancake made from potatoes or buckwheat.

‒ORIGIN French, from Old French *galet* 'pebble.'

game ▶ the flesh of wild mammals or birds, used as food.

ganache /gəˈnäSH/ ▶ a whipped filling or frosting of chocolate and cream, used in desserts such as cakes and truffles.

‒ORIGIN French.

garam masala /ˈgärəm məˈsälə/ ▶ a spice mixture, typically cinnamon, cloves, cardamom, cumin, coriander, and pepper, used in Indian cooking.

‒ORIGIN from Urdu *garam maṣālah*, from *garam* 'hot, pungent' + *maṣālah* 'spice.'

garbanzo (also **garbanzo bean**) ▶ a chickpea.

‒ORIGIN from Spanish.

garibaldi /ˌgarəˈbôldē/ ▶ a small bright orange marine fish found off California.

‒ORIGIN named after Giuseppe *Garibaldi*, Italian military leader.

garlic ▶ the strong-smelling pungent-tasting bulb of a plant related to the onion, used as a flavoring in food.

-ORIGIN Old English *gārlēac*, from *gār* 'spear' (from the resemblance of a clove to the head of a spear) + *lēac* 'leek.'

garnish ▸ to decorate or embellish (food).

▸ a decoration or embellishment for food.

-ORIGIN Middle English: from Old French *garnir* 'warn, equip, garnish.'

gateau /gä'tō/ ▸ chiefly British a rich cake, typically one containing layers of cream or fruit.

-ORIGIN from French *gâteau* 'cake.'

gazpacho ▸ a Spanish-style soup made from tomatoes and other vegetables and spices, served cold.

-ORIGIN Spanish.

gefilte fish /gə'filtə/ ▸ a dish of stewed or baked stuffed fish, or of fish cakes boiled in a fish or vegetable broth and usually served chilled.

-ORIGIN Yiddish, 'stuffed fish,' from *filn* 'to fill' + *fish*.

gelatin ▸ a virtually colorless and tasteless water-soluble protein prepared from collagen and used in food preparation as the basis of jellies.

▢ **gelatinous** /jə'latn-əs/: *gelatinous okra pods.*

-ORIGIN from French *gélatine*, from Italian *gelatina*, from *gelata*, from Latin (see JELLY).

gelato /jə'lätō/ ▸ an Italian-style ice cream.

-ORIGIN Italian.

gemelli /jə'melē/ ▸ pasta in the form of two short rods twisted around each other.

-ORIGIN Italian, literally 'twins.'

génoise /zнän'wäz/ ▸ a light yellow sponge cake made with eggs and butter, used for layer cakes and petits fours.

-ORIGIN French, feminine of *génois* 'of Genoa, Italy.'

ghee /gē/ ▸ clarified butter made from the milk of a buffalo or cow, used in Indian cooking.

-ORIGIN from Hindi *ghī*, from Sanskrit *ghṛtá* 'sprinkled.'

gherkin ▸ a pickle made from a small variety of cucumber, or a young green cucumber.

-ORIGIN from Dutch *augurkje*, *gurkje*, diminutive of *augurk*, *gurk*, from Slavic.

giblets ▶ the liver, heart, gizzard, and neck of a chicken or other fowl, usually removed before the bird is cooked, and often used to make gravy, stuffing, or soup.
–ORIGIN Middle English: from Old French *gibelet* 'game bird stew.'

gigot /'jigət; zHē'gō/ ▶ a leg of mutton or lamb.
–ORIGIN French, diminutive of colloquial *gigue* 'leg,' from *giguer* 'to hop, jump.'

ginger ▶ a hot fragrant spice made from the rhizome of a plant. It is chopped or powdered for cooking, preserved in syrup, or candied.
▶ to flavor with ginger: *gingered chicken wings.*
–ORIGIN Old English *gingifer*, combined in Middle English with Old French *gingimbre*, from medieval Latin *gingiber*, from Greek *zingiberis*, from Pali *singivera*, of Dravidian origin.

ginger ale ▶ a clear, effervescent nonalcoholic drink flavored with ginger extract.

gingerbread ▶ a cake or soft cookie made with molasses and flavored with ginger.
–ORIGIN Middle English (in the sense 'preserved ginger'): from Old French *gingembrat*, from medieval Latin *gingibratum*, from *gingiber* (see **GINGER**). The ending was changed by association with *bread*.

ginger snap ▶ a thin brittle cookie flavored with ginger.

ginseng /'jinseNG/ ▶ a plant tuber used to prepare herbal teas and tonics, especially in the Far East.
–ORIGIN from Chinese *rénshēn*, from *rén* 'man' + *shēn*, a kind of herb (from the supposed resemblance of the forked root to a person).

gizzard ▶ a muscular, thick-walled part of a bird's stomach, used in gravies and stuffings.
–ORIGIN Middle English *giser*: from Old French, based on Latin *gigeria* 'cooked fowl entrails.' The final *-d* was added in the 16th century.

gjetost /'yātōst; 'jetäst/ ▶ a very sweet, firm, golden-brown Norwegian cheese, traditionally made with goat's milk.
–ORIGIN Norwegian, from *gjet, geit* 'goat' + *ost* 'cheese.'

glacé /gla'sā/ ▸ (of fruit) having a glossy surface due to preservation in sugar: *a glacé cherry.*

▸ to glaze with a thin sugar-based coating: *glacéed cape gooseberries.*

-ORIGIN French, literally 'iced,' past participle of *glacer*, from *glace* 'ice.'

glacé icing ▸ icing made with powdered sugar and water.

glaze ▸ a liquid such as milk or beaten egg, used to form a smooth shiny coating on food.

▸ to cover with a glaze: *new potatoes glazed in mint-flavored butter.*

globe artichoke ▸ see ARTICHOKE (sense 1).

Gloucester ▸ a firm and waxy English cheese made in two sizes, single and double. Double Gloucester is about twice as thick as single Gloucester.

-ORIGIN named after *Gloucester*, city in England.

gluten /'glo͞otn/ ▸ a substance present in cereal grains, especially wheat, that is responsible for the elastic texture of dough. It is a mixture of two proteins.

-ORIGIN via French from Latin, literally 'glue.'

gnocchi /'n(y)ôkē/ ▸ (in Italian cooking) small dumplings made from potato, semolina, or flour, usually served with a sauce.

-ORIGIN Italian, plural of *gnocco*, alteration of *nocchio* 'knot in wood.'

gobo /'gō,bō/ ▸ a vegetable root used chiefly in Japanese and Hawaiian cooking.

-ORIGIN Japanese.

golden ▸ colored like gold; light brown: *bake until golden.*

Golden Delicious ▸ a widely grown dessert apple of a greenish-yellow, soft-fleshed variety.

golden syrup ▸ British a thick syrup with a buttery aroma, made from cane sugar.

good ▸ (of beef) of the grade below choice.

goose ▸ the flesh of a large waterbird with a long neck and webbed feet, used as food.

gooseberry ▸ the round edible yellowish-green or reddish berry of a thorny shrub, having a thin translucent hairy skin.

-ORIGIN the first element perhaps from GOOSE, or perhaps based on

Old French *groseille*, altered because of an unexplained association with the bird.

Gorgonzola /ˌgôrgənˈzōlə/ ▸ a type of rich, strong-flavored Italian cheese with bluish-green veins.

‒ORIGIN named after *Gorgonzola*, a village in northern Italy, where it was originally made.

Gouda /ˈgo͞odə/ ▸ a flat round cheese with a yellow rind, originally made in the town of Gouda in the Netherlands.

gougère /go͞oˈzHe(ə)r/ ▸ a puff of choux pastry flavored with cheese (usually Gruyère), often stuffed with a savory filling.

‒ORIGIN French.

goulash /ˈgo͞oläsH/ ▸ a highly seasoned Hungarian soup or stew of meat and vegetables, flavored with paprika.

‒ORIGIN from Hungarian *gulyás-hús*, from *gulyás* 'herdsman' + *hús* 'meat.'

gourmand ▸ a person who enjoys eating and often eats too much.

■ a connoisseur of good food.

‒ORIGIN Middle English: from Old French.

USAGE: The words **gourmand** and **gourmet** overlap in meaning but are not identical. Both mean 'a connoisseur of good food,' but **gourmand** more usually means 'a person who enjoys eating and often overeats.'

gourmet ▸ a connoisseur of good food; a person with a discerning palate.

▸ of a kind or standard suitable for a gourmet: *a gourmet meal.*

‒ORIGIN French, originally meaning 'wine taster,' influenced by GOURMAND.

USAGE: See usage note at GOURMAND.

graham (also **Graham**) ▸ denoting whole-wheat flour, or cookies or bread made from this: *graham crackers.*

‒ORIGIN named after Sylvester *Graham* (1794–1851), American advocate of dietary reform.

gram ▸ chickpeas or other legumes used as food.

‒ORIGIN from Portuguese *grão*, from Latin *granum* 'grain.'

granita /grəˈnētə/ ▸ a coarse, Italian-style flavored ice.

■ a drink made with crushed ice.

-ORIGIN Italian, from feminine of *granito*, past participle of *granire* 'to granulate,' from *grano* 'grain,' from Latin *granum*.

Granny Smith ▸ an eating apple of a bright green variety with crisp, sharp-flavored flesh, originating in Australia.

-ORIGIN named after Maria Ann (*Granny*) Smith (*circa* 1801–1870), who first produced such apples.

granola ▸ a breakfast cereal consisting typically of rolled oats, brown sugar or honey, dried fruit, and nuts.

-ORIGIN (originally a trademark) from *gran-* (representing *granular* or *grain*) + the suffix *-ola*.

grape ▸ a berry, typically green, purple, or black, growing in clusters on a grapevine, eaten as fruit, and used in making wine.

-ORIGIN Middle English: from Old French, 'bunch of grapes,' probably from *graper* 'gather (grapes),' from *grap* 'hook' (used in harvesting grapes), of Germanic origin.

grapefruit ▸ a large, round, yellow citrus fruit with an acid, juicy pulp.

-ORIGIN from GRAPE + FRUIT (probably because the fruits grow in clusters).

grapeseed oil ▸ oil extracted from the residue of grapes that have been juiced.

grate ▸ to reduce (food) to small shreds by rubbing it on a grater: *peel and roughly grate the carrots | grated cheese.*

grater ▸ a device having a surface covered with holes edged by slightly raised cutting edges, used for grating cheese and other foods.

■ a device in which blades are moved manually (by turning a handle), used for grating cheese and other foods.

gratin /ˈgrätn/ ▸ a dish with a light browned crust of breadcrumbs or melted cheese. See also AU GRATIN.

-ORIGIN French, from *gratter*, earlier *grater* 'to grate.'

gratiné /ˌgrätnˈā/ (also **gratinée**) ▸ another term for AU GRATIN.

-ORIGIN French, past participle of *gratiner* 'cook au gratin.'

Gravenstein ▸ a widely grown apple of a large variety having yellow, red-streaked skin, used for cooking and as an eating apple.

-ORIGIN the German form of *Graasten*, village in Denmark formerly in Schleswig-Holstein, Germany.

gravlax /'gräv,läks/ ▸ a Scandinavian dish of dry-cured salmon marinated in herbs.

-ORIGIN Swedish, from *grav* 'trench' + *lax* 'salmon' (from the former practice of burying the salmon in salt in a hole in the ground).

gravy ▸ the fat and juices exuding from meat during cooking.

■ a sauce made from these juices together with stock and other ingredients.

-ORIGIN Middle English: perhaps from a misreading (as *gravé*) of Old French *grané*, probably from *grain* 'spice,' from Latin *granum* 'grain.'

Greek coffee ▸ a rich, strong brew made by boiling finely ground coffee with water, and often sugar, in a tall, narrow pot. The frothy coffee is served in a demitasse cup and the grounds are allowed to settle before drinking.

Greek salad ▸ a salad usually consisting of tomatoes, onions, cucumbers, peppers, olives, and feta cheese, dressed with oil, vinegar, and herbs.

green bean ▸ the immature pod of any of various bean plants, eaten as a vegetable. See also STRING BEAN.

green cheese ▸ unripened or unmatured cheese.

green fat ▸ the green, gelatinous part of a turtle, highly regarded by gourmets.

greengage ▸ a variety of plum with greenish-yellow skin (also called **gage**).

-ORIGIN named after Sir William *Gage* (1657–1727), English botanist who introduced it to England.

Green Goddess ▸ a salad dressing made with mayonnaise, garlic, and anchovies, and colored with parsley and green onions.

green goose ▸ a goose that is killed when under four months old and eaten without stuffing.

green onion ▸ an onion taken from the ground before the bulb has formed, typically eaten raw in salad; a scallion.

green pepper ▸ the unripe fruit of a sweet pepper, which is mild in flavor and widely used in cooking.

green tea ▸ tea that is made from unfermented leaves and is pale in color and slightly bitter in flavor, produced mainly in China and Japan. Compare with BLACK TEA.

green turtle ▸ a sea turtle with an olive-brown shell, often living close to the coast and extensively hunted for food.

griddle ▸ a heavy, flat iron plate that is heated and used for cooking food.
▸ to cook on a griddle: *griddled corn cakes.*
–ORIGIN Middle English: from Old French *gredil,* from Latin *craticula,* diminutive of *cratis* 'hurdle.'

grill ▸ a metal framework used for cooking food over an open fire.
■ a portable device for cooking outdoors, consisting of a such a framework placed over charcoal or gas fuel.
■ a large griddle.
■ a dish of food, especially meat, cooked using a grill.
■ (also **grill room**) a restaurant serving grilled food.
▸ to cook (something) using a grill.
–ORIGIN from French *gril* (noun), *griller* (verb), from Old French *graille* 'gridiron, grille.'
USAGE: See usage note at **MUFFIN**.

grillade /gri'läd/ ▸ (often **grillades**) a kind of stew usually made with beef steak, typical of French regional and Cajun cooking.
–ORIGIN French, literally 'something grilled.'

grind ▸ to reduce (a foodstuff) to small particles or powder by crushing it: *grind some black pepper over the salad | they grind up fish to make fish cakes.*
▸ the size of ground particles, especially ground coffee beans: *only the right grind gives you all the fine flavor.*

grinder ▸ a machine used for grinding something: *a coffee grinder.*
■ another term for **SUBMARINE SANDWICH**.

grissini /gri'sēnē/ ▸ thin, crisp Italian breadsticks.
–ORIGIN Italian.

grist ▸ grain that is ground to make flour.
–ORIGIN Old English, 'grinding,' of Germanic origin.

grits ▸ a dish of coarsely ground corn kernels boiled with water or milk.
■ coarsely ground corn kernels from which this dish is made.
–ORIGIN Old English *grytt, grytte* 'bran, mill dust,' of Germanic origin.

groats ▸ hulled or crushed grain, especially oats.

–ORIGIN Old English *grotan* (plural): related to GRITS.

grounds ▸ solid particles, especially of ground coffee, that form a residue; sediment.

grouper ▸ a large heavy-bodied fish of the sea bass family, found in warm seas.

–ORIGIN from Portuguese *garoupa*, probably from a local term in South America.

grouse ▸ the flesh of a medium to large game bird with a plump body and feathered legs, used as food.

gruel ▸ a thin liquid food of oatmeal or other meal boiled in milk or water.

–ORIGIN Middle English: from Old French, of Germanic origin.

grunt ▸ a dessert made of fruit topped with cookie dough: *blueberry grunt.*

–ORIGIN Old English *grunnettan*, of Germanic origin; probably originally imitative.

Gruyère /grōōˈye(ə)r/ ▸ a firm, tangy Swiss cheese.

–ORIGIN named after *Gruyère*, district in Switzerland, where it was first made.

guacamole /ˌgwäkəˈmōlē/ ▸ a dish or dip of mashed avocado mixed with chopped onion, tomatoes, chili peppers, and seasoning.

–ORIGIN Latin American Spanish, from Nahuatl *ahuacamolli*, from *ahuacatl* 'avocado' + *molli* 'sauce.'

guava ▸ the pale orange fruit of a tropical American tree, with pink, juicy flesh and a strong, sweet aroma.

–ORIGIN from Spanish *guayaba*, probably from Taino.

gumbo ▸ okra, especially the gelatinous pods used in cooking.

■ (in Cajun cooking) a spicy chicken or seafood soup thickened typically with okra or rice.

–ORIGIN from the Angolan word *kingombo* 'okra.'

gunpowder ▸ (also **gunpowder tea**) a fine green China tea of granular appearance.

gyro /ˈyi(ə)rō; ˈjīrō/ ▸ a sandwich made with slices of spiced minced meat cooked on a spit, served with salad in pita bread.

–ORIGIN from modern Greek *guros* 'turning.'

H

Habanero (also **habanero**) /ˌhäbəˈne(ə)rō/ ▸ a small chili pepper that is the hottest variety available.
-ORIGIN Spanish, literally 'of Havana, Cuba.'

haddock ▸ an edible, silvery-gray, bottom-dwelling fish of North Atlantic coastal waters.
-ORIGIN Middle English: from Anglo-Norman French *hadoc*, from Old French *hadot*.

haggis /ˈhagis/ ▸ a Scottish dish consisting of a sheep's or calf's entrails mixed with suet, oatmeal, and seasoning and boiled in a bag, traditionally one made from the animal's stomach.
-ORIGIN Middle English: probably from earlier *hag* 'hack, hew,' from Old Norse *hǫggva*.

halibut ▸ a large, edible fish of northern Atlantic or Pacific waters.
-ORIGIN Middle English: from *haly* 'holy' + obsolete *butt* 'flatfish' (because it was often eaten on holy days).

halloumi /häˈlo͞omē/ ▸ a mild, firm, white Cypriot cheese made from goats' or ewes' milk.
-ORIGIN from Egyptian Arabic *ḥalūm*, probably from Arabic *ḥaluma* 'to be mild.'

halvah (also **halva**) /ˈhälvä/ ▸ a Middle Eastern confection made of sesame flour and honey.
-ORIGIN Yiddish, or from Turkish *helva*, from Arabic and Persian *ḥalwā* 'sweetmeat.'

halwa /ˈhälwä/ (also **halwah**) ▸ a sweet Indian dish consisting of carrots or semolina boiled with milk, almonds, sugar, butter, and cardamom.
-ORIGIN from Arabic *ḥalwā* (see **HALVAH**).

ham ▸ meat from the upper part of a pig's leg, salted and dried or smoked.

hamburger ▸ a round patty of ground beef, fried or grilled and typically served on a bun or roll, and garnished with various condiments.

■ ground beef.

–ORIGIN from German, from *Hamburg*, city in Germany.

hard-boiled ▸ (of an egg) boiled until the white and the yolk are solid.

hard roe ▸ see ROE.

hard sauce ▸ a sauce of butter and sugar, typically with brandy, rum, or vanilla added.

hard wheat ▸ wheat of a variety having a hard grain rich in gluten, used for making bread.

haricot /'hari‚kō/ ▸ the small white seed of any of several bean plants, especially the kidney bean.

–ORIGIN French, perhaps from Aztec *ayacotli*.

haricot vert /'hari‚kō 've(ə)rt/ ▸ a green bean with a very narrow edible pod and very small seeds.

–ORIGIN French, 'green bean.'

harissa /hə'rēsə/ ▸ a hot sauce or paste used in North African cuisine, made from chili peppers, paprika, and olive oil.

–ORIGIN from Arabic.

hash ▸ a dish of cooked meat cut into small pieces and recooked, usually with potatoes.

■ a finely chopped mixture.

–ORIGIN from French *hacher*, from *hache* 'ax.'

hash browns (also **hashed browns**) ▸ cooked potatoes, usually with onions added, that have been chopped into small pieces, formed into patties, and fried until brown.

hazelnut ▸ a round brown hard-shelled nut that is the edible fruit of the hazel tree.

headcheese ▸ meat from a pig's or calf's head that is cooked and pressed into a loaf with aspic.

heart of palm ▸ the edible bud of a palm tree, eaten as a vegetable or in salads.

heavy cream ▸ thick cream that contains from 36 to 40 percent butterfat.

herb ▸ any plant with leaves, seeds, or flowers used for flavoring, food, medicine, or perfume: *bundles of dried herbs.*

■ a part of such a plant as used in cooking: *a potato base topped with tomatoes, cheese, and herbs.*

□ **herbed**: *herbed cream cheese.*

-ORIGIN Middle English: via Old French from Latin *herba* 'grass, green crops, herb.'

Herbs

basil	dandelion	pandanus
bay leaf	dill	parsley
bee balm	feverfew	pennyroyal
black cohosh	fines herbes	peppermint
boldo leaf	horehound	perilla
borage	hyssop	ramson
bouquet garni	Kaffir lime leaf	rice paddy herb
burdock	laurel leaf	rocket
burnet	lavender	rosemary
calamint	lemon balm	rue
calendula	lemon basil	sage
capers	lemon verbena	savory
catnip	lemongrass	saw leaf
chervil	lovage	shiso
Chinese parsley	marjoram	sorrel
chives	Mexican pepperleaf	sweet basil
cicely	mint	tarragon
cilantro	mugwort	Thai basil
costmary	myrtle	thyme
cress	myrtle	wormwood
curry leaf	oregano	yarrow

hero (also **hero sandwich**) ▸ another term for SUBMARINE SANDWICH.

-ORIGIN Middle English (with mythological reference): via Latin from Greek *hērōs.*

herring ▸ a silvery fish that is most abundant in coastal waters and is of great commercial importance as a food fish in many parts of the world.

hibachi ▸ a portable cooking apparatus consisting of a small grill over a brazier.

-ORIGIN Japanese *hibachi, hi-hachi*, from *hi* 'fire' + *hachi* 'bowl, pot.'

high tea ▸ British a meal eaten in the late afternoon or early evening, typically consisting of a cooked dish, bread and butter, and tea.

hijiki /hē'jēkē/ ▸ Japanese seaweed sold in dried black strips.

-ORIGIN Japanese.

hoagie (also **hoagy**) ▸ another term for SUBMARINE SANDWICH.

hock ▸ a knuckle of meat, especially of pork or ham.

hoisin /'hoisin/ (also **hoisin sauce**) ▸ a sweet, spicy, dark red sauce made from soybeans, vinegar, sugar, garlic, and various spices, widely used in southern Chinese cooking.

-ORIGIN from Chinese (Cantonese dialect) *hoisin* 'seafood.'

hollandaise sauce /'hälən,dāz/ ▸ a creamy sauce of melted butter, egg yolks, and lemon juice or vinegar, served especially with fish.

-ORIGIN French *hollandaise*, feminine of *hollandais* 'Dutch,' from *Hollande* 'Holland.'

home fries (also **home-fried potatoes**) ▸ boiled potatoes that are sliced or cubed and fried in butter or oil.

hominy ▸ coarsely ground corn used to make grits: *hominy grits.*

-ORIGIN shortened from Virginia Algonquian *uskatahomen.*

honey ▸ a sweet, sticky, yellowish-brown fluid made by bees and other insects from nectar, used especially as a sweetener.

honeycomb ▸ tripe from the second stomach of a ruminant.

■ a piece of beehive structure that contains honey and can be chewed as a sweet.

honeydew ▸ a melon of a variety with smooth pale skin and sweet green flesh.

hopping john ▸ (in the southern U.S. and Caribbean) a stew of rice with black-eyed peas, often also containing bacon and red peppers.

hors d'oeuvre /ˌôr 'dərv/ ▸ a small savory dish, typically one served as an appetizer at the beginning of a meal.

-ORIGIN French, literally 'outside the work.'

horseradish ▸ the pungent root of a European plant of the cabbage family, which is scraped or grated as a condiment and often made into a sauce.

hot ▸ prepared by heating and served without cooling.

■ containing or consisting of pungent spices or peppers that produce a burning sensation when tasted.

hot cross bun ▸ a bun marked with a cross of white icing and containing dried fruit, traditionally eaten during Lent.

hot dog ▸ a frankfurter or other sausage served hot in a long, soft roll and typically topped with various condiments.

hot plate ▸ a flat heated surface (or a set of these), typically portable, used for cooking food or keeping it hot.

hummus (also **hoummos** or **humous**) /'ho͞oməs; 'həm-/ ▸ a thick paste used as a spread or dip made from ground chickpeas and sesame seeds, olive oil, lemon, and garlic, made originally in the Middle East.

-ORIGIN from Arabic *ḥummuṣ*.

hush puppy ▸ a small cake of cornmeal dough that has been deep-fried.

-ORIGIN from the supposed practice of feeding them to dogs to quiet them.

husk ▸ the dry outer covering of some fruits or seeds.

▸ to remove the husk or husks from: *husked corn*.

-ORIGIN late Middle English: probably from Low German *hūske* 'sheath,' literally 'little house.'

hyson /'hīsən/ ▸ a type of green China tea.

-ORIGIN from Chinese *xīchūn*, literally 'bright spring.'

MOCK FOODS

Mock foods are an insight into America's national heritage. This culinary genre was introduced to colonial America by European cooks, who had a long tradition of artistic presentation and food substitution. American mock foods were created when colonial cooks plied these skills to reconcile Old World recipes with New World ingredients. In the eighteenth and nineteenth centuries American mock foods centered mainly on practical substitutions. In the late nineteenth century creations featured more complicated, showy foods. In the twentieth century mock foods often showcased manufactured products promoted by food companies.

What makes a food "mock" is not a simple question to answer: *mock*, at various times, has meant many different things.

Mock is often used for foods where there is a substitution for a primary ingredient. Perhaps the most famous mock food is mock turtle soup, immortalized by Lewis Carroll in *Alice's Adventures in Wonderland*. Mock goose (leg of pork), mock duck (leg of lamb), and mock oysters (corn fritters) were known to Americans in the nineteenth century. In the twentieth century recipes for mock chicken included pork, peanuts, tuna, or veal. *Mock* can also mean less of a key ingredient. Fannie Farmer's 1923 recipe for mock angel food called for two egg whites rather than eight.

Mock can also be used for foods that taste like something else. The mock apple pie known to most Americans was introduced in the 1930s by the National Biscuit Company (Nabisco) as a promotion for Ritz crackers. This recipe evolved from mid-nineteenth-century imitation apple pies and mock mince pies, which were made with soda crackers, sugar, and spices. Crackers have a history of approximating apple pie in both texture and taste.

Mock foods may look like other foods. Upscale caterers throughout time have used food to create complicated, edible works of art. American culinary artists have been known to disguise entire hams as Easter eggs, create fantastic beasts from bread, and sculpt national icons from pâté. In the twentieth century American homemakers decorated holiday tables with pineapple peacocks and cheese ducks.

Mock foods can also be economical approximations of more expensive foods. Depression-era and wartime cooks relied on mock foods to stretch budgets. American cookbooks printed in these lean years were filled with less-expensive alternatives to traditional favorites. In some cookbooks, the word "mock" was featured in the index, facilitating recipe identification. Fannie Farmer's 1939 *Boston Cooking-School Cook Book* listed nineteen recipes under this heading.

Mock can mean a vegetarian alternative. In the 1920s the American vegetarian movement created mock sausage (puréed lima beans) and mock veal cutlets (lentils and peanuts). Tofu burgers were promoted as healthy protein alternatives in the 1970s. American vegetarians in the 1980s celebrated Thanksgiving with "tofurkey" (tofu shaped like turkey).

Mock foods have been known by other names. In 1796 in a recipe for "a tasty indian pudding" in *American Cookery* (considered the first American cookbook) Amelia Simmons substituted cornmeal for wheat flour. In the 1884 edition of the *Boston Cooking-School Cook Book,* Mrs. D. A. Lincoln provided detailed instructions for meat porcupines (molded meat with bacon quills) and mutton ducks (artfully reconstructed bones and meat). Betty Crocker promoted emergency steak (T-bone–shaped meat loaf) during World War II. In the 1950s residents of Pittsburgh consumed "city chicken" (skewered pork and veal), adopting it as a local favorite.

Here is a short list of some mock foods and their true ingredients:

Mock Foods List

Mock turtle soup—calf's head, 1824

Mock hollandaise—hot cream cheese, egg yolks, lemon juice, and mayonnaise, 1958

Mock maple syrup—brown sugar, water, salt, and vanilla, 1939

Mock chicken—breaded and fried peanuts and sweet potatoes, 1925

Mock chicken drumsticks or "city chicken"—veal and pork on skewers, 1946

Mock duck—shoulder of lamb, the shank shaped to look like a duck's bill, 1884

Mock duck—stuffed tenderloin or flank steak, 1958

Mock sausages—pureed lima beans, cracker crumbs, heavy cream, and spices fried in oil, 1923

Mock veal cutlets—baked lentils, peanuts, graham cracker crumbs, tomatoes, and spices, 1925

Mock venison—mutton served with gravy and currant jelly, 1844

Mock crab sandwich—grated cheese, creamed butter, mustard, and anchovy paste served hot, 1929

Mock crabs—canned corn, cracker crumbs, milk, and spices baked in butter, 1923

Mock oysters—corn fritters shaped like oysters, 1844

Mock oysters—mushrooms dipped in egg and bread crumbs and then fried, 1902

Mock scallops—halibut cut in the shape of scallops, breaded and deep fried, 1939

Mock artichokes—white turnips, 1902

Mock macaroni—crackers soaked in milk and used for casseroles, 1828

Mock olives—unripe plums preserved in brine, 1918

Mock cherry pie—cranberries and raisins, 1923

Mock cream—milk, cornstarch, eggs, and butter, 1910

Mock cream pie—eggs, flour, and milk poured over puff paste and cooked in the oven, 1847

Mock Devonshire cream—cream cheese, cream, and sugar, 1956

Mock pistachio ice cream—vanilla with almond extract and green food coloring, 1931

Mock toasted marshmallows—gelatin, water, sugar, egg whites, vanilla, and stale macaroons, 1939

Mock almonds—stale bread cut in almond shapes, brushed with butter, and baked; croutons, 1923

Mock candy—ground nuts and fruits pressed together and cut like caramels, 1902

Lynne M. Olver

I

ice ▶ a frozen mixture of fruit juice or flavored water and sugar.

▶ to decorate (a cake) with icing.

iceberg lettuce ▶ a lettuce having a dense, round head of crisp, pale leaves.

ice cream ▶ a soft frozen food made with sweetened and flavored milk or cream and butterfat.

■ a serving of this, typically in a bowl or a wafer cone, or on a stick.

–ORIGIN alteration of *iced cream.*

iced ▶ (of a drink or other liquid) cooled in or mixed with pieces of ice: *iced coffee.*

■ (of a cake or cookie) decorated with icing.

ice milk ▶ a sweet frozen food similar to ice cream but containing less butterfat.

icing ▶ a mixture of sugar with liquid or butter, typically flavored and colored, and used as a coating for cakes, pastries, or cookies.

immerse ▶ to dip or submerge in a liquid: *immerse the beans in water for twenty minutes.*

infuse ▶ to soak (tea, herbs, etc.) in liquid to extract the flavor or healing properties.

■ (of tea, herbs, etc.) to be soaked in this way.

□ **infusion**: *an infusion of mint and chamomile makes soothing tea.*

injera /inˈji(ə)rə/ ▶ a white leavened Ethiopian bread made from teff flour, similar to a crepe.

–ORIGIN Amharic.

insalata /ˌinsäˈlätə/ ▶ an Italian-style salad: *insalata verde.*

–ORIGIN Italian.

instant ▶ (of food) processed to allow quick preparation: *instant coffee.*

Irish coffee ▶ coffee mixed with a dash of Irish whiskey and served with cream on top.

Irish stew ▶ a stew made with lamb or other meat, potatoes, and onions.

J

jacket /'jakit/ ▶ the skin of a potato.

jalapeño /ˌhäləˈpānyō/ (also **jalapeño pepper**) ▶ a very hot green chili pepper, used especially in Mexican-style cooking.
-ORIGIN from Mexican Spanish *(chile) jalapeño* '(chili of) Jalapa, Mexico.'

jam ▶ a sweet spread or preserve made from fruit and sugar boiled to a thick consistency.

jambalaya ▶ a Cajun dish of rice with shrimp, chicken, and vegetables.
-ORIGIN Louisiana French, from Provençal *jambalaia*.

jardiniere (also **jardinière**) /ˌjärdnˈi(ə)r/ ▶ a garnish of mixed vegetables.
-ORIGIN from French *jardinière*, literally 'female gardener.'

Jarlsberg /'yärlzˌbərg/ ▶ a kind of hard yellow Norwegian cheese with many holes and a mild, nutty flavor.
-ORIGIN named after the town of *Jarlsberg*, Norway.

jasmine tea ▶ a tea perfumed with dried jasmine blossoms.

jello (also trademark **Jell-O**) ▶ a fruit-flavored gelatin dessert made from a commercially prepared powder.

jelly ▶ a sweet, clear, semisolid, somewhat elastic spread or preserve made from fruit juice and sugar boiled to a thick consistency.
■ a similar clear preparation made with fruit or other ingredients and used as a condiment: *roast pheasant with red currant jelly.*
■ a gelatinous savory preparation made by boiling meat and bones.
■ chiefly British a sweet, fruit-flavored gelatin dessert.
▶ to set (food) as or in a jelly: *jellied cranberry sauce | jellied eels.*
-ORIGIN Middle English: from Old French *gelée*, from Latin *gelata* 'frozen,' from *gelare* 'freeze.'

jelly roll ▸ a cylindrical cake with a spiral cross section, made from a flat sponge cake spread with a filling such as jam and rolled up.

jerk ▸ (**jerked**) to prepare (meat) by marinating it in spices and drying or barbecuing it over a wood fire: *jerked beef.*

▸ meat cooked in this way: *fiery Jamaican jerk* | *jerk chicken.*

–ORIGIN from Latin American Spanish *charquear*, from *charqui*, from Quechua *echarqui* 'dried flesh.'

Jerusalem artichoke ▸ the knobby white-fleshed tuber of a plant related to the sunflower, eaten raw or cooked as a vegetable.

–ORIGIN *Jerusalem*, alteration of Italian *girasole* 'sunflower.'

jicama /ˈhikəmə/ ▸ the crisp, white-fleshed, edible tuber of a Central American climbing plant of the pea family, used especially in Mexican cooking.

–ORIGIN from Mexican Spanish *jícama*, from Nahuatl *xicama.*

johnnycake ▸ cornbread typically baked or fried on a griddle.

–ORIGIN also referred to as *journey cake*, which may be the original form.

jollof rice /ˈjäləf/ ▸ a West African stew made with rice, chili peppers, and meat or fish.

–ORIGIN *jollof*, variant of *Wolof* (an African language).

Jonagold /ˈjänəˌgōld/ ▸ an eating apple of a variety with greenish-gold skin and crisp flesh.

–ORIGIN blend of **JONATHAN** and **GOLDEN DELICIOUS**.

Jonathan ▸ a cooking apple of a red-skinned variety first grown in the U.S.

–ORIGIN named after *Jonathan* Hasbrouk (died 1846), American lawyer.

jordan almond ▸ a high-quality almond of a variety grown chiefly in southeastern Spain.

■ an almond with a hard sugar coating.

–ORIGIN late Middle English: *jordan* apparently from French or Spanish *jardin* 'garden.'

jubilee ▸ (of desserts) flambé: *cherries jubilee.*

jugged ▸ (of a hare or rabbit) stewed or boiled in a covered container.

–ORIGIN perhaps from *Jug*, nickname for the given names *Joan*, *Joanna*, and *Jenny.*

juice ▸ the liquid obtained from or present in fruit or vegetables: *the juice of a lemon.*

▪ a drink made from such a liquid: *orange juice.*

▪ **(juices)** the liquid that comes from meat or other food when cooked.

▸ to extract the juice from (fruit or vegetables).

juicer ▸ an appliance for extracting juice from fruit and vegetables.

julep /'jo͞oləp/ ▸ a sweet flavored drink made from a sugar syrup, sometimes containing alcohol or medication.

-ORIGIN Middle English: from Old French, from medieval Latin *julapium*, via Arabic from Persian *gulāb*, from *gul* 'rose' + *āb* 'water.'

julienne /ˌjo͞olēˈen/ ▸ a portion of food cut into short, thin strips: *a julienne of vegetables.*

▸ **(julienned)** cut into short, thin strips: *julienned leeks | carrots julienne.*

-ORIGIN French, from the male name *Jules* or *Julien.*

junket ▸ a pudding of sweetened and flavored curds of milk, often served with fruit.

-ORIGIN Middle English: from Old French *jonquette* 'rush basket,' from *jonc* 'rush,' from Latin *juncus* (junkets were formerly drained in a rush basket or served on a rush mat).

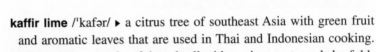

K

kaffir lime /ˈkafər/ ▸ a citrus tree of southeast Asia with green fruit and aromatic leaves that are used in Thai and Indonesian cooking.

kaiser roll ▸ a round, soft bread roll with a crisp crust, made by folding the corners of a square of dough into the center, resulting in a pinwheel shape when baked.

‒ORIGIN Middle English *cayser*, from Old Norse *keisari*, based on Latin *Caesar* 'family name of Julius Caesar.' The modern English form derives from German *Kaiser*.

kale ▸ a hardy variety of cabbage with erect stems and large leaves and no compact head. See also CURLY KALE.

■ the leaves of this plant eaten as a vegetable.

‒ORIGIN Middle English, northern form of *cole* 'cabbage' from Old English *cal*, from Latin *caulis*.

kasha /ˈkäsHə/ ▸ roasted buckwheat groats, cooked until soft.

‒ORIGIN Russian.

katsuobushi /ˌkätswōˈbo͞osHē/ ▸ dried fish prepared in hard blocks from the skipjack tuna and used in Japanese cooking.

‒ORIGIN Japanese.

kebab (also **kabob**) /kəˈbäb/ ▸ a dish of pieces of meat roasted or grilled on a skewer or spit.

■ a dish of any kind of food cooked in pieces in this way: *swordfish kebabs*.

‒ORIGIN from Arabic *kabāb*, partly via Urdu, Persian, and Turkish.

kedgeree /ˈkejəˌrē/ ▸ an Indian dish consisting chiefly of rice, lentils, onions, and eggs.

■ a European dish consisting chiefly of fish, rice, and hard-boiled eggs.

-ORIGIN from Hindi *khichṛī,* from Sanskrit *khiccā,* a dish of rice and sesame.

Keemun /'kē'mo͞on/ ▸ a black tea grown in Keemun, China.

kefir /kə'fi(ə)r/ ▸ a sour-tasting drink make from cow's milk fermented with certain bacteria.

-ORIGIN from Russian.

keftedes /kef'teTHes/ ▸ (in Greek cooking) small meatballs made with herbs and onions.

-ORIGIN from Greek *kephtedes,* plural of *kephtes,* via Turkish from Persian *koftah* (see **KOFTA**).

kelp ▸ a large brown seaweed that has a broad frond divided into strips, used as food and as a nutritional supplement: *dried kelp.*

ketchup (also **catsup**) ▸ a spicy sauce made chiefly from tomatoes and vinegar, used as a condiment.

-ORIGIN perhaps from Chinese (Cantonese dialect) *k'ē chap* 'tomato juice.'

kettle /'ketl/ ▸ a vessel, usually made of metal and with a handle, used for boiling liquids or cooking foods; a pot.
■ a teakettle.

Key lime ▸ a small yellowish lime with yellow flesh.

-ORIGIN named after the Florida *Keys.*

Key lime pie ▸ a custard pie made with the juice of Key limes.

kibbeh /'kibē/ ▸ a Middle Eastern dish of ground lamb with bulgar wheat and seasonings, eaten cooked or raw.

-ORIGIN from Arabic *kubbah.*

kidney bean ▸ a kidney-shaped bean, especially a dark red variety of the common bean plant.

kielbasa /ki(ə)l'bäsə/ ▸ a highly seasoned Polish sausage, typically containing garlic.

-ORIGIN Polish.

kimchi (also **kimchee**) /'kimCHē/ ▸ spicy pickled cabbage, the national dish of Korea.

-ORIGIN Korean.

kipper ▸ a kippered fish, especially a herring.
▸ to cure (a herring or other fish) by splitting it open and salting and drying it in the open air or in smoke: *kippered salmon.*

-ORIGIN Old English *cypera* 'male salmon,' of Germanic origin.

kishke /'kɪsHkə/ ▶ a beef intestine stuffed with a seasoned filling.
–ORIGIN Yiddish, from Polish *kiszka* or Ukrainian *kishka*.

kiss ▶ a small cookie or candy, typically a meringue.

kissel /'kisəl/ ▶ a dessert made from fruit juice or purée, boiled with sugar and water and thickened with potato or cornstarch.
–ORIGIN from Russian *kisel*.

kiwi fruit /'kēwē/ (also **kiwi**) ▶ the fruit of an eastern Asian vine, having a thin hairy skin, green flesh, and black seeds.
–ORIGIN named after the *kiwi*, a flightless New Zealand bird.

knackwurst (also **knockwurst**) /'näk͵wərst/ ▶ a short, fat, highly seasoned German sausage.
–ORIGIN from German *Knackwurst*, from *knacken* 'make a cracking noise' + *Wurst* 'sausage.'

knaidel (also **kneidel**) /'k(ə)nādl/ ▶ a matzoh ball.
–ORIGIN from Yiddish *kneydel*.

knead ▶ to work (moistened flour) into dough or paste with the hands.
■ to make (bread) by such a process.

knish /k(ə)'nisH/ ▶ a dumpling of dough that is stuffed with a filling and baked or fried.
–ORIGIN Yiddish, from Russian *knish, knysh*.

knuckle ▶ a cut of meat consisting of an animal's lower leg joint together with the adjoining parts: *a knuckle of pork*.

kofta /'kôftə/ ▶ (in Middle Eastern and Indian cookery) a spiced meatball.
–ORIGIN from Urdu and Persian, literally 'pounded meat.'

kohlrabi ▶ a variety of cabbage with an edible turniplike swollen stem.
–ORIGIN via German from Italian *cavoli rape*, plural of *cavolo rapa*, from medieval Latin *caulorapa*, from Latin *caulis* 'cabbage' + *rapum, rapa* 'turnip.'

korma ▶ a mildly spiced Indian curry dish of meat or fish marinated in yogurt or curds.
–ORIGIN from Urdu *ḳormā*, from Turkish *kavurma*.

kreplach /'kreplähH/ ▶ (in Jewish cooking) triangular noodles filled with chopped meat or cheese and served with soup.

-ORIGIN from Yiddish *kreplekh*, plural of *krepel*, from German dialect *Kräppel* 'fritter.'

kuchen /ˈkoōkən; -KHən/ ▸ a cake, especially one eaten with coffee.
-ORIGIN from German *Kuchen*.

kugel /ˈkoōgəl/ ▸ (in Jewish cooking) a kind of savory or sweet pudding of noodles, potatoes, or other vegetables.
-ORIGIN Yiddish, literally 'ball.'

kulcha /ˈkoōlCHə/ ▸ a small, round Indian bread made from flour, milk, and butter, typically stuffed with meat or vegetables.
-ORIGIN from Persian *kulīca*.

kulfi /ˈkoōlfē/ ▸ a type of Indian ice cream, typically served in the shape of a cone.
-ORIGIN from Hindi *kulfī*.

kumquat ▸ the small orangelike fruit of an eastern Asian shrub related to the citruses. It has an edible sweet rind and acid pulp and is eaten raw or candied, or used in preserves.
-ORIGIN from Chinese (Cantonese dialect) *kam kwat* 'little orange.'

L

laddu /'lədoo/ ▸ an Indian confection, typically made from flour, sugar, and shortening, that is prepared by frying and then shaping into a ball.
–ORIGIN from Hindi *laḍḍū*.

ladyfinger ▸ a small finger-shaped sponge cake.

laksa /'läksə/ ▸ a Malaysian dish of Chinese origin, consisting of rice noodles served in a curry sauce or hot soup.
–ORIGIN Malay.

lamb ▸ the flesh of a young sheep as food.

lamb's lettuce ▸ the narrow leaves of a herbaceous plant, used in salads (also called **mache**).

langouste /läNG'goost/ ▸ a spiny lobster, especially when prepared and cooked.
–ORIGIN French, from Old Provençal *lagosta*, based on Latin *locusta* 'locust, crustacean.'

langoustine /'laNGgə,stēn/ ▸ a large, commercially important prawn.
–ORIGIN French, from *langouste* (see LANGOUSTE).

lapsang souchong /'lap,saNG 'soo,CHäNG/ ▸ a variety of souchong tea with a smoky flavor.
–ORIGIN from an invented first element + SOUCHONG.

lard ▸ fat from the abdomen of a pig that is rendered and clarified for use in cooking.
▸ to insert strips of fat or bacon in (meat) before cooking.
■ to smear or cover (a foodstuff) with lard or fat, typically to prevent it from drying out during storage.
–ORIGIN Middle English: from Old French, 'bacon,' from Latin *lardum, laridum*.

lardon /'lärdn/ (also **lardoon** /lär'do͞on/) ▸ a chunk or cube of pork belly fat used to lard lean meat.
-ORIGIN late Middle English: from French, from *lard* 'bacon' (see LARD).

lasagna (also **lasagne**) ▸ pasta in the form of wide strips.
■ an Italian dish consisting of this cooked and served layered with meat or vegetables, cheese, and tomato sauce.
-ORIGIN from Italian *lasagna* (plural *lasagne*), based on Latin *lasanum* 'chamber pot,' perhaps also 'cooking pot.'

lassi /'lasē/ ▸ a sweet or savory Indian drink made from a yogurt or buttermilk base with water.
-ORIGIN from Hindi *lassī*.

latke /'lätkə/ ▸ (in Jewish cooking) a pancake, especially one made with grated potato.
-ORIGIN Yiddish.

latte /'lä͵tā/ ▸ short for CAFFÈ LATTE.

lavash /lə'väsн/ ▸ a Middle Eastern crisp flatbread.
-ORIGIN Armenian, from Turkish.

layer cake ▸ a cake of two or more layers with icing or another filling between them.

leaven /'levən/ ▸ (also **leavening**) a substance, usually yeast or baking powder, that is added to dough or batter to make it ferment and rise.
■ dough that is reserved from an earlier batch in order to start a later one fermenting.
▸ to cause (dough or bread) to ferment and rise by adding leaven: *leavened breads are forbidden during Passover.*
-ORIGIN Middle English: from Old French *levain*, based on Latin *levamen* 'relief' (literally 'means of raising'), from *levare* 'to lift.'

leek ▸ a plant related to the onion, with flat overlapping leaves forming an elongated cylindrical bulb that together with the leaves is eaten as a vegetable.
-ORIGIN Old English *lēac*, of Germanic origin.

legume ▸ a seed, pod, or other edible part of any of a large group of plants of the pea family. Beans, lentils, and peas are legumes.
-ORIGIN from French *légume*, from Latin *legumen*, from *legere* 'to pick' (because the fruit may be picked by hand).

Leicester /'lestər/ ▸ (also **Red Leicester**) a kind of mild, firm cheese, typically orange-colored and originally made in Leicestershire, England.

lemon ▸ the yellow, oval fruit of an evergreen citrus tree, with thick skin and fragrant, acidic juice.

■ a drink made from or flavored with lemon juice.

-ORIGIN Middle English: via Old French *limon* (in modern French denoting a lime) from Arabic *līmūn*.

lemonade ▸ a drink made from lemon juice and sweetened water.

lemon curd ▸ a preserve with a thick consistency made from lemons, butter, eggs, and sugar.

lemongrass (also **lemon grass**) ▸ a fragrant tropical grass that yields an oil that smells like lemon, widely used in Asian cooking.

lentil ▸ a high-protein legume that is dried and then soaked and cooked before eating. There are several varieties of lentils, including green ones and smaller orange ones.

-ORIGIN Middle English: from Old French *lentille*, from Latin *lenticula*, diminutive of *lens*, *lent-*.

lettuce ▸ a cultivated plant of the daisy family, with edible leaves that are a usual ingredient of salads. Many varieties of lettuce have been developed with a range of form, texture, and color.

-ORIGIN Middle English: from Old French *letues*, *laitues*, plural of *laitue*, from Latin *lactuca*, from *lac*, *lact-* 'milk' (because of its milky juice).

liaison /'lēə,zän; lē'ā-/ ▸ the binding or thickening agent of a sauce, often based on egg yolks.

-ORIGIN from French, from *lier* 'to bind.'

light ▸ (of a foodstuff) low in fat, cholesterol, sugar, or other rich ingredients: *a light diet.*

■ (of drink) not heavy on the stomach or strongly alcoholic: *light Hungarian wine.*

■ (of food, especially pastry or cake) fluffy or well aerated during cooking.

lima bean ▸ a large bean with a pale green color.

-ORIGIN *lima* from the name of the Peruvian capital *Lima*.

Limburger ▸ a soft white cheese with a characteristic strong smell, originally made in Limburg, a former duchy of Lorraine.

lime ▸ a rounded citrus fruit similar to a lemon but greener, smaller, and with a distinctive acid flavor.

-ORIGIN from French, from modern Provençal *limo*, Spanish *lima*, from Arabic *līma*; compare with LEMON.

limeade ▸ a drink made from lime juice sweetened with sugar.

linguine (also **linguini**) /liNG'gwēnē/ ▸ pasta in the form of narrow ribbons.

-ORIGIN Italian, plural of *linguina*, diminutive of *lingua* 'tongue.'

liqueur /li'kər; -'k(y)ŏŏr/ ▸ a strong, sweet flavored alcoholic liquor, usually drunk after a meal. See word bank at SPIRIT.

-ORIGIN from French, 'liquor.'

liquor ▸ alcoholic drink, especially distilled spirits. See word banks at COCKTAIL and SPIRIT.

■ liquid in which something has been steeped or cooked.

■ liquid that drains from food during cooking.

-ORIGIN Middle English (in the sense 'liquid, drink'): from Old French *lic(o)ur*, from Latin *liquor*; related to *liquare* 'liquefy,' *liquere* 'be fluid.'

litchi (also **lychee** or **lichee**) /'lēCHē/ ▸ a small rounded fruit with sweet white scented flesh, a large central stone, and a thin rough skin. Also called **litchi nut** when dried.

-ORIGIN from Chinese *lìzhī*.

lite ▸ of or relating to low-fat or low-sugar versions of manufactured food or drink products: *lite beer.*

-ORIGIN a deliberate respelling of LIGHT.

liver ▸ the flesh of an animal's liver as food: *calf's liver | liver pâté.*

liverwurst ▸ a seasoned meat paste in the form of a sausage containing cooked liver, or a mixture of liver and pork.

-ORIGIN partial translation of German *Leberwurst* 'liver sausage.'

loaf ▸ a quantity of bread that is shaped and baked in one piece and usually sliced before being eaten.

■ a quantity of other food formed into a particular shape, and often sliced into portions.

-ORIGIN Old English *hlāf*, of Germanic origin.

lobster ▸ any of several large marine crustaceans with a cylindrical body, stalked eyes, and the first of its five pairs of limbs modified as pincers, prized as food.
-ORIGIN Old English *lopustre*, alteration of Latin *locusta* 'crustacean, locust.'

lobster thermidor /ˈTHərmiˌdôr/ ▸ a dish of lobster cooked in a cream sauce, returned to its shell, sprinkled with cheese, and browned under a broiler.
-ORIGIN from *Thermidor*, the 11th month of the calendar used in the French Revolution.

loin ▸ a large cut of meat from the loin of an animal (either side of the spine between the ribs and hips), including the vertebrae of the loin: *loin of pork.*
-ORIGIN Middle English: from Old French *loigne*, based on Latin *lumbus*.

London broil ▸ a grilled steak served in thin slices cut diagonally.

lox /läks/ ▸ smoked salmon.
-ORIGIN from Yiddish *laks*.

lunchmeat /ˈlənCHˌmēt/ (also **luncheon meat**) ▸ meat sold in slices for sandwiches; cold cuts.

lychee /ˈlēCHē/ ▸ variant spelling of LITCHI.

lyonnaise /ˌlīəˈnāz/ ▸ (of food, especially sliced potatoes) cooked with onions or with a white wine and onion sauce.
-ORIGIN French, 'characteristic of the city of Lyons.'

TEN SIGNS OF A BAD RESTAURANT

Just because you're a tourist doesn't mean you should eat like one. How do you know if a place isn't worth your patronage?

1. The name of the restaurant is followed by an exclamation point.

2. It's called Bubba's Down-Home Barbecue—and it's in Boston.

3. Out front, there's a big plastic chef holding a menu.

4. The wine list is bound in tooled leather and has tassels.

5. The cuisine is Chinese, Japanese, and Italian.

6. The review in the window has yellowed and started to curl at the corners.

7. The restaurant revolves.

8. The words "buffet," "all you can eat," or "salad bar" appear in the window.

9. The waiters are carrying pepper mills the size of shoulder-fired rockets.

10. The word "decadent" is used to describe any dessert.

William Grimes

M

macadamia ▸ the edible globular nut of an Australian evergreen tree.

-ORIGIN modern Latin, named after John *Macadam* (1827–65), Australian chemist.

macaroni ▸ a variety of pasta formed in narrow tubes.

-ORIGIN from Italian *maccaroni* (now usually spelled *maccheroni*), plural of *maccarone*, from late Greek *makaria* 'food made from barley.'

macaroon ▸ a light cookie made with egg white, sugar, and usually ground almonds or coconut.

-ORIGIN from French *macaron*, from Italian *maccarone* (see **MACARONI**).

mace ▸ the reddish fleshy outer covering of the nutmeg, dried and ground as a spice.

-ORIGIN Middle English *macis* (taken as plural), via Old French from Latin *macir*.

macédoine /ˌmäsəˈdwän/ ▸ a mixture of vegetables or fruit cut into small dice and served as a salad.

-ORIGIN French, literally 'Macedonia,' with reference to the mixture of peoples in the Macedonian Empire of Alexander the Great.

macerate ▸ to soften or break up (food) by soaking in a liquid.
■ to become softened or broken up by soaking.

-ORIGIN from Latin *macerat-* 'made soft, soaked,' from the verb *macerare*.

mache (also **mâche**) /mäsн/ ▸ another term for **LAMB'S LETTUCE**.

-ORIGIN from French *mâche*.

mackerel /'mak(ə)rəl/ ▸ a migratory surface-dwelling predatory fish, commercially important as a food fish.

–ORIGIN Middle English: from Old French *maquerel*.

macrobiotic ▸ constituting, relating to, or following a diet of whole pure prepared foods that is based on Taoist principles of the balance of yin and yang.

▸ (**macrobiotics**) the use or theory of such a diet.

madeleine /ˌmadl'ān/ ▸ a small rich cake, typically baked in a shell-shaped mold and often decorated with coconut and jam.

–ORIGIN French, probably named after *Madeleine* Paulmier, 19th-century French pastry cook.

madrilene /ˌmadrə'lān/ ▸ a clear soup, usually served cold.

–ORIGIN from French *(consommé à la) madrilène*, literally 'soup in the Madrid style.'

malt ▸ barley or other grain that has been steeped, germinated, and dried, used especially for brewing or distilling and vinegar-making.

■ short for MALTED MILK.

malted milk (also **malted**) ▸ a drink combining milk, a malt preparation, and ice cream or flavoring.

■ the powdered mixture from which this drink is made.

mandoline /'mandlˌin/ ▸ a kitchen utensil consisting of a flat frame with adjustable cutting blades for slicing vegetables, fruits, etc.

–ORIGIN from French, 'mandolin (instrument)' from Italian *mandolino*, from *mandola* 'lute.'

mango ▸ a fleshy yellowish-red tropical fruit that is eaten ripe or used green for pickles or chutneys.

–ORIGIN from Portuguese *manga*, from a Dravidian language.

mangosteen /'maNGgəˌstēn/ ▸ a tropical fruit with sweet juicy white segments of flesh inside a thick reddish-brown rind.

–ORIGIN from Malay *manggustan*, dialect variant of *manggis*.

manicotti /ˌmani'kätē/ ▸ pasta in the shape of large tubes.

■ an Italian dish consisting largely of these stuffed with cheese, typically with tomato sauce.

–ORIGIN Italian, plural of *manicotto* 'muff.'

manioc /'manēˌäk/ ▸ another term for CASSAVA.

–ORIGIN from French, from Tupi *manioca*.

maple sugar ▸ sugar produced by evaporating the sap of certain maples, especially the sugar maple.

maple syrup ▸ syrup produced from the sap of certain maples, especially the sugar maple.

marble cake ▸ a cake with a streaked appearance, made of light and dark (especially chocolate) batter.

Marengo /məˈreNGgō/ ▸ (of chicken or veal) sautéed in oil, served with a tomato sauce, and traditionally garnished with eggs and crayfish: *chicken Marengo.*

-ORIGIN named after the village of *Marengo* in northern Italy, scene of a battle in 1800 in which the French were victorious and after which the dish is said to have been served to Napoleon.

margarine ▸ a butter substitute made from vegetable oils or animal fats.

-ORIGIN from French, from Greek *margaron* 'pearl' (because of the luster of the crystals of margaric acid, a fatty acid incorrectly assumed to be a constituent of animal fats) + the suffix *-ine.*

marinade ▸ a sauce, typically made of oil, vinegar, spices, and herbs, in which meat, fish, or other food is soaked before cooking in order to flavor or soften it.

■ a dish prepared using such a mixture: *a chicken marinade.*

▸ another term for **MARINATE**.

-ORIGIN from French, from Spanish *marinada*, via *marinar* 'pickle in brine' from *marino*, from Latin *marinus* 'of the sea.'

marinara /ˌmarəˈnarə/ ▸ (in Italian cooking) a sauce made from tomatoes, onions, and herbs, served especially with pasta.

▸ served with such a sauce: *spaghetti marinara.*

-ORIGIN from the Italian phrase *alla marinara* 'sailor-style.'

marinate ▸ to soak (meat, fish, or other food) in a marinade: *the beef was marinated in red wine vinegar.*

■ (of food) to undergo such a process.

-ORIGIN from Italian *marinare* 'pickle in brine,' or from French *mariner* (from *marine* 'brine').

marjoram /ˈmärjərəm/ ▸ the leaves of an aromatic southern European plant of the mint family, which are used as a culinary herb.

■ another term for **OREGANO**.

-ORIGIN Middle English: from Old French *majorane*, from medieval Latin *majorana*.

marmalade ▸ a preserve made from citrus fruit, especially bitter oranges, prepared like jam.

-ORIGIN from Portuguese *marmelada* 'quince jam,' from *marmelo* 'quince,' based on Greek *melimēlon* (from *meli* 'honey' + *mēlon* 'apple').

marmite /ˈmärˌmīt/ ▸ an earthenware cooking container.

-ORIGIN French, from Old French *marmite* 'hypocritical,' with reference to the hidden contents of the lidded pot, from *marmotter* 'to mutter' + *mite* 'cat.'

marquise ▸ a chilled dessert similar to a chocolate mousse.

-ORIGIN French, feminine of *marquis* 'nobleman.'.

marron glacé /maˈrôn gläˈsā/ ▸ a chestnut preserved in and coated with sugar.

-ORIGIN French, 'iced chestnut.'

marrow ▸ a soft fatty substance in the cavities of bones. The bones are cooked and the marrow is eaten out of the bone or used in fillings, soups, and sauces. Compare with **MARROWBONE**.

■ (also **vegetable marrow**) British a white-fleshed green-skinned gourd, which is eaten as a vegetable.

USAGE: See usage note at **MUFFIN**.

marrowbone ▸ a bone containing marrow.

marshmallow ▸ a spongy confection made from a soft mixture of sugar, albumen, and gelatin.

marzipan ▸ a sweet, yellowish paste of ground almonds, sugar, and egg whites, often colored and used to make small cakes or confections or as an icing or filling (also called **almond paste**).

■ a confection or cake made of or based on marzipan.

-ORIGIN from Italian *marzapane*, possibly from Arabic. The form *marchpane* (influenced by *March* and obsolete *pain* 'bread') was more usual until the late 19th century.

masa /ˈmäsə/ ▸ (in Latin American cuisine) dough made from corn flour and used to make tortillas, tamales, etc.

-ORIGIN Spanish.

masala /mə'sälə/ ▸ any of a number of spice mixtures ground into a paste or powder for use in Indian cooking.
■ a dish flavored with this: *chicken masala.*
-ORIGIN from Urdu *maṣālaḥ*, based on Arabic *maṣāliḥ* 'ingredients, materials.'

mascarpone /ˌmäskär'pōn(ā)/ ▸ a soft, mild Italian cream cheese.
-ORIGIN from Italian, from Italian dialect *mascarpa* 'cream cheese.'

maté /'mä,tā/ (also **yerba maté**) ▸ an infusion of the leaves of a South American shrub, which is high in caffeine and bitter.
-ORIGIN from Spanish *mate*, from Quechua *mati*.

matelote /ˌmatl'ōt/ ▸ a dish of fish in a sauce of wine and onions.
-ORIGIN French, from *à la matelote*, literally 'mariner-style,' from *matelot* 'sailor.'

mature ▸ (of certain foodstuffs or drinks) ready for consumption.
▸ (with reference to certain foodstuffs or drinks) to become or cause to become ready for consumption: *leave the cheese to mature* | *the Scotch is matured for a minimum of three years.*

matzo /'mätsə/ ▸ a thin, crisp unleavened bread, traditionally eaten by Jews during Passover.
-ORIGIN Yiddish, from Hebrew *maṣṣāh*.

matzo ball ▸ a small dumpling made of seasoned matzo meal bound together with egg and chicken fat, typically served in chicken soup.

matzo meal ▸ meal made from ground matzos.

mayo ▸ short for MAYONNAISE.

mayonnaise ▸ a thick, creamy dressing consisting of egg yolks beaten with oil and vinegar and seasoned.
-ORIGIN French, probably from the feminine of *mahonnais* 'of or from Port *Mahon*,' capital of Minorca.

McIntosh (also **McIntosh red**) ▸ an eating apple of a variety native to North America, with deep red skin.
-ORIGIN named after John *McIntosh* (1777–1845 or 1846), American-born Canadian farmer on whose farm the apple was discovered.

meal[1] ▸ any of the regular occasions in a day when a reasonably large amount of food is eaten, such as breakfast, lunch, or dinner.

■ the food eaten on such an occasion: *a perfectly cooked meal.*

–ORIGIN Old English *mæl* (also in the sense 'measure,' surviving in words such as *piecemeal* 'measure taken at one time'), of Germanic origin. The early sense of *meal* involved a notion of fixed time; compare with Dutch *maal* 'meal, (portion of) time' and German *Mal* 'time,' *Mahl* 'meal.'

Types of Meals

antipasto	continental	prix fixe
appetizer	breakfast	rijstaffel
banquet	crudités	salad bar
barbecue	elevenses	smorgasbord
blue plate	entree	supper
special	fondue	surf'n'turf
breakfast	high tea	table d'hôte
brunch	hors d'oeuvres	tapas
buffet	luncheon	tiffin
clambake	potluck	

meal [2] ▸ the edible part of any grain ground to powder, such as cornmeal.

■ any powdery substance made by grinding: *rice meal.*

–ORIGIN Old English *melu*, *meolo*, of Germanic origin.

meat ▸ the flesh of an animal (especially a mammal) as food. See word bank at **CUT**.

■ the edible part of fruits or nuts.

–ORIGIN Old English *mete* 'food' or 'article of food' (as in *sweetmeat*), of Germanic origin.

meatball ▸ a ball of minced or ground meat, usually beef, with added seasonings.

meat loaf (also **meatloaf**) ▸ minced or ground meat with added seasonings, molded into the shape of a loaf and baked.

médaillon /ˌmādī'yōn/ (also **medallion**) ▸ a small flat round or oval cut of meat or fish: *veal médaillons.*

–ORIGIN French, literally 'medallion.'

Melba sauce ▸ a sauce made from puréed raspberries thickened with powdered sugar.

–ORIGIN named after Dame Nellie *Melba*, Australian soprano.

Meats

alligator	frog legs	pigeon
antelope	game	pork
armadillo	goat	poultry
bear	goose	poussin
beaver	grouse	pullet
beefalo	guinea fowl	rabbit
bison	hare	raccoon
boar	kangaroo	rattlesnake
buffalo	kid	snail
caiman	lamb	squab
capon	llama	squirrel
caribou	moose	turkey
cervena	muscovy duck	turtle
chicken	musk ox	veal
Cornish hen	muskrat	venison
duck	mutton	wild boar
elk	ostrich	wild turkey
emu	partridge	wood pigeon
fowl	pheasant	yak

Melba toast ▸ very thin crisp toast.

–ORIGIN named after Dame Nellie *Melba*, Australian soprano.

melon ▸ the large round fruit of a plant of the gourd family, with sweet pulpy flesh and many seeds.

–ORIGIN Middle English: via Old French from late Latin *melo*, *melon-*, contraction of Latin *melopepo*, from Greek *mēlopepōn*, from *mēlon* 'apple' + *pepōn* 'gourd.'

menudo /məˈnoōdō/ ▸ a spicy Mexican soup made from tripe.

–ORIGIN noun use of a Mexican Spanish adjective meaning 'small.'

meringue ▸ an item of sweet food made from a mixture of well-beaten egg whites and sugar, baked until crisp and typically used as a topping for desserts, especially pies. Individual meringues are often filled with fruit or whipped cream.

–ORIGIN from French.

mesclun /ˈmesklən/ ▸ a salad made from a selection of lettuces with other edible leaves such as dandelion greens, mustard greens, and radicchio.

–ORIGIN Provençal, literally 'mixture,' from *mesclar* 'mix thoroughly.'

mesquite ▸ a spiny tree or shrub of the pea family, native to arid regions of southwestern U.S. and Mexico. The timber is burned in barbecues as flavoring.

-ORIGIN from Mexican Spanish *mezquite*.

meunière /moōn'ye(ə)r/ ▸ (especially of fish) cooked or served in lightly browned butter with lemon juice and parsley: *sole meunière*.

-ORIGIN from French *(à la) meunière* '(in the manner of) a miller's wife.'

meze (also **mezze**) /me'ze/ ▸ in the Mediterranean, an appetizer.

-ORIGIN Turkish and modern Greek.

microwave oven ▸ an oven that uses microwaves to cook or heat food.

milk ▸ the milk of cows (or occasionally goats or ewes) as food for humans.

■ the white juice of certain plants: *coconut milk*.

milk chocolate ▸ solid chocolate made with the addition of milk.

milk shake (also **milkshake**) ▸ a cold drink made of milk, a sweet flavoring such as fruit or chocolate, and typically ice cream, mixed until it is frothy.

mille-feuille /ˌmēl 'fœyə/ ▸ a rich dessert consisting of many very thin layers of puff pastry and such fillings as whipped cream, custard, fruit, etc.

-ORIGIN French, literally 'thousand-leaf.'

millet ▸ a fast-growing cereal plant that is widely grown in warm countries and regions with poor soils. The tiny seeds are used to make flour or alcoholic drinks.

mince ▸ to cut up or grind (food, especially meat) into very small pieces, typically in a machine with revolving blades: *minced beef.*
▸ something minced, especially mincemeat.

■ a quantity of something minced: *a mince of garlic*.

-ORIGIN Middle English: from Old French *mincier*, based on Latin *minutia* 'smallness.'

mincemeat ▸ a mixture of currants, raisins, sugar, apples, candied citrus peel, spices, and suet, typically baked in a pie.

■ minced meat.

mince pie ▸ a small, round pie or tart containing sweet mincemeat, typically eaten at Christmas.

mineral water ▸ water found in nature with some dissolved salts present.

■ chiefly British an artificial imitation of this, especially soda water.

minestrone /ˌminəˈstrōnē/ ▸ a thick soup containing vegetables and pasta.

-ORIGIN Italian.

minneola /ˌminēˈōlə/ ▸ a deep reddish tangelo of a thin-skinned variety.

-ORIGIN named after a town in Florida.

mint ▸ any of various aromatic plants native to temperate regions of the Old World, several kinds of which are used as culinary herbs.

■ the flavor of mint, especially peppermint.

mirepoix /mi(ə)rˈpwä/ ▸ a mixture of sautéed chopped vegetables used in various sauces.

-ORIGIN French, named after the Duc de *Mirepoix* (1699–1757), French general.

mirliton /ˈmərləˌtän/ ▸ a small puff-pastry tart filled with almond cream.

■ another term for CHAYOTE.

-ORIGIN from French, 'reed pipe, tube-shaped pastry.'

miso /ˈmēsō/ ▸ a paste made from fermented soybeans and barley or rice malt, used in Japanese cooking.

-ORIGIN Japanese.

Mississippi mud pie ▸ a type of rich, mousselike chocolate cake or pie.

mixed drink ▸ an alcoholic drink with one or more additional ingredients such as soda or fruit juice. See word bank at COCKTAIL.

mixed grill ▸ a dish consisting of various items of grilled food, typically meats, tomatoes, and mushrooms.

mixer ▸ a machine or device for mixing things, especially an electrical appliance for mixing foods: *a food mixer.*

■ a soft drink that can be mixed with alcohol.

mizuna /məˈzōōnə/ (also **mizuna greens**) ▸ an Asian rape of a variety with finely cut leaves that are eaten as a salad vegetable.

-ORIGIN from Japanese.

mocha /ˈmōkə/ ▸ a fine-quality coffee.

■ a drink or flavoring made with or in imitation of this, typically with chocolate added.

_ORIGIN named after *Mocha*, port on the Red Sea, from where coffee was first shipped.

mochi /ˈmōCHē/ ▸ a short-grained, sweet, glutinous rice with a high starch content, used in Japanese cooking.

_ORIGIN Japanese.

mock turtle soup ▸ imitation turtle soup made from a calf's head.

molasses ▸ thick, dark brown, uncrystallized juice obtained from raw sugar during the refining process.

■ a paler, sweeter version of this used as a table syrup and in baking.

_ORIGIN from Portuguese *melaço*, from late Latin *mellacium* 'must,' based on *mel* 'honey.'

mold [1] ▸ a hollow container used to give shape to liquid foods when they cool and harden.

■ something made in a mold, especially a gelatin dessert or a mousse: *lobster mold.*

_ORIGIN Middle English: apparently from Old French *modle*, from Latin *modulus*, literally 'measure.'

mold[2] ▸ woolly or furry growth of minute fungi occurring especially in moist warm conditions. Certain molds are edible as the ones giving a distinctive taste to some cheeses.

_ORIGIN Middle English: probably from obsolete *mould*, past participle of *moul* 'grow moldy,' of Scandinavian origin.

mole /ˈmōlā/ ▸ a highly spiced Mexican sauce made chiefly from chili peppers and other spices, often including chocolate, served with meat.

_ORIGIN Mexican Spanish, from Nahuatl *molli* 'sauce, stew.'

mollusk ▸ an invertebrate of a large phylum that includes many edible varieties such as snails, mussels, and octopuses. They have a soft, unsegmented body, and most kinds have an external calcareous shell.

_ORIGIN from modern Latin *mollusca*, neuter plural of Latin *molluscus*, from *mollis* 'soft.'

monkfish ▸ a bottom-dwelling anglerfish, used for food.

monosodium glutamate (abbr.: **MSG**) ▸ a compound that occurs naturally as a breakdown product of proteins and is used as a flavor enhancer in food (although itself tasteless). A traditional ingredient in Asian cooking, it was originally obtained from seaweed but is now mainly made from bean and cereal protein.

Monterey Jack (also **Monterey cheese** or **Jack cheese**) ▶ a kind of cheese resembling cheddar.
-ORIGIN named after *Monterey* County, California, where it was first made; the origin of *Jack* is unknown.

moo shu pork ▶ a Chinese dish consisting of shredded pork with vegetables and seasonings, rolled in thin pancakes.

morel ▶ a widely distributed edible fungus that has a brown oval or pointed fruiting body with an irregular honeycombed surface bearing the spores.
-ORIGIN from French *morille*, from Dutch *morilje*; related to German *Morchel* 'fungus.'

morello /mə'relō/ ▶ a sour, dark cherry used in cooking.
-ORIGIN from Italian *morello* 'blackish,' from medieval Latin *morellus*, diminutive of Latin *Maurus* 'Moor.'

mornay (also **Mornay**) ▶ denoting or served in a cheese-flavored white sauce: *mornay sauce | cauliflower mornay.*
-ORIGIN named after *Mornay*, French cook and eldest son of Joseph Voiron, chef of the restaurant Durand at the end of the 19th century and inventor of the sauce.

mortadella /ˌmôrtə'delə/ ▶ a type of light pink, smooth-textured Italian sausage containing pieces of fat, typically served in slices.
-ORIGIN Italian diminutive, formed irregularly from Latin *murtatum* '(sausage) seasoned with myrtle berries.'

moussaka /ˌmo͞osə'kä/ ▶ a Greek dish made of minced lamb, eggplant, and tomatoes, with cheese on top.
-ORIGIN from Turkish *musakka*, based on Arabic.

mousse ▶ a sweet dessert made as a smooth light mass with whipped cream and beaten egg white, flavored with chocolate, fruit, etc., and typically served chilled: *dark chocolate mousse.*
 ■ a light, savory dish made of meat, fish, or vegetables with beaten egg whites and served hot or cold: *lobster mousse.*
-ORIGIN from French, 'moss or froth.'

mousseline /ˌmo͞os(ə)'lēn/ ▶ a soft, light mousse.

■ (also **sauce mousseline**) hollandaise sauce that has been made frothy with whipped cream or egg white, served mainly with fish or asparagus.

-ORIGIN from French, 'muslin,' from Italian *mussolina*, from *Mussolo* 'Mosul (city in Iraq).'

mozzarella ▸ a mild, semisoft white Italian cheese, usually made from cow's milk, often used in Italian cooking as a melted topping, especially on pizzas.

-ORIGIN Italian, diminutive of *mozza*, denoting a kind of cheese, from *mozzare* 'cut off.'

Muenster (also **Munster**) ▸ a mild, semisoft cheese made from whole milk.

-ORIGIN named after *Munster*, a town in the Alsace region of France.

muesli /'m(y)ōozlē/ ▸ a mixture of cereals (especially rolled oats), dried fruit, and nuts, typically eaten with milk at breakfast.

-ORIGIN Swiss German.

muffin ▸ a small domed cake or quick bread made from batter or dough: *blueberry muffins.*

■ short for ENGLISH MUFFIN.

USAGE: The many distinctions between British and American usage can cause confusion. British **muffins** are not the sweet American variety. They are what Americans call **English muffins**. A **biscuit** in Britain refers to any **cracker** or **cookie**, and **corn** refers to any **cereal** grain, such as wheat in England or oats in Scotland. To **grill** in Britain is to **broil** in America. And **marrow** is a **summer squash**, not what is inside a bone.

mug ▸ a large cup, typically cylindrical and with a handle and used without a saucer.

-ORIGIN (originally Scots and northern English, denoting an earthenware bowl): probably of Scandinavian origin.

mull ▸ (**mulled**) to warm (a beverage, especially wine, beer, or cider) and add spices and sweetening to it: *a tankard of mulled ale.*

mullet ▸ a chiefly marine fish that is widely caught for food. See also RED MULLET.

-ORIGIN Middle English: from Old French *mulet*, diminutive of Latin *mullus* 'red mullet,' from Greek *mullos*.

mulligan (also **mulligan stew**) ▸ informal a stew made from odds and ends of food.

-ORIGIN apparently from the surname *Mulligan*.

mulligatawny /ˌməligəˈtônē/ (also **mulligatawny soup**) ▸ a spicy meat soup created in India for the English, usually consisting of chicken or mutton and fried onions in a spicy broth.

-ORIGIN from Tamil *miḻaku-taṇṇi* 'pepper-water.'

multigrain ▸ (of bread) made from more than one kind of grain.

mung bean ▸ a small round green bean commonly grown as a source of bean sprouts.

-ORIGIN from Hindi *mūng*.

muscovado /ˌməskəˈvädō; -ˈvädō/ (also **muscovado sugar**) ▸ unrefined sugar made from the juice of sugar cane by evaporating it and draining off the molasses.

-ORIGIN from Portuguese *mascabado (açúcar)* '(sugar) of the lowest quality.'

mush ▸ thick porridge, especially made of cornmeal.

-ORIGIN apparently a variant of *mash*.

mushroom ▸ a fungal growth that typically takes the form of a domed cap on a stalk. Only some species are edible.

-ORIGIN Middle English: from Old French *mousseron*, from late Latin *mussirio(n-)*.

muskmelon ▸ a melon of a type that has a raised network of markings on the skin and is prized for food. Its many varieties include those with orange, yellow, green, or white juicy flesh.

mussel ▸ any of a number of bivalve mollusks, especially an edible species with a purplish-black shell.

-ORIGIN Old English *mus(c)le*, superseded by forms from Middle Low German *mussel*, Middle Dutch *mosscele*; ultimately from late Latin *muscula*, from Latin *musculus* 'sea mussel, muscle.'

mustard ▸ a pungent-tasting yellow or brown paste made from the crushed seeds of certain Eurasian plants of the cabbage family, typically eaten with meat or used as a cooking ingredient.

-ORIGIN Middle English: from Old French *moustarde*, from Latin *mustum* 'must (unfermented wine),' the condiment being originally prepared with must.

Mushrooms

agaric
almond portobello
armillaria
autumn chanterelle
bearded tooth
beech
beefsteak fungus
black
black trumpet
blewit
blue milky cap
blue oyster
blusher
bolete
bracket fungus
Braunkappe
button
cauliflower fungus
cep
cepe
champignon
chanterelle
chicken of the woods
Chinese
cinnamon cap
clam shell
clitocybe
club fungus
cobweb cap
conifer coral
conifer tuft
coprinus
coral fungus
cordycep
cremini
cup fungus
enoki
enokitake
fairy ring
false morel
field
fly agaric
ganoderma

garden giant
garden oyster
girolle
golden oyster
gray oyster
green-spored
  lepiota
grifola
grisette
guépinie
hedgehog
hericium
himematsutake
honey fungus
hon-shimeji
horn of plenty
horse
huitlacoche
Indian oyster
ink cap
jack o'lantern
jelly fungus
king bolete
king stropharia
king tuber
lentinula
ling zhi
lion's mane
little brown
lobster
maitake
matsutake
milk cap
miller
morchella
morel
morille
mousseron
nameko
Nigerian
oak
oronge
parasol

pearl oyster
phoenix oyster
pholiota
pied de mouton
pine
pink oyster
pioppino
Polish
polypore
pom pom blanc
porcini
poria
portobello/
  portabella
prince
puffball
reishi
russula
shaggy inkcap
shaggy mane
shiitake
sparassis
St. George's
Steinpilz
stinkhorn
stone
straw
sulphur shelf
termite heap
toadstool
tooth fungus
tree ear
tremella
trompette des morts
truffle
turkey tail
wax cap
white
white truffle
wine cap
wood blewit
yellowfoot

mustard greens ▶ the leaves of the mustard plant used in salads or cooked as a vegetable.

mutton ▶ the flesh of sheep, especially mature sheep, used as food: *roast mutton.*

-ORIGIN Middle English: from Old French *moton*, from medieval Latin *multo(n-)*, probably of Celtic origin.

N

nacho ▸ a small crisp piece of a tortilla, typically topped with melted cheese and spices.

-ORIGIN perhaps from Mexican Spanish *Nacho*, nickname for *Ignacio*, given name of the chef credited with creation of the dish. An alternative derivation is from Spanish *nacho* 'flat-nosed.'

nage /näzH/ ▸ an aromatic court bouillon or stock, used for cooking shellfish.

-ORIGIN from French.

nam pla /ˌnäm ˈplä/ ▸ Thai term for FISH SAUCE.

nan (also **naan**) /nän/ ▸ (in Indian cooking) a type of leavened bread, typically of teardrop shape and traditionally cooked in a clay oven.

-ORIGIN from Urdu and Persian *nān*.

napa cabbage ▸ a cabbagelike Chinese plant with long, white leaves that are used in salads and cooking.

napoleon ▸ a rectangular pastry consisting of thin puff-pastry sheets layered with a custard or cream filling.

-ORIGIN named after *Napoleon* Bonaparte.

napped ▸ (of food) served in a sauce or other liquid: *mushrooms napped with melted butter.*

-ORIGIN from French *napper* 'coat with (a sauce),' from *nappe* 'cloth,' figuratively 'pool of liquid,' + the suffix *-ed*.

nasturtium ▸ a South American trailing plant with round leaves and bright orange, yellow, or red edible flowers used in salads or as an edible garnish.

-ORIGIN Old English, from Latin, apparently from *naris* 'nose' + *torquere* 'to twist.'

natural food ▸ food that has undergone a minimum of processing or treatment with preservatives.

navarin /'navərin/ ▸ a stew of lamb or mutton with vegetables.
-ORIGIN French.

neck ▸ meat from an animal's neck: *a stew made with neck of lamb.*

nectar ▸ a thick fruit juice: *peach nectar.*
-ORIGIN via Latin from Greek *nektar.*

nectarine ▸ a peach of a variety with smooth, thin, brightly colored skin and rich firm flesh.

Neufchâtel /ˌnōōsHə'tel/ ▸ a creamy white cheese made from whole or partly skimmed milk in Neufchâtel, France.

New England boiled dinner ▸ a dish of meat (often corned beef), cabbage or other vegetables, and potatoes, prepared by simmering in water.

Niçoise /nē'swäz/ ▸ denoting food that is characteristic of Nice or the surrounding region, typically garnished with tomatoes, capers, and anchovies: *salade Niçoise.*
-ORIGIN French.

noisette /nwä'zet/ ▸ a small round piece of lean meat, especially lamb.
■ a chocolate made with hazelnuts.
-ORIGIN French, diminutive of *noix* 'choice cut of meat, nut,' from Latin *nux.*

noodle ▸ a strip, ring, or tube of pasta or a similar dough, typically made with egg and usually eaten with a sauce or in a soup.
-ORIGIN from German *Nudel.*

Noodles

bean curd	harusame	rice sheet
bean thread	Hokkien	rice stick
cellophane	knodel	rice vermicelli
chasoba	kreplach	Sevian
chow fun	lo mein	shirataki
dang myun	mei fun	soba
dumpling	mung bean	somen
e-fu	naeng myun	spaetzle
egg	pierogi	udon
farfel	quenelle	wheat
glass	ramen	won ton
gooksu	rice	

nopales /nō'päləz/ ▸ the edible fleshy pads of the prickly pear cactus, used as a staple in Mexican cuisine.

–ORIGIN via French and Spanish from Nahuatl *nopalli* 'cactus.'

nori /'nôrē/ ▸ an edible seaweed, eaten either fresh or dried in sheets, especially by the Japanese.

–ORIGIN Japanese.

Norway lobster ▸ another term for LANGOUSTINE.

nouvelle cuisine ▸ a modern style of cooking that avoids rich, heavy foods and emphasizes the freshness of the ingredients and the presentation of the dishes.

–ORIGIN French, literally 'new cooking.'

nuoc cham /nōō'äk 'CHäm/ ▸ a dipping sauce made from nuoc mam, chilies, garlic, sugar, lime juice, and rice vinegar.

–ORIGIN Vietnamese.

nuoc mam /nōō'äk 'mäm/ ▸ Vietnamese term for FISH SAUCE.

–ORIGIN Vietnamese.

nut ▸ a fruit consisting of a hard or tough shell around an edible kernel.

■ the hard kernel of such a fruit.

–ORIGIN Old English *hnutu*, of Germanic origin.

nut loaf ▸ a baked vegetarian dish made from ground or chopped nuts, vegetables, and herbs.

Nuts and Seeds

acorn	coconut	peanut
almond	corozo	pecan
beechnut	dika	pignoli
ben	English walnut	pignut
betel	filbert	pili
black walnut	gabon	pine
Brazil	gingko nut	pistachio
breadnut	grugru	pumpkin seed
bunya nut	hazelnut	sassafras
butternut	hickory	sesame seed
candllenut	horse chestnut	souari nut
cashew	kola	Spanish peanut
chinquapin	litchi	sunflower seed
cobnut	macadamia	walnut
coco de mer	palm	water chestnut

nut meat (also **nutmeat**) ▶ the kernel of a nut, typically edible.

nutmeg ▶ the hard, aromatic, almost spherical seed of a tropical tree, which is grated and used as a spice.

-ORIGIN Middle English *notemuge*, partial translation of Old French *nois muguede*, based on Latin *nux* 'nut' + late Latin *muscus* 'musk.'

O

oat ▸ a cereal plant cultivated chiefly in cool climates and widely used for animal feed as well as human consumption.

■ **(oats)** the grain yielded by this plant, used as food.

oatcake ▸ a thin, unleavened cake made of oatmeal.

oatmeal ▸ meal made from ground oats, used in breakfast cereals or other food.

octopus ▸ an edible mollusk with eight sucker-bearing arms, a soft saclike body, strong beaklike jaws, and no internal shell.

-ORIGIN from Greek *oktōpous*.

USAGE: The standard plural in English of **octopus** is **octopuses**. However, the word **octopus** comes from Greek, and the Greek plural form is **octopodes** (/äk'täpə,dēz/). Modern usage of **octopodes** is so infrequent that many people mistakenly create the erroneous plural form **octopi**, formed according to rules for Latin plurals.

oil ▸ any of various thick, viscous liquids that are insoluble in water and are obtained from animals or plants: *sliced potatoes fried in vegetable oil.*

-ORIGIN Middle English: from Old Northern French *olie*, Old French *oile*, from Latin *oleum* '(olive) oil.'

okra ▸ the immature long ridged seedpods of a plant of the mallow family, eaten as a vegetable and also used to thicken soups and stews. Also called GUMBO.

-ORIGIN a West African word.

oleomargarine ▸ another term for MARGARINE.

olio ▸ another term for OLLA PODRIDA.

-ORIGIN from Spanish *olla* 'stew,' from Latin *olla* 'cooking pot.'

olive ▸ a small oval fruit with a hard pit and bitter flesh, green when unripe and brownish black when ripe, used as a relish and as a source of oil.

-ORIGIN Middle English: via Old French from Latin *oliva*, from Greek *elaia*, from *elaion* 'oil.'

olive oil ▸ an oil pressed from ripe olives, used in cooking.

olla podrida /ˌälə pə'drēdə/ ▸ a highly spiced Spanish-style stew containing a mixture of meat and vegetables.

-ORIGIN Spanish, literally 'rotten pot,' from Latin *olla* 'jar' + *putridus* 'rotten.'

omelet (also **omelette**) ▸ a dish of beaten eggs cooked in a frying pan until firm, often with a filling added while cooking, and usually served folded over.

-ORIGIN French *omelette*, earlier *amelette*, alteration of *alumette*, variant of *alumelle*, from *lemele* 'knife blade,' from Latin *lamella* 'thin plate' (probably with reference to the thin flat shape of an omelet).

onion ▸ an edible bulb with a pungent taste and smell, composed of several concentric layers, widely used in cooking and raw in salads.

-ORIGIN Middle English: from Old French *oignon*, based on Latin *unio(n-)*, denoting a kind of onion.

oolong ▸ a dark-colored China tea made by fermenting the withered leaves to about half the degree usual for black teas.

-ORIGIN from Chinese *wūlóng*, literally 'black dragon.'

orange ▸ a round juicy citrus fruit with a tough bright reddish-yellow rind, eaten fresh or made into juice.

-ORIGIN Middle English: from Old French *orenge* (in the phrase *pomme d'orenge*), based on Arabic *nāranj*, from Persian *nārang*.

orangeade ▸ a drink made with orange juice, sweetener, and water, sometimes carbonated.

orange pekoe /'pēkō/ ▸ a type of black tea made from young leaves.

orecchiette /ˌôri'kyetē/ ▸ small ear-shaped pasta.

-ORIGIN Italian, literally 'little ears.'

oregano ▸ the leaves of an aromatic plant related to marjoram, used fresh or dried as a culinary herb.

-ORIGIN from Spanish, variant of *origanum*, from Latin, 'origanum plant.'

organic ▸ (of food or farming methods) produced or involving production without the use of chemical fertilizers, pesticides, or other artificial agents.

-ORIGIN Middle English: via Latin from Greek *organikos* 'relating to an organ or instrument.'

orzo ▸ a variety of pasta shaped like grains of barley or rice.

-ORIGIN Italian, literally 'barley.'

osso bucco /ˈôsō ˈbo͞okō/ ▸ an Italian dish made with veal shank containing marrowbone, stewed in wine with vegetables and seasonings.

-ORIGIN Italian, literally 'marrowbone.'

oven ▸ an enclosed compartment, as in a stove, for baking, roasting, and heating food.

over easy ▸ (of a fried egg) turned over when the white is nearly done and fried lightly on the other side, so that the yolk remains slightly liquid.

oxtail ▸ meat from the tail of a cow, used especially for making soup.

oyster ▸ any of a number of bivalve mollusks with rough irregular shells. Several kinds are eaten (especially raw) as a delicacy and may be farmed.

■ an oyster-shaped morsel of meat on each side of the backbone in poultry.

-ORIGIN Middle English: from Old French *oistre*, via Latin from Greek *ostreon*; related to *osteon* 'bone' and *ostrakon* 'shell or tile.'

oyster mushroom ▸ a widely distributed edible fungus that has a grayish-brown, oyster-shaped cap and a very short or absent stem, growing on the wood of broad-leaved trees and causing rot.

P

pad thai /'päd 'tī/ ▸ a Thai dish based on rice noodles.
  −ORIGIN Thai.
paella /pä'äyä/ ▸ a Spanish dish of rice, saffron, chicken, seafood,
  etc., cooked and served in a large shallow pan.
  −ORIGIN Catalan, from Old French *paele*, from Latin *patella* 'pan.'
pain perdu /'pän per'dōō/ ▸ French term for **FRENCH TOAST.**
  −ORIGIN French, literally 'lost bread.'
pakora /pə'kôrə/ ▸ (in Indian cooking) a piece of vegetable or meat,
  coated in seasoned batter and deep-fried.
  −ORIGIN from Hindi *pakoṛā*, denoting a dish of vegetables in gram
  flour.
palacsinta /ˌpälət'sintə/ ▸ (in Hungarian cuisine) a thin pancake eaten
  as a dessert, typically with a filling.
  −ORIGIN Hungarian.
palmier /'pä(l)mēˌä/ ▸ a sweet, crisp pastry shaped like a palm leaf.
  −ORIGIN French, literally 'palm tree.'
panada /pə'nädə/ ▸ a simple dish consisting of bread boiled to a pulp
  and flavored.
  −ORIGIN from Spanish and Portuguese, based on Latin *panis*
  'bread.'
pancake ▸ a thin, flat cake of batter, usually fried on both sides in a
  pan. Pancakes are usually eaten with syrup or rolled up with a filling.
pancetta /pan'CHetə/ ▸ Italian cured belly of pork.
  −ORIGIN Italian, diminutive of *pancio* 'belly.'
pandowdy ▸ a kind of spiced apple pie baked in a deep dish.
panettone /ˌpani'tōnē/ ▸ a rich Italian bread made with eggs, fruit,
  and butter and typically eaten at Christmas.

-ORIGIN Italian, from *panetto* 'cake,' diminutive of *pane* 'bread' (from Latin *panis* 'bread').

panforte /panˈfôrtā/ ▸ a dense, spicy Sienese cake containing nuts, candied citrus peel, and honey.

-ORIGIN Italian, from *pane* 'bread' + *forte* 'strong.'

pan-fry ▸ to fry in a pan in a small amount of fat: *pan-fried trout*.

pani puri /ˈpänē ˌpo͞orē/ ▸ (in Indian cooking) a puff-pastry ball filled with spiced mashed potato and tamarind juice and then fried.

-ORIGIN from Hindi *pānī* 'water' and *pūrī* from Sanskrit *pūrikā* 'small, fried wheaten cake.'

panir (also **paneer**) /paˈni(ə)r/ ▸ a type of curd cheese used in Indian, Iranian, and Afghan cooking.

-ORIGIN Hindi and Persian, 'cheese.'

panzanella /ˌpanzəˈnelə/ ▸ a type of Tuscan salad made with anchovies, chopped salad vegetables, and bread soaked in dressing.

-ORIGIN Italian, from *pane* 'bread' + *zanella* 'small basket.'

papain /pəˈpā-in/ ▸ a protein-digesting enzyme obtained from unripe papaya, used to tenderize meat and as a food supplement to aid digestion.

-ORIGIN from PAPAYA + the suffix *-in*.

papaya ▸ a tropical fruit shaped like an elongated melon, with edible orange flesh and small black seeds.

-ORIGIN from Spanish and Portuguese.

pappadam /ˈpäpädəm/ ▸ a thin East Indian bread made with lentil flour.

-ORIGIN from Tamil.

pappardelle /ˌpapärˈdelä/ ▸ pasta in the form of broad flat ribbons, usually served with a meat sauce.

-ORIGIN Italian, from *pappare* 'eat hungrily.'

paprika ▸ a powdered spice with a deep orange-red color and a mildly pungent flavor, made from the dried and ground fruits of certain varieties of sweet pepper.

-ORIGIN from Hungarian.

paratha /pəˈrätə/ ▸ (in Indian cooking) a flat, thick piece of unleavened bread fried on a griddle.

-ORIGIN from Hindi *parāṭhā*.

parboil ▸ to partly cook (food) by boiling.
–ORIGIN Middle English: from Old French *parbouillir*, from late Latin *perbullire* 'boil thoroughly.'

parchment ▸ (also **parchment paper**) a type of stiff translucent paper treated to resemble parchment and used in baking.

parfait ▸ a dessert consisting of layers of ice cream, fruit, etc., served in a tall glass.
■ a rich cold dessert made with whipped cream, eggs, and often fruit.
–ORIGIN from the French adjective *parfait*, literally 'perfect.'

parkin ▸ British a kind of dark gingerbread, typically with a soft, dry texture, made with oatmeal and molasses.
–ORIGIN perhaps from the family name *Parkin*, diminutive of *Per* 'Peter.'

Parma ham ▸ a type of ham that is eaten uncooked.

Parmentier /ˌpärmenˈtyā/ ▸ cooked or served with potatoes: *soups such as potage Parmentier.*
–ORIGIN from the name of Antoine A. *Parmentier* (1737–1813), French agriculturalist who popularized the potato in France.

Parmesan ▸ a hard, dry cheese used in grated form, especially on Italian dishes.
–ORIGIN from French, from Italian *parmigiano* 'of *Parma*, Italy' where it was originally made.

parmigiana /ˌpärməˈzHänə/ ▸ cooked or served with Parmesan cheese: *eggplant parmigiana.*
▸ a dish cooked in this way.
–ORIGIN Italian, feminine of *parmigiano* 'of Parma, Italy.'

USAGE: In French and other Romance languages, the adjective comes after the noun it modifies. These "postpositive" adjectives appear in foreign culinary terms that are partly assimilated into English, so a menu might offer steak bordelaise or veal parmigiana. This feature of grammar has even influenced nonforeign names of dishes, such as chicken tarragon and chicken Maryland.

parsley ▸ a biennial plant with aromatic leaves that are either crinkly or flat and used as a culinary herb, in salads, and for garnishing food.
–ORIGIN Old English *petersilie*, via late Latin based on Greek *petroselinon*, from *petra* 'rock' + *selinon* 'parsley.'

parsnip ▸ a long tapering cream-colored root with a sweet flavor, cooked as a vegetable.
-ORIGIN Middle English: from Old French *pasnaie*, from Latin *pastinaca*. The change in the ending was due to association with *neep* (turnip).

paskha (also **pashka**) /'päsнkə/ ▸ a rich Russian dessert made with soft cheese, dried fruit, nuts, and spices, and traditionally eaten at Easter.
-ORIGIN Russian, literally 'Easter.'

passata /pə'sätə/ ▸ a thick paste made from strained tomatoes and used especially in Italian cooking.
-ORIGIN Italian.

passion fruit (also **passionfruit**) ▸ the edible purple fruit of a kind of passionflower that is grown commercially, especially in tropical America.

pasta ▸ dough made from durum wheat and water, extruded or stamped into various shapes and cooked in boiling water.
■ a dish originally from Italy consisting of this, typically served with a sauce.
-ORIGIN from Italian, literally 'paste.'

paste ▸ a thick, soft, moist substance, usually produced by mixing dry ingredients with a liquid: *beat flour, sugar, and oil to a paste.*
-ORIGIN Middle English: from Old French, from late Latin *pasta* 'square-shaped medicinal preparation,' probably from Greek *pastē* 'barley porridge.'

pastitsio /pä'stētsyō/ ▸ a Greek dish consisting of macaroni, ground lamb, grated cheese, and tomatoes topped with a béchamel sauce.
-ORIGIN from modern Greek, literally 'hodgepodge.'

pastrami ▸ highly seasoned smoked beef, typically served in thin slices.
-ORIGIN Yiddish.

pastry ▸ a dough of flour, shortening, and water, used as a base and covering in baked dishes such as pies.
■ an item of food made of sweet dough, often with a cream, jam, or fruit filling.
-ORIGIN Middle English: from PASTE, influenced by Old French *pastaierie*.

Pasta

acomo pepe	gnocchetti	quadrefiore
anelli	gnocchi	quadrettini
angel hair	gramigna	quadrucci
bavette	grattugiata	radiatore
bavettine	igomiti	ravioli
bucatini	lasagne	riccioli
campanelle	linguine	rigatoni
cannaroni	lumache	riso
cannelloni	lumaconi	rotelle
capelli d'Angelo	macaroni	rotelli
capellini	macceroni	rotini
cappelletti	mafalda	ruote
casarecci	malloreddus	sedani rigati
cavatappi	maltagliati	sedanini rigati
cavatelli	manicotti	seme di mellone
conchiglie	margherite	spaghetti
conchiglioni	margheritine	spaghettini
coralli	maruzze	spiralini
creste di galli	maruzzelle	stelle
ditali	mezze penne	stellini
ditalini	midollini	strozzapreti
eliche	millerighe	tagliarini
elicodali	mostaccioli	tagliatelle
farfalle	occhi di lupo	tagliolini
fedelini	orecchiette	tonnarelli
fettucce	orsetti	torchio
fettuccine	orzo	tortellini
fettucelle	pansotti	tortelloni
fideo	pappardelle	tortiglioni
fischietti	pastina	trenne
fusilli	penne	trennette
fusilli col buco	pennette	tripolini
garganelli	perciatelli	troffiette
gemelli	pezzoccheri	tubetti
gigantoni	pipe rigate	vermicelli
gigli	pipette rigate	ziti

pastry cream ▶ a thick, creamy custard used as a filling for cakes and pastries.

pasty /ˈpastē/ ▶ chiefly British a folded pastry case filled with seasoned meat and vegetables.

Pastries

almond horn	danish	pain au chocolat
baklava	eclair	pate a choux
beggar's purse	elephant ear	petit four
cannoli	feuilletee	profiterole
cornet	finanacier	schnecken
craquelin	frangipane	sfogliatelle
cream puff	kringle	strudel
croissant	madeleine	vol-au-vent
croquembouche	mille-feuille	
crumpet	napoleon	

-ORIGIN Middle English: from Old French *paste(e)*, based on late Latin *pasta* 'paste.'

pâté /pä'tā/ ▸ a rich, savory paste made from finely minced or mashed ingredients, typically seasoned meat or fish.

-ORIGIN French, from Old French *paste* 'pie of seasoned meat.'

pâté de campagne /pä'tā də käm'pänyə/ ▸ coarse pork and liver pâté.

-ORIGIN French, literally 'country pâté.'

pâté de foie gras /pä'tā də ˌfwä 'grä/ ▸ a smooth rich paste made from fatted goose liver.

-ORIGIN French.

patisserie /pə'tisərē/ ▸ a shop where French pastries and cakes are sold.

■ French pastries and cakes collectively.

-ORIGIN from French *pâtisserie*, from medieval Latin *pasticium* 'pastry,' from *pasta* 'paste.'

patty ▸ a small flat cake of minced or finely chopped food, especially meat.

■ a small, round, flat chocolate-covered peppermint candy.

■ chiefly British a small pie or turnover.

-ORIGIN alteration of French *pâté*, by association with PASTY.

paupiette /pō'pyet/ ▸ a long, thin slice of fish or meat, rolled and stuffed with a filling.

-ORIGIN French, probably from Italian *polpetta*, from Latin *pulpa* 'pulp.'

pavlova /päv'lōvə; 'pavləvə/ ▸ a dessert consisting of a meringue base or shell filled with whipped cream and fruit.

-ORIGIN named after Anna *Pavlova*, Russian ballerina.

pawpaw ▸ another term for PAPAYA.

-ORIGIN from Spanish and Portuguese *papaya*, of Carib origin. The change in spelling is unexplained.

pea ▸ the spherical green seed from the pod of a climbing plant, widely eaten as a vegetable.

■ any of a number of edible spherical seeds of the pea family, for example, the CHICKPEA and BLACK-EYED PEA. See word bank at BEAN.

-ORIGIN back-formation from Middle English *pease* (interpreted as plural), from Old English *pise* 'pea,' via Latin from Greek *pison*.

peaberry ▸ a coffee berry containing one rounded seed instead of the usual two, through nonfertilization of one ovule or subsequent abortion. Such beans are esteemed for their fine, strong flavor.

peach ▸ a round stone fruit with juicy yellow flesh and downy pinkish-yellow skin.

-ORIGIN Middle English: from Old French *pesche*, from medieval Latin *persica*, from Latin *persicum (malum)*, literally 'Persian apple.'

peach Melba ▸ a dessert of ice cream and peaches with raspberry liqueur or sauce.

-ORIGIN named after Dame Nellie *Melba*, Australian soprano.

pea flour ▸ flour made from dried split peas.

peanut ▸ the oval seed of a South American plant, used or for its oil, or roasted and made into peanut butter or eaten as a snack.

peanut butter ▸ a paste of ground roasted peanuts, usually eaten spread on bread.

peanut oil ▸ oil produced from peanuts and used mainly for culinary purposes.

pear ▸ a yellowish- or brownish-green edible fruit that is typically narrow at the stalk and wider toward the tip, with sweet, slightly gritty flesh.

pearl barley ▸ barley reduced to small round grains by grinding.

pearl onion ▸ a very small onion used especially for pickling.

pea soup ▸ soup made from peas, especially a thick, yellow or green soup made from dried split peas.

pecan ▸ a smooth brown nut with an edible kernel similar to a walnut.

-ORIGIN from French *pacane*, from Illinois (American Indian language).

pecorino /ˌpekəˈrēnō/ ▸ an Italian cheese made from ewes' milk.

-ORIGIN Italian, from *pecorino* 'of ewes,' from *pecora* 'sheep.'

pectin ▸ a soluble gelatinous substance that is present in ripe fruits and is extracted for use as a setting agent in jams and jellies.

-ORIGIN from Greek *pektos* 'congealed' (from *pēgnuein* 'make solid') + the suffix *-in*.

peel ▸ a flat, shovellike implement used by a baker for carrying loaves, pies, etc., into or out of an oven: *a wooden pizza peel*.

■ the outer covering or rind of a fruit or vegetable.

▸ to remove the outer covering or skin from (a fruit, vegetable, or shrimp): *peel an apple*.

■ to remove (the outer covering or skin) from a fruit or vegetable: *peel off the skins and slice the potatoes*.

■ (of a fruit or vegetable) to have a skin that can be removed: *oranges that peel easily*.

Peking duck ▸ a Chinese dish consisting of strips of roast duck served with shredded vegetables and a sweet sauce.

pekoe /'pēkō/ ▸ a high-quality black tea made from young leaves.

-ORIGIN from Chinese dialect *pekho*, from *pek* 'white' + *ho* 'down' (the leaves being picked young when covered with down).

pelau /pə'lou/ ▸ a spicy dish consisting of meat (typically chicken), rice, and pigeon peas.

-ORIGIN from French Creole *pêlao*.

penne /'penā/ ▸ pasta in the form of short wide tubes.

-ORIGIN Italian, plural of *penna* 'quill.'

pepper ▸ a climbing vine with berries that are dried as black or white peppercorns.

■ a pungent, hot-tasting powder prepared from dried and ground peppercorns, commonly used as a spice or condiment to flavor food.

■ See also CAYENNE.

■ a capsicum, especially a sweet pepper.

■ a reddish and typically hot-tasting spice prepared from various forms of capsicum.

▢ **peppery**: *a peppery stew*

-ORIGIN Old English *piper*, *pipor*, of West Germanic origin, from Greek *peperi*, from Sanskrit *pippalī*.

peppercorn ▸ the dried berry of the pepper plant, used whole as a spice or crushed or ground to make pepper.

peppermint ▸ the aromatic leaves of a plant of the mint family, or an essential oil obtained from them, used as a flavoring in food.

■ a candy flavored with such oil.

pepperoni (also **peperoni**) ▸ a dried beef and pork sausage seasoned with pepper.

-ORIGIN from Italian *peperone* 'cayenne pepper plant.'

pepper pot ▸ a West Indian dish consisting of stewed meat or fish with vegetables, typically flavored with cassareep.

perch ▸ an edible freshwater fish with a high spiny dorsal fin, dark vertical bars on the body, and orange lower fins.

percolator ▸ a pot or machine for making coffee, consisting of a pot in which boiling water is circulated through a small chamber that holds the ground beans.

☐ **percolate**: *let it percolate for five minutes.*

perilla /pə'rilə/ ▸ an Asian plant of the mint family with medicinal and culinary uses. Perilla is often called by its Japanese name, SHISO.

perk ▸ informal (of coffee) to percolate.

■ to percolate (coffee).

perogi /pə'rōgē/ ▸ variant spelling of PIROGI.

persimmon ▸ an edible fruit that resembles a large tomato and has very sweet flesh.

-ORIGIN alteration of Algonquian *pessemmins.*

pesto ▸ a sauce of crushed basil leaves, pine nuts, garlic, Parmesan cheese, and olive oil, typically served with pasta.

-ORIGIN Italian, from *pestare* 'pound, crush.'

petit four /'petē 'fôr/ ▸ a very small fancy cake, cookie, or confection, typically made with marzipan and traditionally served after a meal.

-ORIGIN French, literally 'little oven.'

petits pois /pe'tē 'pwä/ ▸ young peas that are picked before they are grown to full size; small, fine peas.

-ORIGIN French, literally 'small peas.'

pe-tsai /'bā 'tsī/ ▸ Chinese cabbage of a pale variety that resembles lettuce.

-ORIGIN from Chinese (Cantonese dialect) *báicài*, literally 'white vegetable.'

Philadelphia cheese steak (also **Philly cheese steak**) ▸ see CHEESE STEAK.

phyllo (also **filo**) /ˈfēlō/ ▸ a kind of dough that can be stretched into thin sheets, used in layers to make pastries, especially in eastern Mediterranean cooking: *phyllo pastry.*
–ORIGIN from modern Greek *phullo* 'leaf.'

picante /piˈkäntä/ ▸ (of food) spicy.
–ORIGIN Spanish, literally 'pricking, biting.'

piccalilli ▸ a relish of chopped vegetables, mustard, and hot spices.
–ORIGIN probably from a blend of PICKLE and CHILI.

pickle ▸ a small cucumber preserved in vinegar, brine, or a similar solution.
■ any food preserved in this way and used as a relish.
■ the liquid used to preserve food or other perishable items.
▸ to preserve (food or other perishable items) in vinegar, brine, or a similar solution: *green tomatoes pickled in brine.*
–ORIGIN Middle English (denoting a spicy sauce served with meat): from Middle Dutch, Middle Low German *pekel.*

pie ▸ a baked dish of fruit, or meat and vegetables, typically with a top and base of pastry.
■ a pizza.
–ORIGIN Middle English: probably the same word as *pie* 'magpie,' the various combinations of ingredients being compared to objects randomly collected by this bird.

pie crust (also **piecrust**) ▸ the baked pastry crust of a pie.
■ the dough used to make pie crusts.

pierogi /pəˈrōgē/ ▸ variant spelling of PIROGI.

pigeon pea ▸ a dark red tropical pealike seed.

pignoli /pinˈyōlē/ ▸ pine nuts.
–ORIGIN Italian, plural of *pignolo*, from *pigna* 'pine cone,' from Latin *pinea.*

piki /ˈpēkē/ ▸ cornmeal bread in the form of very thin sheets, made by the Hopi Indians of the southwestern U.S.
–ORIGIN Hopi.

pilaf (also **pilaff** or **pilau**) /piˈläf; ˈpēläf/ ▸ a Middle Eastern or Indian

Pies, Tarts, and Turnovers

apple pie	pecan pie	pasteis de nata
banana cream pie	pierogy/piroshki	bitter tart
Banbury tart	pot pie	french silk pie
bierrock	pumpkin pie	lemon chiffon pie
bisteeya	quesadilla	Washington pie
black bottom pie	quiche lorraine	jam tart
bridie	ricotta pie	dumpling
buttermilk pie	runza	roly poly
calzone	shepherd's pie	wonton
cherry pie	shoofly pie	shu mai
chess pie	spanakopita	whoopie pie
coconut cream pie	steak and kidney pie	derby pie
Cornish pasty	strawberry rhubarb pie	pot sticker
empanada	sweet potato pie	boureki
grasshopper pie	tarte au sucre	mezzaluna
key lime pie	tarte Tatin	momo
lemon meringue	tiropita	pyrizhky
millionaire pie	torta	samosa
mincemeat pie	tortilla	borek
Mississippi mud pie	tourtiere	rustici
moon pie	onion tart	sambusak

dish of rice or wheat, with vegetables and spices, typically having added meat or fish.

–ORIGIN from Turkish *pilâv*.

pilchard /'pilCHərd/ ▸ a small, edible, commercially valuable marine fish of the herring family.

pili /pēˈlē/ ▸ the edible seed of a Phillipine tree, which tastes like a sweet almond.

–ORIGIN from Tagalog.

pimiento (also **pimento**) ▸ a red sweet pepper.

■ a piece of pimiento used as a garnish, especially stuffed inside a pitted green olive.

–ORIGIN from Spanish, from medieval Latin *pigmentum* 'spice,' from Latin, 'pigment.'

pineapple ▸ a large juicy tropical fruit consisting of aromatic edible yellow flesh surrounded by a tough segmented skin and topped with a tuft of stiff leaves.

-ORIGIN Middle English (denoting a pine cone): from *pine* (tree) + *apple* (from the fruit's resemblance to a pine cone).

pine nut ▸ the edible seed of various pine trees. Pine nuts are often referred to by their Italian name, PIGNOLI.

pinole /pi'nōlē/ ▸ a sweetened flour made from ground dried corn mixed with flour made of mesquite beans, sugar, and spices.

-ORIGIN from Latin American Spanish, from Nahuatl *pinolli*.

piñon /'pinyən/ ▸ a pine nut obtained from certain pine trees.

-ORIGIN from Spanish, from Latin *pinea* 'pine cone.'

pinto bean ▸ a medium-sized speckled variety of kidney bean.

-ORIGIN from *pinto* 'piebald horse.'

piping ▸ ornamentation on food consisting of lines of icing, whipped cream, etc.

pippin ▸ a red and yellow eating apple.

-ORIGIN Middle English: from Old French *pepin*.

piquant ▸ having a pleasantly sharp taste or appetizing flavor.

-ORIGIN from French, literally 'stinging, pricking,' present participle of *piquer*.

piri-piri /'pi(ə)rē 'pi(ə)rē/ (also **pil-pil** /'pēl ‚pēl/) ▸ Portuguese term for hot chilis or the hot sauce made from them.

pirog /pi'rōg/ ▸ a large Russian pie.

-ORIGIN Russian.

pirogi (also **perogi**) /pi'rōgē/ ▸ a dough dumpling stuffed with a filling such as potato or cheese, typically served with onions or sour cream.

-ORIGIN from Polish *pieróg* or Ukrainian *pyrih*.

piroshki /pi'rôsнkē/ ▸ small Russian pastries or patties, filled with meat or fish and rice.

-ORIGIN from Russian *pirozhki*, plural of *pirozhok*, diminutive of *pirog* (see PIROG).

pissaladière /pē‚säläd'ye(ə)r/ ▸ a Provençal open tart resembling pizza, typically made with onions, anchovies, and black olives.

-ORIGIN French, from Provençal *pissaladiero*, from *pissala* 'salt fish.'

pistachio ▸ (also **pistachio nut**) the edible pale green seed of an Asian tree.

–ORIGIN Middle English *pistace*, from Old French, superseded in the 16th century by forms from Italian *pistaccio*, via Latin from Greek *pistakion*, from Old Persian.

pita /ˈpētə/ ▸ flat hollow bread that can be split open to hold a filling.

–ORIGIN modern Greek, literally 'cake or pie.' Compare with Turkish *pide*, in a similar sense.

pizza ▸ a dish of Italian origin consisting of a flat, round base of dough baked with a topping of tomato sauce and cheese, typically with added meat or vegetables.

–ORIGIN Italian, literally 'pie.'

plank ▸ to cook and serve (meat or fish) on a seasoned wooden plank.

plantain /ˈplant(ə)n/ ▸ a fruit related to the banana containing high levels of starch and little sugar, harvested green and widely used as a cooked vegetable in the tropics.

–ORIGIN from Spanish *plá(n)tano*, probably by assimilation of a South American word to the Spanish *plá(n)tano* 'plane tree.'

plat du jour /ˌplä də ˈzHŌŌr/ ▸ a dish specially prepared by a restaurant on a particular day, in addition to the usual menu.

–ORIGIN French, literally 'dish of the day.'

pluck ▸ to pull the feathers from (a bird's carcass) to prepare it for cooking.

▸ the heart, liver, and lungs of an animal as food.

plum ▸ the oval fleshy fruit of a deciduous tree. The juicy fruit has purple, reddish, or yellow skin when ripe and contains a flattish pointed pit.

–ORIGIN Old English *plūme*, from medieval Latin *pruna*, from Latin *prunum* (see **PRUNE**).

plum pudding ▸ a rich boiled or steamed pudding containing raisins, currants, and spices.

–ORIGIN so named because the pudding was originally made with plums.

poach ▸ to cook (an egg), without its shell, in or over boiling water: *poached egg and grilled bacon.*

■ to cook by simmering in a small amount of liquid: *poach the salmon in white wine.*

-ORIGIN Middle English: from Old French *pochier,* earlier in the sense 'enclose in a bag,' from *poche* 'bag, pocket.'

poacher ▶ a pan for cooking food by poaching.

poi ▶ a Hawaiian dish made from the fermented root of the taro, which has been baked and pounded to a paste.

-ORIGIN of Polynesian origin.

polenta /pōˈlentə/ ▶ cornmeal as used in Italian cooking.

■ a paste or dough made from cornmeal, which is boiled and typically then fried or baked.

-ORIGIN Italian, from Latin, 'pearl barley.'

polonaise /ˌpäləˈnāz/ ▶ (of a dish, especially a vegetable dish) garnished with chopped hard-boiled egg yolk, breadcrumbs, and parsley.

-ORIGIN from French, feminine of *polonais* 'Polish,' from medieval Latin *Polonia* 'Poland.'

pomegranate ▶ the orange-sized fruit of a tree native to North Africa and western Asia. The fruit has a tough reddish outer skin and sweet red, crisp, gelatinous flesh containing many seeds.

-ORIGIN Middle English: from Old French *pome grenate,* from *pome* 'apple' + *grenate* 'pomegranate' (from Latin *(malum) granatum* '(apple) having many seeds').

pomelo /ˈpämə,lō/ ▶ variant spelling of **PUMMELO.**

pommes frites /ˌpäm ˈfrēt/ ▶ (especially in recipes or on menus) French fries.

-ORIGIN French, from *pommes de terre frites,* literally 'fried potatoes.'

pompano ▶ an edible butterfish that lives in shoals along the east coast of North America.

-ORIGIN from Spanish *pámpano,* perhaps from *pámpana* 'vine leaf,' because of its shape.

Pont l'Évêque /ˌpôN ləˈvek/ ▶ a kind of creamy soft cheese made originally at Pont l'Évêque in Normandy, France.

ponzu /ˈpônzōo/ ▶ a mixture of citrus juice and soy sauce, used in Japanese cooking as a dipping sauce.

-ORIGIN Japanese.

poor boy (also **poor-boy** or **po'boy**) ▸ another term for SUBMARINE SANDWICH.

poori (also **puri**) /'pŏorē/ ▸ (in Indian cooking) a small, round, flat bread, deep-fried and served with meat or vegetables.
–ORIGIN from Sanskrit.

pop (also **soda pop**) ▸ see SODA.

popcorn ▸ corn of a variety with hard kernels that swell up and burst open with a pop when heated.
▪ these kernels when popped, typically buttered and salted and eaten as a snack.

popover ▸ a light muffin made from a thin batter, which rises to form a hollow shell when baked.

poppyseed ▸ the tiny, round seed of the poppy plant, used as a topping or in fillings for baked goods
–ORIGIN Old English *popig*: from a medieval Latin alteration of Latin *papaver*.

porcini /pôr'CHēnē/ ▸ the cèpe (a wild mushroom), especially as an item on a menu.
–ORIGIN Italian, literally 'little pigs.'

pork ▸ the flesh of a pig used as food, especially when uncured.
–ORIGIN Middle English: from Old French *porc*, from Latin *porcus* 'pig.'

porridge ▸ a dish consisting of oatmeal or another meal or cereal boiled in water or milk.
–ORIGIN (originally denoting soup thickened with barley): alteration of POTTAGE.

porterhouse steak (also **porterhouse**) ▸ a choice steak cut from the thick end of a sirloin.

portobello /ˌpôrtə'belō/ (also **portobello mushroom**) ▸ a large mature edible mushroom with an open flat cap.

Port Salut /ˌpôr sə'lōo/ ▸ a pale, mild type of cheese.
–ORIGIN named after the Trappist monastery in France, where it was first produced.

potage /pô'täzH/ ▸ thick soup.
–ORIGIN from French, from Old French *potage* 'that which is put into a pot.'

potato ▸ a starchy plant tuber that is one of the most important food crops, cooked and eaten as a vegetable.

■ see **SWEET POTATO**.

-ORIGIN from Spanish *patata*, variant of Taino *batata* 'sweet potato.'

potato chip ▸ a wafer-thin slice of potato fried until crisp and eaten as a snack.

potato pancake ▸ a small flat cake of grated potatoes mixed with flour and egg and fried.

potato salad ▸ a side dish consisting of cold cooked potatoes sliced or chopped and mixed with a dressing and seasonings.

pot-au-feu /ˌpôt ō ˈfœ/ ▸ a French soup of meat, typically boiled beef, and vegetables cooked in a large pot.

-ORIGIN French, literally 'pot on the fire.'

pot cheese ▸ a type of cottage cheese with large curds.

potherb ▸ any herb grown for culinary use.

pot liquor ▸ liquid in which meat, fish, or vegetables have been boiled; stock.

pot pie ▸ a meat and vegetable pie baked in a deep dish, often with a top crust only.

■ a stew with dumplings.

pot roast ▸ a piece of meat cooked slowly in a covered pot.

▸ (**pot-roast**) to cook (a piece of meat) slowly in a covered pot.

pottage /ˈpätij/ ▸ archaic a soup or stew.

-ORIGIN Middle English *potage*: from Old French, 'that which is put into a pot.' Compare with **POTAGE** and **PORRIDGE**.

potted ▸ chiefly British (of food, especially meat or fish) preserved in a sealed pot or jar: *potted smoked trout.*

pouchong /ˈpōōˈCHÔNG/ ▸ a kind of China tea made by fermenting the withered leaves only briefly, typically scented with rose petals.

-ORIGIN Chinese.

pound cake ▸ a rich cake containing a pound, or equal weights, of each chief ingredient, typically flour, butter, and sugar.

poussin /pōōˈsan/ ▸ a chicken killed young for eating.

-ORIGIN French.

powdered sugar ▸ another term for **CONFECTIONERS' SUGAR**.

prairie oyster ▶ a drink made with a raw egg and seasoning, drunk as a cure for a hangover.

■ (**prairie oysters**) the testicles of a calf cooked and served as food.

praline /'prā,lēn; 'prä-/ ▶ a smooth, sweet substance made by boiling nuts in sugar and grinding the mixture, used especially as a filling for chocolates.

■ a crisp or semicrisp candy made by a similar process and typically consisting of butter, brown sugar, and pecans.

-ORIGIN from French, named after Marshal de Plessis-*Praslin* (1598–1675), the French soldier whose cook invented it.

prawn ▶ a marine crustacean that resembles a large shrimp.

preparation ▶ the process of getting food ready for eating, as by combining ingredients or cooking food in a certain style or way: *the preparation of a meal.*

■ a substance that is specially made up and usually sold, especially a medicine or food.

presentation ▶ the manner or style in which food is offered or displayed: *the presentation of foods is designed to stimulate your appetite.*

preservative ▶ a substance used to preserve foodstuffs.

preserve ▶ to treat or refrigerate (food) to prevent its decomposition or fermentation.

■ to prepare (fruit) for long-term storage by boiling it with sugar: *preserved fruits.*

▶ (usually **preserves**) food made with fruit preserved in sugar, such as jam or marmalade.

preserved lemon ▶ lemons or lemon slices preserved in salt and lemon juice, used as an ingredient in Moroccan cooking.

press ▶ to extract (juice or oil) by crushing or squeezing fruit, vegetables, etc.: *freshly pressed grape juice.*

■ to squeeze or crush (fruit, vegetables, etc.) to extract the juice or oil.

▶ a device for applying pressure to something in order to flatten or shape it or to extract juice or oil: *a wine press.*

pressure cooker ▶ an airtight pot in which food can be cooked quickly under steam pressure.

Methods of Preparation

al dente	en papillote	nesselrode
al forno	espagnole	Newburg
Alfredo	escabeche	Niçoise
alla taormina	estragon	normande
alla vodka	étouffée	parmigiana
almondine	farci	périgord
amandine	flambé	parmentier
anglaise	Florentine	piccata
argenteuil	forestière	pilaf
au bleu	fra diavolo	Pittsburgh style
au fromage	francese	Provençale
au gratin	Frenched	puttanesca
au jus	fricassee	ranchero
au naturel	garni	rare
Bolognese	gratiné	relleno
bourguignon	grecque	ripieno
bénaise	hollandaise	roulade
cacciatore	indienne	scallopine
carbonara	jardinière	stroganoff
chiffonade	jerk	subgum
clamart	julienne	sunny side up
country fried	lyonnaise	tandoori
Crécy	marinara	tempura
creole	marinière	tikka
curried	masala	Véronique
dauphine	medium	vindaloo
en brochette	medium rare	well done
en croûte	meunière	

pretzel ▸ a crisp roll baked in the form of a knot or stick and flavored with salt.
  ‑ORIGIN from German *Pretzel*.

prickly pear ▸ a cactus having large pear-shaped, prickly fruits that are edible.

prime ▸ of the best possible quality; excellent: *prime provisions*.
  ■ (of beef) of the highest grade.
  ‑ORIGIN Middle English, via Old French from Latin *primus* 'first.'

prime rib ▸ a roast or steak cut from the seven ribs immediately before the loin.

profiterole /prəˈfitəˌrōl/ ▸ a small hollow choux pastry typically filled with cream and covered with chocolate sauce.

–ORIGIN French, diminutive of *profit* 'profit.'

proof ▸ to activate (yeast) by the addition of liquid.

■ to knead (dough) until light and smooth.

prosciutto /prəˈsHo͞otō/ ▸ Italian ham cured by drying and typically served in very thin slices.

–ORIGIN Italian.

prove ▸ (of bread dough) to become aerated by the action of yeast; rise.

provençale /ˌprōvənˈsäl/ ▸ denoting a dish cooked in a sauce made with tomatoes, garlic, and olive oil: *chicken provençale.*

–ORIGIN from French *à la provençale* 'in the Provençal style.'

provolone ▸ an Italian soft smoked cheese made from cow's milk and having a mellow flavor.

–ORIGIN Italian, from *provola* 'buffalo-milk cheese.'

prune ▸ a plum preserved by drying, having a black, wrinkled appearance.

–ORIGIN Middle English: from Old French, via Latin from Greek *prou(m)non* 'plum.'

pudding ▸ a dessert with a creamy consistency: *chocolate pudding* | *rice pudding.*

■ chiefly British any dessert.

■ chiefly British the dessert course of a meal.

■ a sweet or savory steamed dish made with flour: *plum pudding.* See word bank at CAKE.

■ the intestines of a pig or sheep stuffed with oatmeal, spices, and meat and boiled. See also BLACK PUDDING.

–ORIGIN Middle English (denoting a sausage): apparently from Old French *boudin* 'black pudding,' from Latin *botellus* 'sausage, small intestine.'

pufferfish (also **puffer**, **puffer fish**) ▸ a stout-bodied marine or freshwater fish that typically has spiny skin and inflates itself like a balloon when threatened. It is sometimes used as food, but some parts are highly toxic.

puff pastry ▸ light flaky pastry, used for pie crusts, canapés, etc.

pulp ▸ a soft, wet, shapeless mass of material: *boiling with soda will reduce your peas to pulp.*

■ the soft fleshy part of a fruit.

▸ to crush into a soft, shapeless mass.

■ to remove the pulp from (fruit).

□ **pulpy**: *tomatoes and other pulpy fruits.*

‑ORIGIN Middle English: from Latin *pulpa.*

pulse ▸ (usually **pulses**) the edible seeds of various legumes, for example, CHICKPEAS, LENTILS, and BEANS. See word bank at BEAN.

‑ORIGIN Middle English: from Old French *pols*, from Latin *puls* 'porridge of meal or pulse.'

pummelo /ˈpəməˌlō/ ▸ the largest of the citrus fruits, with a thick yellow skin and bitter pulp that resembles grapefruit in flavor.

pumpernickel ▸ dark, dense German bread made from coarsely ground whole-grain rye.

‑ORIGIN transferred use of German *Pumpernickel* 'lout, bumpkin.'

pumpkin ▸ a large rounded orange-yellow fruit with a thick rind, edible flesh, and many seeds.

‑ORIGIN from obsolete French *pompon*, via Latin from Greek *pepōn* 'large melon.'

punch ▸ a drink made with fruit juices, soda, spices, and sometimes liquor, typically served in small cups from a large bowl.

‑ORIGIN apparently from Sanskrit *pañca* 'five, five kinds of' (because the drink had five ingredients).

pungent ▸ having a sharply strong taste or smell: *the pungent smell of frying onions.*

‑ORIGIN from Latin *pungent-* 'pricking,' from the verb *pungere.*

purée /pyo͝oˈrā/ ▸ a smooth, creamy substance made of liquidized or crushed fruit or vegetables: *tomato purée.*

▸ to make a purée of (fruit or vegetables).

‑ORIGIN French, literally 'purified,' feminine past participle of *purer.*

puri (also **poori**) /ˈpo͝orē/ ▸ (in Indian cooking) a small, round, flat piece of bread made of unleavened wheat flour, deep-fried and served with meat or vegetables.

‑ORIGIN via Hindi from Sanskrit *pūrikā.*

purslane /ˈpərslən; -ˌlān/ ▸ a small fleshy-leaved edible plant that grows in damp sand along coastal shores, eaten in salads.

-ORIGIN Middle English: from Old French *porcelaine*, probably from Latin *porcil(l)aca*, variant of *portulaca*, influenced by French *porcelaine* 'porcelain.'

HOG OR DOG?
THAT'S THE QUESTION

Sausages, served hot or cold, boiled or fried, on a bun or with kraut, have existed for centuries, but the term "hot dog" is clouded in folk etymologies.

The short, true, version of *hot dog* is this: jokes were often made about dog meat in sausages. Dog meat *was* sometimes used in sausages, illegal though it may have been. These sausages were sold by vendors with trolleys. In their irreverence, college kids and others called the sausages "dogs" and the trolleys "dog wagons." The sausages were served hot, and sometimes called "all hots," so a natural blend occurred: the sausages were called "hot dogs."

Everything else you've heard or read about the origins of hot dog is either secondary, subsequent, or untrue. This is in part because in getting to the bottom of the origins of the term *hot dog,* it is important to separate it from the history of the food item itself.

One thing which becomes evident when reading the hot dog work of word researchers David Schulman, Gerald Cohen, and Barry Popik, is that jokes about dog meat going into the making of sausages were commonplace even as early as the mid-nineteenth century, when what we call *hot dogs* went by other names.

An article in the *New York Commercial Advertiser* of July 6, 1838, joked, "Sausages have fallen in price one half, in New York, since the dog killers have commenced operations. Thus speaks an Eastern editor. We presume he will be here in a day or two, with flocks of his readers, to take advantage of the market."

Later that year, the *Boston Times* of Sept. 18 comments on a competing newspaper, "The Methuen gazette editor 'infers' that dog-meat sausages is a new article of food. Bless you[r] soul man—it's as old as *your granny*."

It wasn't just dogs—people were worried about all kinds of disgusting meats in their sausages. An 1845 article in the New York City newspaper *Subterranean* tells of a man who was "in the habit of making sausages and Bologna puddings out of dead rats, cats, dogs, and even horses." He was accosted by fellow citizens, stripped, tarred, and feathered. He fled town, his neighbors nipping at his heels.

The dogs-in-sausages rumors and stories were widespread: in New York, Boston, New Orleans, Baltimore, and in New Jersey, where articles from 1843 recount the horrific details of a scandal involving "dog sandwiches" and commented that no canine should cross the Hudson for fear of never returning. An 1870 cartoon read, "Please Do Not Whistle Near Sausidge (sic) Stand," hinting, perhaps, that the tube steaks might all leap up and follow.

Whether dogs were actually being slaughtered for sausages or not—and there was plenty of evidence that they were—by 1900, the idea of dogs in *sassengers,* as they were often spelled, though still scandalous and abhorrent, was downright ordinary.

The first recorded instance of *hot dog* in print so far found appeared in the *Yale Record*—a humor newspaper at that university—of Oct. 19, 1895. It's in a yarn about a night when students hijacked the dog wagon and rode on its roof "in great state down Chapel street, amid frantic cheers from the awakened residents," to the chapel.

There, the story says, the students "contentedly munched hot dogs during the whole service." It's clear those "hot dogs" in the hijacked dog wagon story were the same sort of sausages we call hot dogs today.

In 1904, the newspaper published these lines:

Mary had a little dog,
It played a naughty trick;
Just think—it bit poor Mary so,
The mustard was too thick.

Juvenile, yes, but more to the point, it's just one of many examples of dogs and sausages being linked (as it were) in the minds of college students. Issue after issue of that newspaper mentions the Dog Wagon, and the "all hots" and the "dogs" it sold, and the Kennel Club, a popular all-night student hangout which featured the "Frankfort" on its menu.

Since the first recorded use of "hot dog" sausages appeared in 1895, we can dismiss several popular hot dog theories as false. We know, as a result, hot dogs did not first appear at Coney Island in 1916, and that they were not first named by Harry Stevens at New York's Polo Grounds in 1906 (nor in 1902).

Further, a bit of doggerel in the Yale newspaper from Oct. 5, 1895, shows that even a hot dog on a bun was known nine years before the 1904 St. Louis World's Fair, where it is sometimes claimed hot dogs were invented or named.

The rhyme, titled, "Echoes From The Lunch Wagon," goes like this:

" 'Tis dogs' delight to bark and bite,"
    Thus does the adage run.
But I delight to bite the dog
    When placed inside a bun.

Because of all the instances of *hot dog* which can be found in print between 1895 and 1906, we also know that cartoonist Thomas Aloysius Dorgan (usually known as Tad) did not coin the term *hot dog*. Dorgan is usually said to have drawn a cartoon showing dachshunds in buns, at New York's Polo Grounds, in 1902.

However, no such cartoon has ever been found, even though libraries, newspaper morgues, and microfilm have been scrutinized by researcher Leonard Zwilling and others. Anyway, Tad did not arrive in New York City until 1903, and so could not very well have been at the Polo Grounds in 1902.

He did use the term in two 1906 cartoons, but as *hot dog* was well established by then—and even before 1902—he can hardly be said to have been the coiner or the popularizer.

A survey published in 1900 shows that *hot dog* already meant sausage to students around the country (and that they also called them *bow-wows, dogs,* and *doggies*). We can also trace a different kind of *hot dog* to college students: a snazzy, well-dressed man was also a hot dog, the forerunner for our modern non-food *hot dog*—someone who shows off.

We are past the age when dogs might be found in a butcher's wagon, or when a bounty of fifty cents a head might be offered for strays, but the dogs-as-food joke continues. Who wouldn't still appreciate this joke from 1897?

FRANK FORT: Why do they have these skins on the hot dogs?
ALL HOTSIR: That's the bark.

Grant Barrett is the Project Editor of the *Oxford Historical Dictionary of American Slang,* and the editor of *Hatchet Jobs and Hardball: The Oxford Dictionary of American Political Slang.*

Q

quark ▸ a type of low-fat curd cheese.

-ORIGIN from German *Quark* 'curds.'

queen cake ▸ a small, soft, typically heart-shaped currant cake.

queen of puddings ▸ a pudding made with bread, jam, and meringue.

quenelle /kə'nel/ ▸ (usually **quenelles**) a small seasoned ball of pounded fish or meat.

-ORIGIN French, probably from Alsatian German *knödel*.

quesadilla /ˌkāsə'dēyə/ ▸ a tortilla filled with cheese and heated.

-ORIGIN Spanish.

queso blanco /'kāsō 'bläNGkō/ ▸ a fresh white cow's milk cheese used in Latin American cooking.

-ORIGIN Spanish, 'white cheese.'

queso fresco /'kāsō 'freskō/ ▸ a semisoft fresh Mexican cheese, white in color, typically served shredded over hot foods.

-ORIGIN Spanish, 'fresh cheese.'

quiche /kēSH/ ▸ a baked flan or tart with a savory filling thickened with eggs.

-ORIGIN French, from Alsatian dialect *Küchen*; related to German *Kuchen* 'cake.'

quince /kwins/ ▸ a hard, acidic, pear-shaped fruit used in preserves or as flavoring.

-ORIGIN Middle English (originally a collective plural): from Old French *cooin*, from Latin *(malum) cotoneum*, variant of *(malum) cydonium* 'apple of *Cydonia* (= Canea, in Crete).'

quinoa /'kēnwä/ ▸ the edible starchy grainlike seeds of a plant found in the Andes. It is cooked like rice.

-ORIGIN Spanish spelling of Quechua *kinua, kinoa*.

R

rack ▸ a cut of meat, typically lamb, that includes the front ribs.

raclette /ra'klet/ ▸ a Swiss dish of melted cheese, typically eaten with potatoes.

–ORIGIN French, literally 'small scraper,' referring to the practice of holding the cheese over the heat and scraping it on to a plate as it melts.

radicchio /ra'dēkē‚ō/ ▸ chicory of a variety that has dark red leaves, eaten raw in salads.

–ORIGIN Italian.

USAGE: See usage note at ENDIVE.

radish ▸ a swollen pungent-tasting edible root, especially a variety that is small, spherical, and red, and eaten raw with salad.

–ORIGIN Old English *rædic*, from Latin *radix, radic-* 'root.'

ragout /ra'gōō/ ▸ a highly seasoned dish of meat cut into small pieces and stewed with vegetables.

–ORIGIN from French *ragoût*, from *ragoûter* 'revive the taste of.'

raise ▸ to cause (bread) to rise, especially by the action of yeast: *raised doughnuts.*

–ORIGIN Middle English: from Old Norse *reisa*.

raisin ▸ a partially dried grape.

–ORIGIN Middle English: from Old French, 'grape,' from an alteration of Latin *racemus* 'grape bunch.'

raita /'rītə/ ▸ an Indian side dish of yogurt containing chopped cucumber or other vegetables, and spices.

–ORIGIN from Hindi *rāytā*.

rambutan /ram'bōōtn/ ▸ a red, plum-sized tropical fruit with soft spines and a slightly acidic taste.

-ORIGIN from Malay *rambūtan*, from *rambut* 'hair,' with allusion to the fruit's spines.

ramekin /'ramikin/ ▸ a small dish for baking and serving an individual portion of food.

■ a quantity of food served in such a dish, in particular a small quantity of cheese baked with breadcrumbs, eggs, and seasoning.
-ORIGIN from French *ramequin*, of Low German or Dutch origin; compare with obsolete Flemish *rameken* 'toasted bread.'

ramen /'rämən/ ▸ (in Asian cuisine) quick-cooking noodles, typically served in a broth with meat and vegetables.
-ORIGIN Japanese, from Chinese *lā* 'to pull' + *miàn* 'noodles.'

rape ▸ a plant of the cabbage family with bright yellow, heavily scented flowers, especially a variety grown for its oil-rich seed and as stockfeed.
-ORIGIN Middle English (originally denoting the turnip plant): from Latin *rapum, rapa* 'turnip.'

rare ▸ (of meat) lightly cooked, so that the inside is still red.
-ORIGIN variant of obsolete *rear* 'half-cooked.'

rarebit (also **Welsh rarebit**) ▸ a dish of melted and seasoned cheese on toast, sometimes with other ingredients.
-ORIGIN alteration of *rabbit* in *Welsh rabbit*.

rasam /'rəsəm/ ▸ a thin, very spicy southern Indian soup served with other dishes, typically as a drink.
-ORIGIN Tamil.

rasher ▸ a thin slice of bacon.
■ a serving of several such slices.

raspberry ▸ an edible soft reddish-pink fruit related to the blackberry.
-ORIGIN from dialect *rasp*, abbreviation of obsolete *raspis* 'raspberry' + BERRY.

ratatouille /ˌratə'tōō-ē/ ▸ a vegetable dish consisting of onions, zucchini, tomatoes, eggplant, and peppers, sautéed and stewed in oil and sometimes served cold.
-ORIGIN a French dialect word.

ravigote (also **ravigotte**) /ˌrävi'gôt/ ▸ a mixture of chopped chervil, chives, tarragon, and shallots, used to give piquancy to a sauce or as a base for an herb butter.

–ORIGIN French, from *ravigoter* 'invigorate.'

ravioli ▸ small pasta envelopes containing ground meat, cheese, or vegetables.

■ a dish consisting of this, typically served with a sauce.

–ORIGIN Italian.

raw ▸ (of food) uncooked: *raw eggs | salsify can be eaten raw in salads or cooked.*

■ unrefined: *raw sugar.*

raw sugar ▸ the residue left after sugarcane has been processed to remove the molasses and refine the sugar crystals. The flavor is similar to that of brown sugar.

reamer ▸ another term for JUICER.

rebaked ▸ another term for TWICE-BAKED.

reblochon /rəblô'shōn/ ▸ a soft French cheese, made originally and chiefly in Savoy.

–ORIGIN French.

réchauffé /ˌrāshō'fā -'shō,fā/ ▸ a dish of warmed-up food left over from a previous meal.

–ORIGIN French, literally 'reheated,' past participle of *réchauffer.*

red currant ▸ a small, sweet, edible red berry.

Red Delicious ▸ a widely grown eating apple of a soft-fleshed red-skinned variety.

red-eye gravy ▸ gravy made by adding liquid to the fat from cooked ham.

red flannel hash ▸ a type of hash made with beets.

red herring ▸ a dried smoked herring, which is turned red by the smoke.

red meat ▸ meat that is red when raw, for example beef or lamb. Often contrasted with WHITE MEAT.

red mullet ▸ an elongated fish living in warmer seas, widely valued as a food fish.

red pepper ▸ the ripe red fruit of a sweet pepper. Compare with GREEN PEPPER.

■ another term for CAYENNE.

reduction ▸ a thick and concentrated liquid or sauce made by boiling.

□ **reduce**: *reduce the liquid so that it will coat the back of a spoon.*

refined ▸ with impurities or unwanted elements having been removed by processing: *refined sugar.*

refried beans ▸ pinto beans boiled and mashed in advance and re-heated when required, used especially in Mexican cooking. Refried beans are often called by their Spanish name, FRIJOLES REFRITOS.

relish ▸ a condiment or savory food eaten with a meal to add flavor.
■ chopped sweet pickles used as such a condiment.
–ORIGIN Middle English: alteration of obsolete *reles*, from Old French, 'remainder,' from *relaisser* 'to release.'

relleno /rel'yānō/ ▸ short for CHILE RELLENO.

rémoulade (also **remoulade**) /ˌrāmə'läd/ ▸ salad or seafood dressing made with hard-boiled egg yolks, oil, and vinegar, and flavored with mustard, capers, and herbs.
–ORIGIN French, from Italian *remolata.*

render ▸ to melt down (fat), typically in order to clarify it.

rennet /'renit/ ▸ an extract from the stomach of an unweaned calf, used in curdling milk for cheese.

restaurant ▸ a place where people pay to sit and eat meals that are prepared and served on the premises.
–ORIGIN from French, from *restaurer* 'provide food for' (literally 'restore to a former state').

restaurateur /ˌrestərə'tər/ ▸ a person who owns and manages a res-taurant.
–ORIGIN French, from the verb *restaurer* (see RESTAURANT).

USAGE: Despite its close relation to *restaurant*, there is no *n* in **res-taurateur**, either in its spelling or in its pronunciation.

rhubarb ▸ the thick leaf stalks of a cultivated plant of the dock fam-ily, which are reddish or green and eaten as a fruit after cooking.
–ORIGIN Middle English: from Old French *reubarbe*, from a short-ening of medieval Latin *rheubarbarum*, alteration of *rhabarbarum* 'foreign rhubarb,' from Greek *rha* 'rhubarb') + *barbaros* 'foreign.'

rib ▸ a cut of meat having one or more ribs with meat adhering to it.

rib eye (also **ribeye** or **rib-eye steak**) ▸ a cut of beef from the outer side of the ribs.

rice ▸ a swamp grass that is widely cultivated as a source of food, especially in Asia.

Restaurants

auberge	pub	Cuban
bakery	public house	French
bar	rathskeller	German
bar & grill	raw bar	Greek
barbecue	relais	health food
bistro	sandwich shop	Hungarian
brasserie	shabu-shabu	Indian
buffet	smorgasbord	Indonesian
café	steak house	Italian
cafeteria	supper club	Jamaican
charcuterie	sushi bar	Japanese
cantina	sweet shop	Korean
chip shop	tapas bar	Lebanese
chophouse	taqueria	Malaysian
churrascaria	tavern	Middle Eastern
coffee shop	tea room	Moroccan
coffeehouse	trattoria	Nuevo Latino
delicatessen	Afghan	Persian
diner	American, new	Peruvian
enoteca	American, traditional	Polish
fast food	Argentinean	Portuguese
gin joint	Austrian	Russian
luncheonette	Belgian	soul food
malt shop	Brazilian	Southern
noodle shop	Burmese	Spanish
osteria	cajun/creole	Tex-Mex
oyster bar	Caribbean	Thai
paninoteca	Chinese	Turkish
patisserie	Colombian	vegetarian
pizzeria	Continental	Vietnamese

- the grains of this cereal used as food.
- ▸ to force (cooked potatoes or other vegetables) through a sieve or ricer.

  _ORIGIN Middle English: from Old French *ris*, from Italian *riso*, from Greek *oruza*.

ricer ▸ a utensil with small holes through which boiled potatoes or other soft food can be pushed to form particles of a similar size to grains of rice.

rich ▸ having (a particular thing) in large amounts: *many vegetables and fruits are rich in antioxidant vitamins* | *a protein-rich diet.*

■ (of food) containing a large amount of fat, spices, sugar, etc.: *dishes with wonderfully rich sauces.*

■ (of drink) full-bodied: *a rich, hoppy beer.*

■ (of a smell or taste) pleasantly smooth and mellow: *Basmati rice has a rich aroma.*

ricotta ▸ a soft white unsalted Italian cheese.

–ORIGIN Italian, literally 'recooked, cooked twice.'

rigatoni /ˌrigəˈtōnē/ ▸ pasta in the form of short hollow fluted tubes.

–ORIGIN Italian.

rijsttafel /ˈrīˌstäfəl/ ▸ a meal of Southeast Asian food consisting of a selection of traditional dishes and condiments served with rice.

–ORIGIN Dutch, from *rijst* 'rice' + *tafel* 'table.'

rillettes /rēˈyet/ ▸ pâté made of minced pork or poultry, seasoned and combined with fat.

–ORIGIN French, diminutive (plural) of Old French *rille* 'strip of pork.'

rind ▸ the tough outer skin of certain fruit, especially citrus fruit.

■ the hard outer edge of cheese or bacon, usually removed before eating.

ripe ▸ (of fruit or grain) developed to the point of readiness for harvesting and eating.

■ (of a smell or flavor) rich, intense, or pungent.

risotto /riˈzôtō/ ▸ an Italian dish of rice cooked in stock with other ingredients such as meat and vegetables.

–ORIGIN Italian, from *riso* 'rice.'

rissole /riˈsōl/ ▸ a compressed mixture of meat and spices, coated in breadcrumbs and fried.

–ORIGIN from French, from Old French dialect *ruissole*, from a feminine form of late Latin *russeolus* 'reddish,' from Latin *russus* 'red.'

roast ▸ to cook (food, especially meat) by prolonged exposure to heat in an oven or over a fire.

■ process (a foodstuff) by subjecting it to intense heat: *coffee beans are roasted and ground.*

▸ (of food) having been cooked in an oven or over an open fire: *a plate of cold roast beef.*

▸ a cut of meat that has been roasted or that is intended for roasting: *carving the Sunday roast.*

■ a dish or meal of roasted food.

■ an outdoor party at which meat, especially of a particular type, is roasted: *a pig roast.*

■ the process of roasting something, especially coffee, or the result of this.

■ a particular type of roasted coffee: *continental roasts.*

–ORIGIN Middle English: from Old French *rostir*, of West Germanic origin.

roaster ▸ a container, oven, furnace, or apparatus used for roasting.

■ a foodstuff that is particularly suitable for roasting, especially a chicken.

■ a person or company that processes coffee beans.

robusta /rō'bəstə/ ▸ coffee or coffee beans from a widely grown kind of coffee plant. Beans of this variety are often used in the manufacture of instant coffee. Compare with ARABICA.

–ORIGIN modern Latin, feminine of Latin *robustus* 'robust.'

rocket ▸ an edible Mediterranean plant of the cabbage family, eaten in salads. See also ARUGULA.

–ORIGIN from French *roquette*, from Italian *ruchetta*, diminutive of *ruca*, from Latin *eruca* 'downy-stemmed plant.'

roe ▸ (also **hard roe**) the mass of eggs contained in the ovaries of a female fish or shellfish, typically including the ovaries themselves, especially when ripe and used as food.

■ (also **soft roe**) the ripe testes of a male fish, especially when used as food.

rogan josh /'rōgən 'jäsH/ ▸ an Indian dish of curried meat, typically lamb, in a rich tomato-based sauce.

–ORIGIN from Urdu *roġan još.*

roll ▸ an item of food that is made by wrapping a piecet of meat, or fish around a savory filling: *salmon and rice rolls.*

■ a pastry or dessert made by wrapping a flat sheet of dough or cake around a sweet filling: *a jelly roll.*

■ a very small loaf of bread, typically eaten with butter or a filling: *assorted dinner rolls.*

–ORIGIN Middle English: from Old French *rolle* (noun), *roller* (verb), from Latin *rotulus* 'a roll,' variant of *rotula* 'little wheel,' diminutive of *rota*.

rolled oats ▸ oats that have been husked and crushed.

romaine ▸ a lettuce of a variety with crisp narrow leaves that form a tall head.
-ORIGIN from French, feminine of *romain* 'Roman.'

Romano /rō'mänō/ ▸ a strong-tasting hard cheese, originally made in Italy.
-ORIGIN Italian, literally 'Roman.'

root ▸ the underground part of a plant.
■ (also **root vegetable**) the fleshy enlarged root of a plant used as a vegetable, for example, a CARROT, RUTABAGA, or BEET.
-ORIGIN Old English *rōt*, from Old Norse *rót*.

root beer ▸ an effervescent drink made from an extract of the roots and bark of certain plants.

Roquefort /'rōkfərt/ ▸ a soft blue cheese made from ewes' milk. It is ripened in limestone caves and has a strong flavor.
-ORIGIN from the name of a village in southern France.

rosemary ▸ the narrow leaves of an evergreen aromatic shrub of the mint family, used as a culinary herb.
-ORIGIN Middle English *rosmarine*, based on Latin *ros marinus*, from *ros* 'dew' + *marinus* 'of the sea.'

rose water ▸ scented water made with rose petals, used in pastries.

roti ▸ (in Indian cooking) bread, especially a flat round bread cooked on a griddle.
-ORIGIN from Hindi *roṭī*.

rotini /rō'tēnē/ ▸ pasta in short pieces with a helical shape.
-ORIGIN Italian, literally 'spirals.'

rotisserie ▸ a cooking appliance with a rotating spit for roasting and barbecuing meat.
-ORIGIN from French *rôtisserie*, from *rôtir* 'to roast.'

rouget /roo'ZHä/ ▸ French term for RED MULLET, used especially in cooking.
-ORIGIN French.

rouille /'roo-ē(yə)/ ▸ a Provençal sauce made from pounded red chilies, garlic, breadcrumbs, and other ingredients blended with stock, typically added to bouillabaisse.

–ORIGIN French, literally 'rust,' with reference to the color.

roulade /roo'läd/ ▸ a dish cooked or served in the form of a roll, typically made from a flat piece of meat or fish spread with a soft filling and rolled up into a spiral.

–ORIGIN French, from *rouler* 'to roll.'

round ▸ a circular piece of a particular substance: *cut the pastry into rounds.*

■ a thick disk of beef cut from the haunch of an animal.

roux /roo/ ▸ a mixture of fat (usually butter) and flour used in making sauces.

–ORIGIN from French *(beurre) roux* 'browned (butter).'

royal icing ▸ chiefly British hard white icing made from confectioners' sugar and egg whites, typically used to decorate fruitcakes.

rugalach (also **rugelach**) /'rəgələкн/ ▸ a bite-size cookie made with cream-cheese dough rolled around a filling of nuts, poppy seed paste, chocolate, or jam.

–ORIGIN Yiddish, literally 'little twists.'

rump ▸ a cut of beef or veal from the hind part of an animal, but not the leg: *a rump roast.*

–ORIGIN Middle English: probably of Scandinavian origin.

rusk ▸ a light, dry piece of twice-baked bread.

–ORIGIN from Spanish or Portuguese *rosca* 'twist, coil, roll of bread.'

russet ▸ an eating apple of a variety with a slightly rough greenish-brown skin.

■ (also **russet potato**) a variety of potato with a rough brown skin.

–ORIGIN Middle English: from an Anglo-Norman French variant of Old French *rousset*, diminutive of *rous* 'red,' from Provençal *ros*, from Latin *russus* 'red.'

Russian salad ▸ a salad of mixed diced vegetables with mayonnaise.

Russian tea ▸ tea laced with rum and typically served with lemon.

rutabaga ▸ a large, round, yellow-fleshed root that is eaten as a vegetable.

–ORIGIN from Swedish dialect *rotabagge*.

rye ▸ a hardy, widely-cultivated cereal plant.

■ grains of this, used mainly for making bread or whiskey.

■ short for RYE BREAD: *pastrami on rye.*

–ORIGIN Old English *ryge*, of Germanic origin.

rye bread ▸ bread made with all or part rye flour, often with caraway seeds added.

S

---

sabayon /ˌsäbīˈōn/ ▸ French term for ZABAGLIONE.

Sachertorte /ˈzäkHərˌtôrt(ə)/ ▸ a rich chocolate cake with apricot jam filling and chocolate icing.

–ORIGIN German, from the name of Franz *Sacher*, pastry chef who created it, + *Torte* 'tart, pastry.'

saddle ▸ a cut of meat consisting of the two loins.

safflower ▸ a thistlelike Eurasian plant. Its seeds yield an edible oil and its orange flowers are sometimes dried and used as a saffron substitute.

■ **(safflower oil)** the oil obtained from the seeds of this plant.

–ORIGIN Middle English: from Dutch *saffloer* or German *Saflor*, via Old French and Italian from Arabic *asfar* 'yellow.' The spelling has been influenced by *saffron* and *flower*.

saffron /ˈsafrən/ ▸ an orange-yellow flavoring and food coloring made from the dried stigmas of a crocus.

–ORIGIN Middle English: from Old French *safran*, based on Arabic *zaʿfarān*.

saganaki /ˌsägəˈnäkē/ ▸ a Greek dish consisting of breaded or floured cheese fried in butter, served as an appetizer.

–ORIGIN modern Greek, denoting a small two-handled frying pan, in which the dish is traditionally made.

sage ▸ the grayish-green leaves of an aromatic plant native to the Mediterranean, used as a culinary herb.

–ORIGIN Middle English: from Old French *sauge*, from Latin *salvia* 'healing plant,' from *salvus* 'safe.'

sago /ˈsāgō/ ▸ edible starch that is obtained from a palm and is a staple food in parts of the tropics. The pith inside the trunk is scraped out, washed, and dried to produce a flour or processed to produce the granular sago used in the West.

■ (also **sago pudding**) a sweet dish made from sago and milk.

-ORIGIN: from Malay *sagu* (originally via Portuguese).

salad ▸ a cold dish of various mixtures of raw or cooked vegetables, usually seasoned with oil and vinegar, or other dressing, and sometimes accompanied by meat, fish, or other ingredients: *a green salad.*

■ a mixture containing a specified ingredient dressed with mayonnaise: *a red pepper filled with tuna salad.*

■ a vegetable suitable for eating raw.

-ORIGIN late Middle English: from Old French *salade*, from Provençal *salada*, based on Latin *sal* 'salt.'

salad dressing ▸ see DRESSING.

salamander ▸ a metal plate heated and placed over food to brown it.

-ORIGIN Middle English (mythological reptile that was resistant to fire): from Old French *salamandre*, via Latin from Greek *salamandra.*

salami ▸ a type of highly seasoned sausage, originally from Italy, usually eaten cold in slices.

-ORIGIN Italian, plural of *salame*, from a late Latin word meaning 'to salt.'

salep /'saləp/ ▸ a starchy preparation of the dried tubers of various orchids, used as a thickener in cooking.

-ORIGIN from French, from Turkish *sālep*, from Arabic (*ḵuṣa-'t-) ta'lab.*

Sally Lunn ▸ a sweet, light teacake, typically served hot.

-ORIGIN said to be from the name of a woman selling such cakes in Bath, England, *circa* 1800.

salmagundi ▸ a dish of chopped meat, anchovies, eggs, onions, and seasoning.

-ORIGIN from French *salmigondis.*

salmi ▸ a ragout or casserole of game stewed in a rich sauce: *a pheasant salmi.*

-ORIGIN French, abbreviation of *salmigondis* (see SALMAGUNDI).

salmon ▶ a large edible fish that is a popular game fish, much prized for its pink flesh.

-ORIGIN Middle English *samoun*, from Anglo-Norman French *saumoun*, from Latin *salmo, salmon-*.

salpicon ▶ a mixture of finely chopped ingredients bound in a thick sauce and used as a filling or stuffing.

-ORIGIN via French from Spanish, from *salpicar* 'sprinkle (with salt).'

salsa ▶ (especially in Latin American cooking) a condiment made with chopped fruit or tomatoes, onions, chilis, and herbs.

-ORIGIN Spanish, literally 'sauce.'

salsa verde /'verdā/ ▶ an Italian sauce made with olive oil, garlic, capers, anchovies, vinegar or lemon juice, and parsley.

■ a Mexican sauce of finely chopped onion, garlic, coriander, parsley, and hot peppers.

-ORIGIN Spanish, literally 'green sauce.'

salsify /'salsəfē/ ▶ an edible European plant of the daisy family, with a long root like that of a parsnip (also called **oyster plant**).

■ the root of this plant eaten raw in salads or cooked as a vegetable.

-ORIGIN from French *salsifis*, from obsolete Italian *salsefica*.

salt ▶ a white crystalline mineral, sodium chloride, that gives seawater its characteristic taste and is used for seasoning or preserving food. See SEA SALT.

■ table salt mixed with a specified seasoning: *garlic salt.*

▶ impregnated with, treated with, or tasting of salt: *salt pork.*

▶ to season or preserve with salt: *cook the carrots in boiling salted water.*

-ORIGIN Old English *sealt* (noun), *sealtan* (verb), of Germanic origin; from an Indo-European root shared by Latin *sal*, Greek *hals* 'salt.'

salt fish ▶ fish, especially cod, that has been preserved in salt.

saltimbocca /ˌsältim'bōkə/ ▶ a dish consisting of rolled pieces of veal or poultry cooked with herbs, bacon, and other flavorings.

-ORIGIN Italian, literally 'leap into the mouth.'

saltine ▶ a thin, crisp, savory cracker sprinkled with salt.

salty ▶ tasting of, containing, or preserved with salt.

salumi /sä'lōōmē/ ▸ cured meats that are sliced and served as an appetizer in an Italian meal.
–ORIGIN Italian.

sambal /'sämbäl/ ▸ (in southeast Asian cooking) hot relish made with vegetables or fruit and spices.
–ORIGIN Malay.

sambhar /'sämbər/ ▸ a spicy southern Indian dish consisting of lentils and vegetables.
–ORIGIN from Tamil *cāmpār*, via Marathi from Sanskrit *sambhāra* 'collection, materials.'

samosa /sə'mōsə/ ▸ a triangular savory pastry fried in ghee or oil, containing spiced vegetables or meat.
–ORIGIN from Persian and Urdu.

sancoche /san'kôCHä/ ▸ (in South America and the Caribbean) a thick soup consisting of meat and root vegetables.
–ORIGIN from Latin American Spanish *sancocho* 'a stew.'

sandwich ▸ an item of food consisting of two pieces of bread with meat, cheese, or other filling between them, eaten as a light meal.
–ORIGIN named after the 4th Earl of *Sandwich* (1718–92), English nobleman said to have ordered food in this form so as not to leave the gaming table.

sardine ▸ a young or small herringlike fish, eaten fresh or processed and canned.
–ORIGIN Middle English: from French, or from Latin *sardina*, from *sarda*, from Greek, probably from *Sardō* 'Sardinia.'

sarsaparilla ▸ a preparation of the dried rhizomes of various plants, used to flavor some drinks and medicines and formerly as a tonic.
■ a soft drink flavored with this.
–ORIGIN from Spanish *zarzaparilla*, from *zarza* 'bramble' + a diminutive of *parra* 'vine.'

sashimi /sä'sHēmē/ ▸ a Japanese dish of bite-sized pieces of raw fish eaten with soy sauce and horseradish paste: *tuna sashimi*.
–ORIGIN Japanese.

sassafras ▸ a North American tree with aromatic leaves and bark. The leaves are infused to make tea or ground into filé.

Sandwiches

arepa
bacon butty
bagel
barbecue beef
biscuit
BLT
boat
bologna
burrito
California club
calzone
canapé
chicken salad
chilaquile
chili dog
chimichanga
club
Coney Island
corndog
corned beef
Cornish pasty
crepe
croissant
croque madame
croque monsieur
Cuban
cucumber
Dagwood
Dagwood
deviled ham
eggplant parmigiana
egg salad
empanada
enchilada

fajita
finger
flauta
fluffernutter
focaccia
focaccia
french dip
fried peanut butter and
  banana
gordita
grilled cheese
grinder
gyro
ham and cheese
hamburger
hero
hoagie
hobo
hot brown
hot dog
hot pastrami
Italian
kidney pie
meat loaf
meatball
Monte Cristo
muffuletta
open-faced
oyster loaf
pan bagnat
panino
peanut butter and jelly
Philly cheese steak
pig in a blanket

pinwheel
pistolette
pita pocket
poor boy
pocket
pork bun
pulled pork
quesadilla
Rachel
Reuben
roast beef
sausage and
  pepper
shawarma
sliced steak
sloppy joe
smoked salmon
stromboli
sub
submarine
taco
tea
tongue
torpedo
torta
triple-decker
tuna melt
tuna salad
watercress
wedge
Welsh rarebit/rabbit
Western
wrap

-ORIGIN from Spanish *sasafrás*, based on Latin *saxifraga* 'saxifrage.'

satay (also **saté**) /ˈsäˌtā/ ▶ an Indonesian and Malaysian dish consisting of small pieces of meat grilled on a skewer and usually served with spiced sauce.
-ORIGIN from Malay *satai*, Indonesian *sate*.

sauce ▶ a thick liquid served with food, usually savory dishes, to add moistness and flavor: *tomato sauce.*

■ stewed fruit, especially apples, eaten as dessert or used as a garnish.

▶ to provide a sauce for (something); season with a sauce.

-ORIGIN Middle English: from Old French, based on Latin *salsus* 'salted,' past participle of *salere* 'to salt,' from *sal* 'salt.' Compare with SALAD.

sauce mousseline /ˌmo͞os(ə)'lēn/ ▶ see MOUSSELINE.

saucepan ▶ a deep cooking pan, typically round and made of metal with one long handle and a lid.

saucier /sôs'yā/ ▶ a chef who prepares sauces.

-ORIGIN French.

saucisson /ˌsōsē'sôN/ ▶ a large, thick French sausage, typically firm in texture and flavored with herbs.

-ORIGIN French, literally 'large sausage.'

sauerbraten ▶ a dish of German origin consisting of beef that is marinated in vinegar with peppercorns, onions, and other seasonings before cooking.

-ORIGIN from German, from *sauer* 'sour' + *Braten* 'roast meat.'

sauerkraut ▶ shredded cabbage that has been pickled in brine.

-ORIGIN from German, from *sauer* 'sour' + *Kraut* 'vegetable.'

sausage ▶ a short cylindrical tube of minced pork, beef, or other meat encased in a skin, typically sold raw to be cooked before eating.

■ a cylindrical tube of minced pork, beef, or other meat seasoned and cooked or preserved, sold mainly to be eaten cold in slices: *smoked German sausage.*

-ORIGIN Middle English: from Old Northern French *saussiche*, from medieval Latin *salsicia*, from Latin *salsus* 'salted' (see SAUCE).

sauté ▶ cooked or browned quickly in a little hot fat: *sauté potatoes.*

▶ a dish cooked in such a way.

▶ to cook in a small amount of fat: *sauté the onions in the olive oil.*

-ORIGIN French, literally 'jumped,' past participle of *sauter.*

savarin ▶ a light ring-shaped cake made with yeast and soaked in liqueur-flavored syrup.

-ORIGIN named after Anthelme Brillat-*Savarin* (1755–1826), French gastronome.

savory[1] ▸ an aromatic plant of the mint family, used as a culinary herb.

-ORIGIN Middle English: perhaps from Old English *sætherie*, or via Old French, from Latin *satureia*.

savory[2] ▸ (of food) belonging to the category that is salty or spicy rather than sweet.

▸ chiefly British a savory dish, especially a snack or an appetizer.

-ORIGIN Middle English (in the sense 'pleasing to the sense of taste or smell'): from Old French *savoure* 'tasty, fragrant,' based on Latin *sapor* 'taste.'

savoy (also **savoy cabbage**) ▸ a cabbage of a hardy variety with densely wrinkled leaves.

-ORIGIN from *Savoy* in southeastern France.

scald ▸ to heat (milk or other liquid) to near boiling point.

■ to immerse (something) briefly in boiling water for various purposes, such as to facilitate the removal of skin from fruit or to preserve meat.

scallion ▸ a long-necked onion with a small bulb, in particular a shallot or green onion.

-ORIGIN late Middle English: from Anglo-Norman French *scaloun*, based on Latin *Ascalonia (caepa)* '(onion) of *Ascalon*,' a port in ancient Palestine.

scallop ▸ an edible bivalve mollusk with a ribbed fan-shaped shell.

■ a small pan or dish shaped like a scallop shell and used for baking or serving food.

■ another term for ESCALOPE.

▸ to bake with milk or a sauce: *scalloped potatoes*.

-ORIGIN Middle English: shortening of Old French *escalope*, probably of Germanic origin.

scaloppine /ˌskälə'pēnē/ (also **scallopini**) ▸ (in Italian cooking) thin, boneless slices of meat, typically veal, sautéed or fried.

-ORIGIN Italian, plural of *scaloppina*, diminutive of *scaloppa* 'envelope.'

scampi ▸ large shrimp or prawns, especially when prepared or cooked.

■ a dish of shrimp or prawns, typically sautéed in garlic and butter and often topped with breadcrumbs.

-ORIGIN Italian.

scarlet runner (also **scarlet runner bean**) ▸ the very long flat edible pod and seed of a twining bean plant.

schnitzel ▸ a thin slice of veal or other light meat, coated in breadcrumbs and fried.

-ORIGIN from German *Schnitzel*, literally 'slice.'

scone ▸ a small unsweetened or lightly sweetened biscuitlike cake made from flour, fat, and milk and sometimes having added fruit.

-ORIGIN (originally Scots): perhaps from Middle Dutch *schoon(broot)* 'fine (bread).'

Scotch broth ▸ a traditional Scottish soup made from beef or mutton stock with pearl barley and vegetables.

Scotch egg ▸ a hard-boiled egg enclosed in sausage meat, rolled in breadcrumbs, and fried.

scrambled eggs ▸ eggs prepared by beating them with a little liquid and then cooking and stirring gently in a pan.

scrapple ▸ scraps of pork or other meat stewed with cornmeal and shaped into loaves for slicing and frying.

-ORIGIN diminutive of the noun *scrap.*

scrod ▸ a young cod, haddock, or similar fish, especially one prepared for cooking.

scungille (also **scungile**) /skoͦn'jēlē/ ▸ a mollusk (especially with reference to its meat eaten as a delicacy).

-ORIGIN from Italian dialect *scunciglio*, probably an alteration of Italian *conchiglia* 'seashell.'

sea bass ▸ any of a number of edible marine fishes that are related to or resemble the common perch.

sea cucumber ▸ an edible echinoderm that has a thick, wormlike body. See also BÊCHE DE MER.

seafood ▸ fish and shellfish, prepared and served as food.

Fish and Seafood

abalone	barbel	bluefish
akule	barracuda	bluefish
albacore	basa	bonito
amberjack	bass	branzino
anchovy	blackfish	bream
angelfish	blenny	brill
anglerfish	blowfish	brisling
bacalao	blue crab	buffalo fish

Fish and Seafood (continued)

burbot
butterfish
calamari
carp
catfish
caviar
char
clam
cockle
cod
codfish
conch
conger eel
coral
crab
crappie
crawdad
crawfish
crayfish
cusk
cuttlefish
dogfish
dolphin fish
dorade
dover sole
eel
escargot
finnan haddie
flounder
fluke
flying fish
fugu
geoduck
goby
gravlax
grouper
grunion
grunt
haddock
hake
halibut
herring
jellyfish

John Dory
king crab
kingfish
kipper
lamprey
langoustine
lemon sole
limpet
lobster
lotte
lox
lutefisk
mackerel
mahimahi
mako shark
milt
monkfish
moray eel
mussel
octopus
orange roughy
orata
oyster
parrotfish
perch
periwinkle
pilchard
pollack
pompano
prawn
pulpo
quahog
rainbow trout
ray
razor clam
red mullet
red snapper
rockfish
roe
rouget
sable
salmon
salt cod

sand dab
sardine
scallop
scrod
scungilli
sea anemone
sea bass
sea bream
sea cucumber
sea trout
sea urchin
shad
shark
shrimp
skate
smelt
snail
snapper
snow crab
softshell crab
sole
sprat
squid
stone crab
striped bass
sturgeon
sunfish
surimi
swordfish
tarpon
teal
terrapin
tilapia
tilefish
trout
tuna
turbot
wahoo
whelk
whitefish
wrasse
yellowtail

sea lettuce ▶ an edible seaweed with green fronds that resemble lettuce leaves.

sear ▶ to brown (food) quickly at a high temperature so that it will retain its juices in subsequent cooking: *seared chicken livers.*

sea salt ▶ salt produced by the evaporation of seawater.

season ▶ the time of year when a particular fruit, vegetable, or other food is plentiful and in good condition: *the pies are made with fruit that is in season* | *lobster season.*

▶ to add salt, herbs, pepper, or other spices to (food): *season the soup to taste with salt and pepper* | *seasoned flour.*

■ to prepare (a cast-iron or other metal pan) for use by rubbing vegetable oil into its surface.

seasoning ▶ salt, herbs, or spices added to food to enhance the flavor. See word banks at **HERB** and **SPICE**.

sea urchin ▶ a marine echinoderm that has a spherical or flattened shell covered in mobile spines. Many species are harvested for food.

seed ▶ a flowering plant's unit of reproduction, capable of developing into another such plant.

■ certain seeds used for food, eaten as they are or ground into meal or flour: *roasted pumpkin seeds* | *sesame seed candy.* See word bank at **NUT**.

▶ to remove the seeds from (vegetables or fruit): *stem and seed the chilies.*

-ORIGIN Old English *sǣd*, of Germanic origin; related to Dutch *zaad*, German *Saat.*

seed cake ▶ a cake containing caraway or other seeds as flavoring.

self-rising flour ▶ flour that has a leavening agent already added.

seltzer (also **seltzer water**) ▶ soda water.

■ medicinal mineral water from Niederselters in Germany.

-ORIGIN alteration of German *Selterser*, from *(Nieder)selters.*

semisweet ▶ slightly sweetened, but less so than normal: *semisweet chocolates.*

semolina ▶ the hard grains left after the milling of flour, used in puddings, bread, and pasta.

-ORIGIN from Italian *semolino*, diminutive of *semola* 'bran,' from Latin *simila* 'flour.'

server ▸ a large utensil for serving food: *a silver pie server.*

■ a waiter or waitress.

serving ▸ a quantity of food suitable for or served to one person: *a large serving of spaghetti.*

sesame ▸ a tall annual herbaceous plant of tropical and subtropical areas of the Old World.

■ (**sesame seed**) the edible seeds of this plant, which are used whole or have the oil extracted.

-ORIGIN late Middle English: via Latin from Greek *sēsamon*, *sēsamē*; compare with Arabic *simsim*.

sev /sāv; sev/ ▸ an Indian snack consisting of long, thin strands of gram flour, deep-fried and spiced.

-ORIGIN Hindi.

seviche /səˈvēCHā/ ▸ variant spelling of CEVICHE.

sevruga /səˈvroōgə/ ▸ caviar obtained from a migratory sturgeon found only in the basins of the Caspian and Black Seas.

-ORIGIN from Russian *sevryuga.*

shabu-shabu /ˈSHäboō ˈSHäboō/ ▸ a Japanese dish of pieces of thinly sliced beef or pork cooked quickly with vegetables in boiling water and then dipped in sauce.

-ORIGIN Japanese.

shallot ▸ a small bulb that resembles an onion and is used for pickling or as a substitute for onion.

-ORIGIN shortening of *eschalot*, from French *eschalotte*, alteration of Old French *eschaloigne* (in Anglo-Norman French *scaloun*: see SCALLION).

shank ▸ a cut of meat from the lower part of an animal's foreleg: *baked lamb shanks.*

shashlik /ˈSHäSH‚lik/ ▸ a kebab, typically of lamb or beef, or in Asia and eastern Europe, of mutton. See also SHISH KEBAB.

-ORIGIN from Russian *shashlyk*, based on Turkish *şiş* 'spit, skewer'.

shchi /SH-CHē/ ▸ a type of Russian cabbage soup.

-ORIGIN Russian.

shell ▸ something resembling or likened to a shell because of its shape or its function as an outer case: *pasta shells | baked pastry shells filled with cheese.*

▸ to remove the shell or pod from (a nut or seed): *they were shelling peas* | *shelled Brazil nuts.*

shellfish ▸ an aquatic shelled mollusk (for example, an OYSTER) or a crustacean (for example, a CRAB or SHRIMP), especially one that is edible.

■ such mollusks or crustaceans as food. See word bank at SEAFOOD.

shepherd's pie ▸ a dish of seasoned ground meat under a layer of mashed potato.

sherbet ▸ a frozen dessert made with fruit juice added to milk or cream, egg white, or gelatin.

■ a frozen fruit juice and sugar mixture served as a dessert or between courses of a meal to cleanse the palate.

■ (especially in Arab countries) a cooling drink of sweet diluted fruit juices.

■ British a flavored sweet effervescent powder eaten alone or made into a drink.

-ORIGIN from Turkish *şerbet*, Persian *šerbet*, from Arabic *šarba* 'drink,' from *šariba* 'to drink.' Compare with SYRUP.

USAGE: The tendency to insert an *r* into the second syllable of **sherbet** is very common. Frequency of misuse has not changed the fact that the spelling **sherbert** and the pronunciation /'sHərbərt/ are wrong and should not be considered acceptable variants. Also see usage note at FLAN.

shiitake /sHē'täkē/ (also **shiitake mushroom**) ▸ an edible mushroom that grows on fallen timber, cultivated in Japan and China.

-ORIGIN from Japanese, from *shii*, denoting a kind of oak, + *take* 'mushroom.'

shin ▸ a cut of beef from the lower part of a cow's leg.

shirr ▸ to bake (an egg) without its shell.

shish kebab /'sHisH kə,bäb/ ▸ a dish of pieces of marinated meat and vegetables cooked and served on skewers.

-ORIGIN from Turkish *şiş kebap*, from *şiş* 'skewer' + *kebāp* 'roast meat.'

shiso /'sHēsō/ ▸ Japanese term for PERILLA.

shoestring potatoes ▸ potatoes cut into long thin strips and deep-fried.

shoo-fly pie (also **shoofly pie**) ▸ a rich pie made with molasses and topped with crumbs.

-ORIGIN from the interjection *shoo-fly* (referring to the need to wave flies away from the sweet molasses).

short ▸ (of pastry) containing a high proportion of fat to flour and therefore crumbly.

shortbread ▸ a crisp, rich, crumbly type of cookie made with butter, flour, and sugar.

-ORIGIN *short* in the sense 'easily crumbled.'

shortcake ▸ a small cake made of biscuit dough or sponge cake and typically served with fruit and whipped cream as a dessert.

■ a dessert made from shortcake topped with fruit, typically strawberries, and whipped cream.

-ORIGIN see **SHORTBREAD**.

shortening ▸ butter or other solid fat used for making pastry or bread.

short ribs ▸ a narrow cut of beef containing the ends of the ribs near to the breastbone.

shoulder ▸ a cut of meat from the upper foreleg and shoulder blade of an animal: *a shoulder of lamb.*

shoyu /ˈSHōyōō/ ▸ a type of Japanese soy sauce.

-ORIGIN from Japanese *shōyu.*

shred ▸ to tear or cut into long narrow pieces: *shredded cabbage.*

shrimp ▸ a small free-swimming crustacean with an elongated body, typically marine, and prized for food.

-ORIGIN Middle English: probably related to Middle Low German *schrempen* 'to wrinkle,' Middle High German *schrimpfen* 'to contract.'

shuck ▸ an outer covering such as a husk or pod, especially the husk of an ear of corn.

■ the shell of an oyster or clam.

▸ to remove the shucks from corn or shellfish.

side /sīd/ ▸ either of the lateral halves of the body of a butchered animal, or an animal or fish prepared for eating: *a side of beef.*

■ (also **side dish**) a dish served as subsidiary to the main one: *sides of German potato salad and red cabbage.*

sieve ▸ a utensil consisting of a wire or plastic mesh held in a frame, used for straining solids from liquids, for separating coarser from finer particles, or for reducing soft solids to a pulp.

▸ to put (a food substance or other material) through a sieve.

-ORIGIN Old English *sife* (noun), of West Germanic origin.

simmer ▸ (of water or food that is being heated) to stay just below boiling point while bubbling gently.

■ to keep (something) at such a point when cooking or heating it: *simmer the sauce until thickened.*

▸ a state or temperature just below boiling point: *bring the water to a simmer.*

-ORIGIN alteration of dialect *simper* (in the same sense), perhaps imitative.

sippet ▸ a small piece of bread or toast, used to dip into soup or sauce or as a garnish.

-ORIGIN apparently a diminutive of *sop.*

sirloin ▸ the choicer part of a loin of beef: *sirloin steaks.*

-ORIGIN Middle English: from Old French, from *sur-* 'above' + *loigne* (see LOIN).

skate ▸ a large edible marine fish of the ray family with a cartilaginous skeleton and a flattened diamond-shaped body.

-ORIGIN Middle English: from Old Norse *skata.*

skewer ▸ a long piece of wood or metal used for holding pieces of food, typically meat, together during cooking.

▸ to fasten together or pierce with a pin or skewer: *skewered chunks of fish.*

skillet ▸ a frying pan.

-ORIGIN Middle English: perhaps from Old French *escuelete*, diminutive of *escuele* 'platter,' from late Latin *scutella.*

skim milk (also **skimmed milk**) ▸ milk from which the cream has been removed.

skyr /ski(ə)r/ ▸ an Icelandic dish consisting of curdled milk.

-ORIGIN Icelandic.

slaw ▸ coleslaw.

■ a similar salad containing a specified shredded or chopped vegetable: *carrot slaw.*

-ORIGIN from Dutch *sla*, shortened from *salade* 'salad.'

slice ▸ a thin, broad piece of food, such as bread, meat, or cake, cut from a larger portion.
■ a utensil with a broad, flat blade for lifting foods such as cake and fish.
▸ to cut (food) into slices.
□ **slicer**: *a small electric meat slicer.*

Slim Jim ▸ a long thin variety of smoked sausage.

sloppy joe ▸ a sandwich with a filling of ground beef that has been seasoned with a sauce of tomatoes and spices.

slotted spoon ▸ a large spoon with slots or holes for draining liquid from food.

slow cooker ▸ a large electric pot used for cooking food, especially stews, at a very low temperature for long periods.

smelt ▸ a small edible silvery fish that lives in both marine and fresh water and is sometimes fished commercially.

Smithfield ham ▸ a dry-cured ham produced near Smithfield, Virginia, from hogs that have fed on hickory nuts, acorns, and peanuts.

smoke ▸ to cure or preserve (meat or fish) by exposure to smoke: *smoked salmon.*

smokebox ▸ an oven for smoking food

smoothie ▸ a thick, smooth drink of fresh fruit puréed with milk, yogurt, or ice cream.

smorgasbord ▸ a buffet offering a variety of hot and cold meats, salads, hors d'oeuvres, etc.
–ORIGIN Swedish, from *smörgås* '(slice of) bread and butter' (from *smör* 'butter' + *gås* 'goose, lump of butter') + *bord* 'table.'

smother ▸ to cook (meat) in a covered pan or pot, typically with a sauce and vegetables on top: *smothered fried chicken.*
–ORIGIN Middle English (as a noun in the sense 'stifling smoke'): from the base of Old English *smorian* 'suffocate.'

snack ▸ a small amount of food eaten between meals.
■ a light meal that is eaten in a hurry or in a casual manner.
–ORIGIN (originally in the sense 'snap, bite'): from Middle Dutch *snac(k)*, from *snacken* 'to bite,' variant of *snappen.*

snail ▸ an edible mollusk with a single spiral shell into which the whole body can be withdrawn.
–ORIGIN Old English *snæg(e)l*, of Germanic origin.

snap bean /'snap ˌbēn/ ▶ a bean of a variety grown for its edible pods. –ORIGIN so named because the pods are broken into pieces to be eaten.

snow ▶ a dessert or other dish resembling snow: *vanilla snow.*

snowball ▶ a dessert resembling a ball of snow, especially one containing or covered in ice cream.

snow crab ▶ an edible crab found off the eastern seaboard of Canada.

snow pea ▶ a pea of a variety with an edible pod, eaten when the pod is young and flat. Compare with SUGAR SNAP.

soba /'sōbə/ ▶ Japanese noodles made from buckwheat flour. –ORIGIN Japanese.

soda ▶ (also **soda water** or **club soda**) carbonated water (originally made with sodium bicarbonate) drunk alone or with liquor or wine: *a whiskey and soda.*

■ (also **soda pop**) a carbonated soft drink: *a can of soda.* See word bank at SOFT DRINK.
–ORIGIN Middle English: from medieval Latin, from Arabic *suwwad* 'saltwort.'

soda bread ▶ bread leavened with baking soda.

soda cracker ▶ a thin, crisp cracker leavened with baking soda.

sofrito /sō'frētō/ ▶ a Caribbean and Latin American sauce of tomatoes, onions, peppers, garlic, and herbs.
–ORIGIN American Spanish, from past participle of Spanish *sofreír* 'to fry.'

soft drink ▶ a nonalcoholic drink, especially one that is carbonated.

soft roe ▶ see ROE.

soft-shell clam (also **softshell clam**) ▶ a marine bivalve mollusk with a thin shell and a long siphon, inhabiting the east coast of North America and valued as food (also called **steamer**).

soft-shell crab (also **softshell crab**) ▶ an edible crab, especially a blue crab, that has recently molted and has a new shell that is still soft and edible.

soft wheat ▶ wheat of a variety having a soft grain rich in starch, used for cakes and pastries.

sole ▶ a marine flatfish of almost worldwide distribution, important as a food fish.
–ORIGIN Middle English: from Old French, from Provençal *sola*, from Latin *solea*, named from its shape.

Soft Drinks, Sodas, Pops, and other Non-Alcoholic Beverages

ambrosia	float	Mountain Dew
atole	frappe	nectar
batido	fruit juice	orangeade
birch beer	fruit punch	orange soda
bubble tea	ginger ale	Orangina
café au lait	ginger beer	Pepsi
café latte	grape soda	pop
cappuccino	green tea	refresco
chai	guarana	ristretto
cherry cola	horchata	root beer
chocolate milk	iced coffee	Russian tea
cider	iced tea	sarsaparilla
club soda	kava	seltzer
Coca-Cola	kefir	7–Up
coconut milk	kumiss	Shirley Temple
coffee	lemonade	slush
cola	lemon-lime	smoothie
cream soda	lime rickey	soy milk
diet	limeade	spritzer
Dr. Pepper	malted	tea
egg cream	maté	tisane
eggnog	milkshake	tonic water
espresso	mineral water	Turkish coffee
flip	mochaccino	wassail

sopaipilla /ˌsōpīˈpēyə/ ▶ a deep-fried pastry, typically square, eaten with honey or sugar or as a bread, originating in the southwestern U.S.

–ORIGIN American Spanish.

sorbet ▶ a dessert consisting of frozen fruit juice or flavored water and sugar.

–ORIGIN from French, from Italian *sorbetto*, from Turkish şerbet, based on Arabic *šariba* 'to drink'; compare with SHERBET.

sorghum ▶ a widely cultivated cereal native to warm regions of the Old World. It is a major source of grain.

■ a syrupy sweetener made from it.

–ORIGIN modern Latin, from Italian *sorgo*, perhaps based on a variant of Latin *syricum* 'Syrian.'

sorrel ▶ a European plant of the dock family, with arrow-shaped leaves that are used in salads and cooking for their acidic flavor.

-ORIGIN late Middle English: from Old French *sorele*, of Germanic origin.

soubise /soo'bēz/ ▶ a thick white sauce made with onion purée and often served with fish or eggs.

-ORIGIN named after Charles de Rohan *Soubise* (1715–87), French general and courtier.

souchong /'soo'chäNG/ ▶ a fine black variety of China tea.

-ORIGIN from Chinese *siŭ* 'small' + *chúng* 'sort.'

soufflé ▶ a light, spongy baked dish made by adding cheese, fish, or other ingredients combined with egg yolks to stiffly beaten egg whites.

■ any of various light dishes made with beaten egg whites.

-ORIGIN French, literally 'blown,' past participle of *souffler*.

soul food ▶ traditional African-American food that originated in the rural South.

soup ▶ a liquid dish, typically made by boiling meat, fish, vegetables, etc., in stock or water: *tomato soup*.

-ORIGIN Middle English: from Old French *soupe* 'sop, broth (poured on slices of bread),' from late Latin *suppa*, of Germanic origin.

sour ▶ having an acid taste like lemon or vinegar.

■ (of food, especially milk) spoiled because of fermentation.

▶ to make or become sour: *water soured with tamarind | soured cream | a bowl of milk was souring in the sun*.

sour cream ▶ cream that has been deliberately fermented by the addition of certain bacteria.

sourdough ▶ leaven for making bread, consisting of fermenting dough, typically that left over from a previous batch.

■ bread made using such leaven.

souse ▶ to put (gherkins, fish, etc.) in a pickling solution or a marinade: *soused herring*.

▶ liquid, typically salted, used for pickling.

■ pickled food, especially a pig's head.

-ORIGIN Middle English (as a noun denoting pickled meat): from Old French *sous* 'pickle,' of Germanic origin; related to **SALT**.

sous vide /'sooz 'vēd/ ▶ a method of treating food by partial cooking followed by vacuum-sealing and chilling.

▶ (of food or cooking) involving such preparation: *a convection oven can be used in sous vide operations* | *cuisine sous vide.*
–ORIGIN French, literally 'under vacuum.'

southern-fried ▶ (of food, especially chicken) coated in flour, egg, and breadcrumbs and then deep-fried.

souvlaki /sōōv'läkē/ ▶ a Greek dish of pieces of meat grilled on a skewer: *a generous plate of souvlaki* | *souvlakia in pita.*
–ORIGIN modern Greek.

soy ▶ another term for SOYBEAN.
–ORIGIN from Japanese *shō-yu*, from Chinese *shi-yu*, from *shi* 'salted beans' + *yu* 'oil.'

soybean ▶ the seed of a legume native to Asia, used in a variety of foods, especially as a replacement for animal protein.

soy milk (also **soybean milk**) ▶ the liquid obtained by suspending soybean flour in water, used as a fat-free substitute for milk.

soy sauce ▶ a sauce made with fermented soybeans, used in Chinese and Japanese cooking.

spaetzle /'sHpetslə/ ▶ small dumplings of a type made in southern Germany and Alsace, consisting of seasoned dough poached in boiling water.
–ORIGIN from German dialect *Spätzle*, literally 'little sparrows.'

spaghetti ▶ pasta made in long, slender, solid strings.
■ an Italian dish consisting largely of this, typically with a sauce.
–ORIGIN Italian, plural of the diminutive of *spago* 'string.'

spaghetti bolognese ▶ spaghetti served with a sauce of ground beef, tomato, onion, and herbs.
–ORIGIN Italian, literally 'spaghetti of Bologna.'

spaghettini ▶ pasta in the form of strings of thin spaghetti.
–ORIGIN Italian, diminutive of *spaghetti* 'little strings' (see SPA-GHETTI).

spaghetti squash ▶ an edible squash of a variety with slightly stringy flesh which when cooked has a texture and appearance like that of spaghetti.

spanakopita /ˌspänä'kôpētä/ ▶ (in Greek cooking) phyllo pastry stuffed or layered with spinach, cheese, eggs, and seasonings.

-ORIGIN modern Greek, literally 'spinach pie.'

Spanish omelet ▸ an omelet containing chopped vegetables, often served open rather than folded.

Spanish onion ▸ a large cultivated onion with a mild flavor.

Spanish rice ▸ a dish of rice with onions, peppers, and tomatoes, often colored and flavored with saffron.

spareribs (also **spare ribs**) ▸ closely trimmed ribs of pork or sometimes beef.

-ORIGIN probably from Middle Low German *ribbesper* (by transposition of the syllables), and associated with the adjective *spare*.

spatula ▸ an implement with a broad, flat, blunt blade, used for spreading, turning, or serving foods.

-ORIGIN from Latin, variant of *spathula*, diminutive of *spatha* 'broad blade.'

spearmint ▸ the common garden mint, used as a culinary herb and to flavor candy, chewing gum, etc.

spice ▸ an aromatic or pungent vegetable substance used to flavor food, for example, CLOVES or PEPPER.

-ORIGIN Middle English: shortening of Old French *espice*, from Latin *species* 'sort, kind,' in late Latin 'wares.'

spicy ▸ flavored with or fragrant with spice: *a spicy tomato sauce.*

■ peppery or pungent: *too spicy for American tastes.*

spinach ▸ a widely cultivated Asian plant of the goosefoot family, with large, dark green leaves that are eaten raw or cooked as a vegetable.

-ORIGIN Middle English: probably from Old French *espinache*, via Arabic from Persian *aspānāk̲.*

spiny lobster ▸ a large edible crustacean with a spiny shell and long heavy antennae, but lacking the large claws of true lobsters.

spirit ▸ (usually **spirits**) strong distilled liquor such as brandy, whiskey, gin, or rum.

-ORIGIN Middle English: from Anglo-Norman French, from Latin *spiritus* 'breath, spirit,' from *spirare* 'breathe.'

spit ▸ a long, thin metal rod pushed through meat in order to hold and turn it while it is roasted over an open fire.

▸ to put a spit through (meat) in order to roast it over an open fire.

Spices

achiote	curry powder	pepper
ajwain	dill seed	pepper flakes
allspice	dukka	pickling spice
angelica	epazote	pimento
anise	epices fines	pomegranate
aniseed	fennel seed	poppy seed
annatto	fenugreek	pumpkin seed
arrowroot	filé	ras el hanout
asafetida	fingerrot	red pepper
benne seed	finochio	safflower
berbere	flaxseed	saffron
black pepper	galangal	salt
cacao	garam masala	sansho
caraway seed	garlic powder	sassafras
cardamom	ginger	sesame seed
carob	grains of paradise	Sichuan pepper
cassia	green peppercorn	St John's bread
cayenne	horseradish	star anise
celery seed	juniper	sumac
chicory	licorice	tonka bean
chili pepper	mace	turmeric
chili powder	mahaleb	valerian
cinnamon	mastic	vanilla
cloves	mustard seed	wasabi
coriander	nigella	white pepper
cubeb	nutmeg	zahtar
cumin	paprika	zedoary

spit-roast ▸ (**spit-roasted**) to cook (a piece of meat) on a spit: *spit-roasted lamb*.

split pea ▸ a pea dried and split in half for cooking.

sponge ▸ raised yeast dough.

■ British (also **sponge pudding**) a steamed or baked pudding of fat, flour, and eggs.

■ short for SPONGE CAKE.

sponge cake ▸ a very light sweet cake of spongelike consistency, made with little or no fat.

spoon bread ▸ soft cornbread served with a spoon.

spotted dick ▸ British a suet pudding containing currants or sultanas.

spread ▸ to apply (a substance) in an even layer: *spreading jam on a croissant*.

Spirits and Liqueurs

absinthe	crème de cassis	mezcal
Advocat	crème de menthe	Midori
amaretto	curaçao	ouzo
amarula	Damiana	pastis
Amarula	Drambuie	Pernod
anisette	Dubonnet	Pimm's
aquavit	eau de vie	pisco
arak	fortified wine	raki
armagnac	Galliano	Rémy Martin
B & B	gin	Ricard
Benedictine	Glayva	rum
bitters	Goldwasser	sambuca
bourbon	grain spirit	schnapps
brandy	Grand Marnier	scotch
cachaça	grappa	single malt
Calvados	Irish cream	Slivovitz
Campari	Jagermeister	Southern Comfort
Carolans	Kahlúa	tequila
Chambord	Kummel	Tia Maria
chartreuse	Lillet	triple sec
cognac	limoncello	vermouth
Cointreau	maraschino	vodka
Courvoisier	marc	whiskey
crème de cacao	Martel	

■ to cover (a surface) in such a way: *spread each slice with mayonnaise.*

■ to be able to be applied in such a way: *the whipped butter spreads easily.*

■ archaic to lay (a table) for a meal.

▶ a soft paste that can be applied in a layer to bread or other food.

■ a large and impressively elaborate meal.

spring chicken ▶ a young chicken for eating (originally available only in spring).

springerle /SHpriNGərlə/ ▶ a German anise-flavored Christmas cookie with an embossed design on top made with a special rolling pin.

-ORIGIN German dialect *Springerle*, literally 'little jumping horses.'

spring onion ▶ British term for GREEN ONION.

spring roll ▶ an Asian snack consisting of rice paper filled with minced vegetables and usually meat, rolled into a cylinder and fried.

sprinkles ▶ tiny sugar shapes, typically strands and balls, used for decorating cakes and desserts.

sprout ▶ (**sprouts**) young plant shoots eaten as a vegetable, especially the shoots of alfalfa, mung beans, or soybeans.

■ short for BRUSSELS SPROUT.

spumoni (also **spumone**) ▶ a kind of ice cream with different colors and flavors in layers, and often made with bits of fruit and nuts.

-ORIGIN from Italian *spumone*, from *spuma* 'foam.'

squab ▶ a young unfledged pigeon.

■ the flesh of such a bird as food: *roast squab.*

squash ▶ an edible fruit of the gourd family, the flesh of which is cooked and eaten as a vegetable. See also SUMMER SQUASH, WINTER SQUASH.

-ORIGIN abbreviation of Narragansett *asquutasquash.*

squid ▶ an elongated cephalopod mollusk with ten arms (technically, eight arms and two long tentacles), used as food.

star anise ▶ a small star-shaped fruit with one seed in each arm. It has an aniseed flavor and is used unripe as a spice in Asian cooking.

star fruit (also **starfruit**) ▶ another term for CARAMBOLA.

steak ▶ high-quality beef taken from the hindquarters of the animal, typically cut into thick slices that are cooked by broiling or grilling.

■ a thick slice of such beef or other high-quality meat or fish: *a salmon steak.*

■ poorer-quality beef that is cubed or ground and cooked more slowly by braising or stewing.

-ORIGIN Middle English: from Old Norse *steik*; related to *steikja* 'roast on a spit' and *stikna* 'be roasted.'

steak au poivre ▶ steak coated liberally with crushed peppercorns before cooking.

-ORIGIN French, literally 'steak with pepper.'

steak Diane ▶ a dish consisting of thin slices of steak sautéed with seasonings, especially Worcestershire sauce.

steak tartare /tär'tär/ ▶ a dish consisting of raw ground steak mixed with raw egg, onion, and seasonings.

steam ▶ to cook (food) by heating it in steam from boiling water: *steam the vegetables until just tender.*

■ (of food) to cook in this way.

steamer ▶ a type of utensil or saucepan in which food can be steamed.

■ (also **steamer clam**) another term for SOFT-SHELL CLAM.

steam table ▶ (in a cafeteria or restaurant) a table with slots to hold food containers that are kept hot by steam circulating beneath them.

stew ▶ a dish of meat and vegetables cooked slowly in liquid in a closed dish or pan: *lamb stew*.

▶ to cook (meat, fruit, or other food) slowly in liquid in a closed dish or pan.

■ (of meat, fruit, or other food) to be cooked in such a way.

□ **stewed**: *stewed beef with onions.*

–ORIGIN Middle English (in the sense 'cauldron'): from Old French *estuve* (related to *estuver* 'heat in steam.'

stifado /sti'fädō/ ▶ a Greek dish of meat stewed with onions and sometimes wine or tomatoes.

–ORIGIN from modern Greek *stiphado*.

Stews and Casseroles

adobo	cioppino	lobscouse
baked ziti	colcannon	lobster Newburg
beef Bourguignonne	coquilles St. Jacques	macaroni and cheese
beef en daube	curry	manicotti
beef pilau	dal	matelote
beef stew	daube	Mongolian hot pot
beef stroganoff	eggplant	moussaka
blanquette de veau	parmigiana	mulligatwny
bobotie	fricassee	olla podrida
bouillabaisse	frikadeller	oyster stew
Brunswick stew	ful medames	paella
burgoo	goulash	peperonata
calaloo	groundnut stew	pepper pot
carne guisada	gumbo	potage
cassoulet	hasenpfeffer	pot-au-feu
chicken and dumplings	hunter's stew	ragout
chicken cacciatore	Irish stew	ratatouille
chicken Marengo	jager-eintopf	stifado
chicken paprika	jambalaya	Swedish meatballs
chili	kedgeree	tikka
cholent	kugel	tuna casserole
chop suey	lamb stew	vindaloo
choucroute garni	lasagne	waterzooi

Stilton /'stiltn/ ▸ a kind of strong rich cheese, often with blue veins, originally made at various places in Leicestershire, England.

–ORIGIN so named because it was formerly sold to travelers at a coaching inn in Stilton, England.

stir-fry ▸ to cook (meat, fish, or vegetables) rapidly, in a large pan or wok, over a high heat while stirring briskly: *stir-fried beef.*

▸ a dish cooked by such a method.

stock ▸ liquid made by cooking bones, meat, fish, or vegetables slowly in water, used as a basis for the preparation of soup, gravy, or sauces: *chicken stock.*

stollen /'SHtōlən/ ▸ a rich German fruit and nut bread.

–ORIGIN from German *Stollen.*

stone crab ▸ a large, heavy, edible crab of the Gulf of Mexico and Caribbean area.

stracciatella /ˌsträCHēə'telə/ ▸ an Italian soup containing eggs and cheese.

–ORIGIN Italian.

strawberry ▸ a sweet soft red fruit with a seed-studded surface.

–ORIGIN Old English *strēa(w)berige, strēowberige* (*straw*, with reference to the fruit's achenes).

streusel ▸ a crumbly topping or filling made from fat, flour, sugar, and often cinnamon.

■ a cake or pastry with such a topping.

–ORIGIN from German *Streusel*, from *streuen* 'sprinkle.'

string ▸ a tough piece of fiber in vegetables, meat, or other food, such as a tough elongated piece connecting the two halves of a bean pod.

▸ to remove the strings from (a bean).

string bean ▸ any of various beans eaten in their fibrous pods, such as scarlet runners.

striped bass ▸ a large edible bass of North American coastal waters, with dark horizontal stripes along the upper sides.

stroganoff /'strôgəˌnôf/ ▸ a dish in which the central ingredient, typically strips of beef, is cooked in a sauce containing sour cream.

–ORIGIN named after Count Pavel *Stroganov* (1772–1817), Russian diplomat.

strudel ▸ a confection of thin pastry rolled up around a fruit filling and baked.
–ORIGIN from German *Strudel*, literally 'whirlpool.'
stuff ▸ to fill (poultry, rolled or hollowed vegetables, etc.) with a savory or sweet mixture, especially before cooking.
□ **stuffer**: *a sausage-stuffer.*
stuffing ▸ a mixture used to stuff poultry or meat before cooking.
sturgeon ▸ a very large primitive fish occurring in temperate waters of the northern hemisphere, especially central Eurasia. It is of commercial importance for its caviar and flesh.
–ORIGIN Middle English: from Anglo-Norman French, of Germanic origin.
submarine sandwich (also **sub**) ▸ a sandwich made of a long roll typically filled with meat, cheese, and vegetables such as lettuce, tomato, and onions (also called **grinder**, **hero**, **hoagie**, **poor boy**).
succotash ▸ a dish of corn and lima beans cooked together.
–ORIGIN from Narragansett *msícquatash* (plural).
suet ▸ the hard white fat on the kidneys and loins of cattle, sheep, and other animals, used to make foods including puddings, pastry, and mincemeat.
–ORIGIN Middle English: from Anglo-Norman French, from the synonymous word *su*, from Latin *sebum* 'tallow.'
sugar ▸ a sweet crystalline substance obtained from various plants, especially sugar cane and sugar beet, consisting essentially of sucrose, and used as a sweetener in food and drink.
■ a lump or teaspoonful of this, used to sweeten tea or coffee: *I'll have mine black with two sugars.*
▸ to sweeten, sprinkle, or coat with sugar.
□ **sugary**: *sugary tea.*
–ORIGIN Middle English: from Old French *sukere*, from Italian *zucchero*, probably via medieval Latin from Arabic *sukkar*.
sugaring ▸ (also **sugaring off**) the boiling down of maple sap until it thickens into syrup or crystallizes into sugar.
sugarplum ▸ a small round candy of flavored boiled sugar.
sugar snap (also **sugar snap pea**) ▸ a snow pea, especially of a variety with distinctively thick and rounded pods.

Types of Sugar

barley	dextrose	muscovado
beet	fructose	palm
birch	galactose	panela
blackstrap molasses	golden syrup	piloncillo
brown	granulated	powdered
candy	gur	preserving
cane	honey	raw
caramel	icing	sorghum
caster	jaggery	spun
coffee	lactose	sucrose
confectioners'	loaf	superfine
corn syrup	maltose	treacle
cube	manna	turbinado
dark brown	maple	
demerara	molasses	

sukiyaki /ˌso͞okēˈyäkē/ ▶ a Japanese dish of sliced meat, especially beef, cooked rapidly with vegetables and sauce.
–ORIGIN Japanese.

sultana ▶ a small, light brown, seedless raisin used in foods such as puddings and cakes.
–ORIGIN from Italian, feminine of *sultano* 'sultan,' from Arabic.

summer sausage ▶ a type of hard dried and smoked sausage that is similar to salami in preparation and can be kept without refrigeration.

summer squash ▶ a squash that is eaten before the seeds and rind have hardened. Unlike winter squash, summer squash does not keep well. Compare with WINTER SQUASH.

sundae ▶ a dish of ice cream with added ingredients such as fruit, nuts, syrup, and whipped cream.
–ORIGIN perhaps an alteration of *Sunday*, either because the dish was made with ice cream left over from Sunday and sold cheaply on Monday, or because it was sold only on Sundays, a practice devised (according to some accounts) to circumvent Sunday legislation.

sun-dry ▶ to dry (food) in the sun, as opposed to using artificial heat: *sun-dried tomatoes.*

sunflower seed ▶ the hard-shelled edible seed of a plant of the daisy family, yielding an oil used in cooking and margarine.

sunny side up ▶ (of an egg) fried on one side only.

superfine sugar ▶ finely granulated white sugar that dissolves quickly and is used in cold drinks and baking.

supplement ▶ a substance taken to remedy the deficiencies in a person's diet.

■ (also **food supplement**) an extract or concentrate of a food, used as a supplement.

supreme (also **suprême**) /səˈprem/ ▶ a rich cream sauce.

■ a dish served in such a sauce: *chicken supreme.*

–ORIGIN from French *suprême*, from Latin *supremus*, superlative of *superus* 'that is above,' from *super* 'above.'

sushi ▶ a Japanese dish consisting of small balls or rolls of vinegar-flavored cold cooked rice served with a garnish of vegetables, egg, or raw seafood.

–ORIGIN Japanese.

sweat ▶ (of food) to ooze or exude beads of moisture onto its surface: *cheese stored at room temperature will quickly begin to sweat.*

■ to heat (chopped vegetables) slowly in a pan with a small amount

Sushi

aji (horse mackerel)	kazunoko (herring roe)
ama-ebi (raw shrimp)	maguro (tuna)
anago (sea eel)	masago (smelt roe)
awabi (abalone)	masu (trout)
ebi (boiled shrimp)	mekajiki (swordfish)
hamachi (yellowtail)	mirugai (surf clam)
hamaguri (clam)	saba (mackerel)
hamo (sea eel)	sake (salmon)
hirame (flounder)	sawara (Spanish mackerel)
hokkigai (surf clam)	suzuki (sea bass)
hotategai (scallop)	tai (sea bream)
ika (squid)	tairagai (razor-shell clam)
ikura (salmon roe)	tako (octopus)
kaibashira (scallop)	tamago (sweet egg omelet)
kajiki (swordfish)	tobiko (flying fish roe)
kani (crab or surimi)	toro (fatty tuna)
karei (flatfish)	unagi (freshwater eel)
katsuo (bonito)	uni (sea urchin roe)

of fat, so that they cook in their own juices: *sweat the celery and onions with olive oil and seasoning.*

■ (of chopped vegetables) to be cooked in this way: *let the chopped onion sweat gently for five minutes.*

Swede British ▸ a rutabaga.

sweet ▸ having the pleasant taste characteristic of sugar or honey; not salty, sour, or bitter.

■ fresh; not smoked, salted, or dried: *sweet sausages.*

▸ British a small shaped piece of confectionery made with sugar. See word bank at CANDY.

■ British a sweet dish forming a course of a meal; a dessert.

▢ **sweeten**: *oatmeal sweetened with honey.*

sweet-and-sour ▸ (especially of Chinese-style food) cooked in a sauce containing sugar and either vinegar or lemon.

sweetbread ▸ the thymus gland (or, rarely, the pancreas) of an animal, especially as used for food.

sweet butter ▸ unsalted butter made from fresh pasteurized cream.

sweet corn ▸ corn of a variety with tender kernels that have a high sugar content.

sweet pepper ▸ a large green, yellow, orange, or red variety of capsicum that has a mild or sweet flavor and is often eaten raw (also called **bell pepper**).

sweet potato ▸ an edible tropical tuber with pinkish orange or pale yellow, slightly sweet flesh.

USAGE: The words **sweet potato** and **yam** are used interchangeably but are actually two different species. In the U.S. what is commonly labeled a yam, as fresh produce and in cans, is actually a sweet potato. Real yams are not as common and are not particularly sweet.

Swiss chard ▸ see CHARD.

Swiss cheese ▸ cheese of a style originating in Switzerland, typically containing large holes.

swordfish ▸ a large edible marine fish with a streamlined body and a long flattened swordlike snout.

syllabub /ˈsiləˌbəb/ ▸ a dessert made with whipped cream flavored with white wine or sherry.

syrup ▶ a thick sweet liquid made by dissolving sugar, and sometimes flavorings, in boiling water, often used for preserving fruit.
■ a similar preparation made with fruit or fruit juice, water, and sugar.
■ a thick sticky liquid derived from a sugar-rich plant, especially sugar cane, corn, and maple.
–ORIGIN late Middle English: from Old French *sirop* or medieval Latin *siropus*, from Arabic *šarāb* 'beverage.'

SLANG WITH BITE:
AN EATIMOLOGY

Chances are you began the day with a "mug of murk," some "elephant dandruff" or even "two dots and a dash." In other words: a cup of coffee, a bowl of cornflakes, or two fried eggs with a strip of bacon. Although not many are familiar with it today, this serving of classic American breakfast lingo is still impressive for its inventive spirit.

"Quick bite" meals and the eatery slang that followed them were created in response to a growing need to get food to the customer fast. Surprisingly, it has been with us since the 1840s, and, by the turn of the last century, when ice cream sodas and hot dogs charmed their way into our hearts, these cleverly coded catchwords were already hard at work.

The role this resourceful jargon played helped to transform the otherwise thankless process of taking orders and serving meals into a quick, manageable task. This was often carried out with the addition of humorously concealed observations, including cutting asides about the quality of the dishes and the goings-on within the particular eatery, fostering a unique camaraderie among the waiting and cooking staff.

Let's imagine it's 1938. You've just pulled up to a cozy little neon-lit diner. As you grab a counter seat and eyeball the menu, the age-old question greets you from the other side: "So, what'll it be?" You place your order and hear the "beanery queen" shout into the kitchen "Wax a high hat on a cable car, go heavy on the barn paint and carnations!" Just like that, this "call" gets you an open-faced cheeseburger, smothered in ketchup and onions, pronto.

For these versatile "slingers," short-order shorthand was a valuable showpiece. During the 1920s, 30s, and 40s, talented jargon jockeys got work wherever they went, because they brought in steady customers and kept everything in those "grab joints" moving. Diner slang was good for business.

Today, when you order your eggs "over easy" or ask for a "burger with the works" in a diner, you're using enduring examples of this smart and sassy language that was routinely dished out in main street soda fountains, corner luncheonettes, and roadside diners all across the country.

Unfortunately, the heyday of slinging slang has slipped away, but witty, irreverent words like these deserve to be relished once again. Here are some of the most over-the-top terms you'll ever encounter. Some may startle you with their bluntness (and, in some cases, racism and general intolerance), others may impress you with how long they've been around, but all this "Eatimology" speaks volumes about our fast-food culture.

Arkansas wedding cake	white bread
axle grease	margarine
bad breath	onions
baled hay	Shredded Wheat cereal
Boston strawberries	baked beans (also called *whistleberries*)
California breakfast	a cigarette and an orange (also called a *Mexican breakfast*)
cannibal	steak tartare
communist	ketchup (also called *hemorrhage*)
dead eyes	poached eggs (*dead eyes down* was poached eggs on toast)
Guinea football	a jelly doughnut
Hebrew enemies	pork chops

Jayne Mansfield	a large stack of six pancakes
Jack Benny	a grilled American cheese and bacon sandwich
John Wayne	a steak well-done
looseners	prunes
midget from Harlem	a scoop of chocolate ice cream
Mormon candy	carrots (also called *Irish cherries*)
nervous pudding	Jell-O
Pope's nose	the rear end of any cooked fowl (also called the *parson's nose*, or the *bishop's nose*)
radio sandwich	a tuna fish sandwich
synagogue twins	fried ham and eggs
twist it, choke it, and make it cackle	a chocolate malted milkshake with an egg
Watson, the needle	Coca Cola (a reference to Sherlock Holmes and his penchant for a 7% solution of cocaine, combined with the rumor that Coca-Cola still contained cocaine)

John Clarke has collected nearly 5000 diner slang terms and phrases, and is working on a book-length collection.

T

Tabasco (also **Tabasco sauce**) ▸ a pungent sauce made from the fruit of a capsicum pepper.

–ORIGIN named after the state of *Tabasco* in Mexico.

tabbouleh (also **tabouli**) /tə'bo͞olē/ ▸ an Arab salad of cracked wheat mixed with finely chopped ingredients such as tomatoes, onions, and parsley and dressed with olive oil and lemon juice.

–ORIGIN from Arabic *tabbūla*.

tablespoon ▸ a large spoon for serving food.

■ (abbr.: **tbsp.** or **tbs.**) a measurement in cooking, equivalent to ½ fluid ounce, three teaspoons, or 15 ml.

taco ▸ a Mexican dish consisting of a fried tortilla, typically folded, filled with various mixtures, such as seasoned meat, cheese, beans, lettuce, and tomatoes.

–ORIGIN Mexican Spanish, from Spanish, literally 'plug, wad.'

taco chip ▸ a fried fragment of a taco, flavored with spices and eaten as a snack.

taffy ▸ a candy similar to toffee, made from sugar or molasses, boiled with butter and pulled until glossy.

–ORIGIN earlier form of **TOFFEE**.

tagine /tə'zHēn/ ▸ a North African stew of spiced meat and vegetables traditionally prepared by slow cooking in a shallow earthenware cooking dish with a tall, conical lid.

–ORIGIN from Moroccan Arabic: *ṭazin* from Arabic *ṭājin* 'frying pan.'

tagliatelle /ˌtälyə'telē/ ▸ pasta in long ribbons.

–ORIGIN Italian, from *tagliare* 'to cut.'

tahini /tə'hēnē/ ▸ a Middle Eastern paste or sauce made from ground sesame seeds.
-ORIGIN from modern Greek *takhini*, based on Arabic *ṭaḥana* 'to crush.'

tai /tī/ ▸ a deep red-brown fish, the Pacific sea bream, eaten as a delicacy in Japan.
-ORIGIN from Japanese.

taleggio /tə'lejē‚ō/ ▸ a type of soft Italian cheese made from cows' milk.
-ORIGIN named after the *Taleggio* valley in Lombardy.

tamale /tə'mälē/ ▸ a Mexican dish of seasoned meat wrapped in cornmeal dough and steamed or baked in corn husks.
-ORIGIN from Mexican Spanish *tamal*, plural *tamales*, from Nahuatl *tamalli*.

tamari /tə'märē/ (also **tamari sauce**) ▸ a variety of rich, naturally fermented soy sauce.
-ORIGIN Japanese.

tamarillo /‚tamə'rilō/ ▸ the edible egg-shaped red fruit of a tropical South American plant of the nightshade family.
-ORIGIN an invented name, perhaps suggested by Spanish *tomatillo*, diminutive of *tomate* 'tomato.'

tamarind /'tamə‚rind/ ▸ the sticky brown acidic pulp from the pod of a tree of the pea family, widely used as a flavoring in Asian cooking.
-ORIGIN Middle English: from medieval Latin *tamarindus*, from Arabic *tamr hindī* 'Indian date.'

tandoor /tan'do͞or/ ▸ a clay oven of a type used originally in northern India and Pakistan.
-ORIGIN from Urdu *tandūr*, from Persian *tanūr*, based on Arabic *tannūr* 'oven.'

tandoori /tan'do͞orē/ ▸ denoting or relating to a style of Indian cooking based on the use of a tandoor: *tandoori chicken.*
▸ food or cooking of this type.
■ a restaurant serving such food.
-ORIGIN from Urdu and Persian *tandūri*, from *tandūr* (see TANDOOR).

tangelo ▸ a hybrid of the tangerine and grapefruit.
-ORIGIN blend of TANGERINE and POMELO.

tangerine ▸ a small citrus fruit with a loose skin, especially one of a variety with deep orange-red skin.

-ORIGIN from *Tanger* (former name of *Tangier*, Morocco) + the suffix -*ine*. The fruit, exported from Tangier, was originally called the *tangerine orange*.

tapas /'täpəs/ ▸ small Spanish savory dishes, typically served with drinks at a bar.

-ORIGIN Spanish, literally 'cover, lid' (because the dishes were given free with the drink, served on a dish balanced on, therefore "covering," the glass).

tapenade /ˌtäpəˈnäd/ ▸ a Provençal paste or dip, made from black olives, capers, and anchovies.

-ORIGIN French, from Provençal.

tapioca ▸ a starchy substance in the form of hard white grains, obtained from cassava and used in cooking puddings and other dishes.

-ORIGIN from Tupi-Guarani *tipioca*, from *tipi* 'dregs' + *og, ok* 'squeeze out.'

taramasalata /ˌtärəˌmäsəˈlätə/ ▸ a Greek pinkish paste or dip, made from the roe of certain fish mixed with olive oil, lemon juice, and seasonings.

-ORIGIN from modern Greek *taramas* 'roe' (from Turkish *tarama*, denoting a preparation of soft roe or red caviar) + *salata* 'salad.'

taro ▸ a tropical Asian plant of the arum family that has edible starchy corms and edible fleshy leaves, especially a variety with a large central corm grown as a staple in the Pacific. Compare with **EDDO**.

■ the corm of this plant.

-ORIGIN of Polynesian origin.

tarragon ▸ the narrow aromatic leaves of a perennial plant of the daisy family, used as a culinary herb.

-ORIGIN representing medieval Latin *tragonia* and *tarchon*, perhaps from an Arabic alteration of Greek *drakōn* 'dragon' (by association with *drakontion* 'green dragon').

tart ▸ sharp or acid in taste.

▸ an open pastry shell containing a filling. See word bank at **PIE**.

❑ **tartlet**: *individual tartlets.*

-ORIGIN Middle English (denoting a savory pie): from Old French *tarte* or medieval Latin *tarta*.

tartare /tär'tär/ ▶ (of fish) served raw, typically seasoned and shaped into small cakes: *tuna tartare*. See also STEAK TARTARE.

-ORIGIN French, literally 'Tartar.'

tartar sauce ▶ a cold sauce, typically eaten with fish, consisting of mayonnaise mixed with chopped pickles, capers, etc.

tarte Tatin /'tärt ta'taN/ ▶ a type of upside-down apple tart consisting of pastry baked over slices of fruit arranged in caramelized sugar, served fruit side up after baking.

-ORIGIN French, from *tarte* 'tart' + *Tatin*, the surname of the sisters said to have created the dish.

tartufo /tär'to͞ofō/ ▶ an edible fungus, especially the white truffle.

■ an Italian dessert, containing chocolate, of a creamy mousselike consistency.

-ORIGIN Italian, literally 'truffle.'

taster ▶ a person employed to test food or drink for quality by tasting it.

■ an instrument for extracting a small sample from within a cheese.

T-bone ▶ (also **T-bone steak**) a large choice piece of loin steak containing a T-shaped bone.

tbsp. (also **tbs.**) ▶ abbreviation of tablespoon.

tea ▶ a hot drink made by infusing the dried, crushed leaves of the tea plant in boiling water.

■ the dried leaves used to make such a drink.

■ (also **iced tea**) such a drink served cold with ice cubes.

■ a hot drink made from the infused leaves, fruits, or flowers of other plants: *herbal tea* | *fruit teas*. See word bank at SOFT DRINK.

■ chiefly British a light afternoon meal consisting typically of sandwiches and cakes with tea to drink.

■ British a cooked evening meal. See also HIGH TEA.

-ORIGIN probably via Malay from Chinese (Min dialect) *te*; related to Mandarin *chá*.

teacake ▶ British a light yeast-raised sweet bun with dried fruit, typically served toasted and buttered.

■ a small cake, cookie, etc. for serving with tea.

teakettle ▶ a typically metal container with a lid, spout, and handle, used for boiling water.

Teas

Assam	green	oolong
black	gunpowder	pearl
blackcurrant	Gyokuro Asahi	pekoe
Caravan	herbal	peppermint
Ceylon	Hubei	pinhead
chai	Huo Mountain	Pu-erh
chamomile	infusion	red
chrysanthemum	Irish breakfast	Rooibos
dagonwell	jasmine	sage
Darjeeling	Kashmiri	sencha
dragon phoenix	Keemun	tisane
Earl Grey	kukicha	white
English breakfast	Lapsang Souchong	Yunnan
genmai	matcha	Zhufeng
ginseng	Nilgiri	

teapot ▸ a typically china or ceramic pot with a handle, spout, and lid, in which tea is brewed and from which it is poured.
■ a teakettle.

teaspoon ▸ a small spoon used typically for adding sugar to and stirring hot drinks or for eating some soft foods.
■ (abbreviation: **tsp.**) a measurement used in cooking, equivalent to $^1/_6$ fluid ounce, $^1/_3$ tablespoon, or 4.9 ml.

tea strainer ▸ a small device incorporating a fine mesh for straining tea.

teff ▸ an African cereal that is cultivated almost exclusively in Ethiopia, used mainly to make flour.
-ORIGIN from Amharic *ṭêf*.

tempeh /'tempā/ ▸ a deep-fried fermented soybean cake with a nutty flavor, popular in Asian cooking, and often used as a meat substitute.
-ORIGIN from Indonesian *tempe*.

tempura /tem'pŏŏrə/ ▸ a Japanese dish of fish, shellfish, or vegetables, fried in batter.
-ORIGIN Japanese, probably from Portuguese *tempêro* 'seasoning.'

tenderizer ▸ a thing used to make meat tender, in particular:
■ a substance such as papain that is rubbed onto meat or used as a marinade to soften the fibers.
■ a small hammer with teeth on the head, used to beat meat.

tenderloin ▸ the tenderest part of a loin of beef, pork, etc., taken from under the short ribs in the hindquarters.

■ the undercut of a sirloin.

teppan-yaki /'tepän 'yäkē/ ▸ a Japanese dish of meat, fish, or both, fried with vegetables on a hot steel plate forming the center of the dining table.

-ORIGIN Japanese, from *teppan* 'steel plate' + *yaki* 'to fry.'

teriyaki ▸ a Japanese dish consisting of fish or meat marinated in soy sauce and grilled.

■ (also **teriyaki sauce**) a mixture of soy sauce, sake, ginger, and other flavorings, used in Japanese cooking as a marinade or glaze for such dishes.

-ORIGIN Japanese.

terrine /tə'rēn/ ▸ a meat, fish, or vegetable mixture that has been cooked or otherwise prepared in advance and allowed to cool or set in its container, typically served in slices.

■ a container used for such a dish, typically of an oblong shape and made of earthenware.

-ORIGIN from French, literally 'large earthenware pot,' from *terrin* 'earthen.'

Tex-Mex ▸ (of cooking) having a blend of Mexican and southern American features originally characteristic of the border regions of Texas and Mexico.

▸ cooking of such a type.

-ORIGIN blend of *Texan* and *Mexican*.

textured vegetable protein ▸ a type of protein obtained from soybeans and made to resemble minced meat.

Thousand Island dressing ▸ a dressing for salad or seafood consisting of mayonnaise with ketchup and chopped gherkins.

thyme ▸ the small leaves of a low-growing aromatic plant of the mint family, used as a culinary herb.

-ORIGIN Middle English: from Old French *thym*, via Latin from Greek *thumon*, from *thuein* 'burn, sacrifice.'

tian /tyan/ ▸ a dish of finely chopped vegetables cooked in olive oil and then baked au gratin.

■ a large oval earthenware cooking pot traditionally used in Provence.

−ORIGIN Provençal, based on Greek *tēganon* 'frying pan.'

tiger shrimp ▶ a large edible shrimp marked with dark bands, found in the Indian and Pacific oceans.

tikka ▶ an Indian dish of small pieces of meat or vegetables marinated in a spice mixture: *chicken tikka.*

−ORIGIN from Punjabi *ṭikkā.*

tilapia /təˈläpēə/ ▶ an African freshwater fish that has been widely introduced to many areas for food.

−ORIGIN modern Latin.

Tilsit ▶ a semihard mildly flavored cheese.

−ORIGIN named after the town in East Prussia (now Sovetsk, Russia) where it was first produced.

timbale /timˈbal/ ▶ a dish of finely minced meat or fish cooked with other ingredients in a pastry shell or in a mold.

−ORIGIN French, 'drum' (with reference to the shape of the prepared dish).

tiramisu (also **tiramisù**) /ˌtirəˈmēso͞o; -miˈso͞o/ ▶ an Italian dessert consisting of layers of sponge cake soaked in coffee and brandy or liqueur with powdered chocolate and mascarpone cheese.

−ORIGIN Italian, from the phrase *tira mi sù* 'pick me up.'

tisane /tiˈzan/ ▶ an herbal tea, consumed especially for its medicinal properties.

−ORIGIN from French.

toad-in-the-hole ▶ British a dish consisting of sausages baked in batter.

toast ▶ sliced bread browned on both sides by exposure to radiant heat.
▶ to cook or brown (food, especially bread or cheese) by exposure to a grill, fire, or other source of radiant heat.

■ (of food) to cook or become brown in this way.

−ORIGIN Middle English: from Old French *toster* 'roast,' from Latin *torrere* 'parch.'

toffee ▶ a kind of firm or hard candy that softens when sucked or chewed, made by boiling together sugar and butter, often with other ingredients or flavorings added.

■ a small shaped piece of such candy.

−ORIGIN alteration of TAFFY.

tofu ▸ curd made from mashed soybeans, used chiefly in Asian and vegetarian cooking.

-ORIGIN from Japanese *tōfu*, from Chinese *dòufu*, from *dòu* 'beans' + *fŭ* 'rot, turn sour.'

tomalley ▸ the digestive gland of a lobster, which turns green when cooked. It is sometimes considered a delicacy.

-ORIGIN from French *taumalin*, from Carib *taumali*.

tomatillo /ˌtōmə'tē(l)yō/ ▸ a small edible fruit that is purplish or yellow when ripe, but is most often used when green for salsas and preserves.

-ORIGIN from Spanish, diminutive of *tomate* 'tomato.'

tomato ▸ a glossy red, or occasionally yellow, pulpy edible fruit that is typically eaten as a vegetable, in salad, or made into sauce.

-ORIGIN from French, Spanish, or Portuguese *tomate*, from Nahuatl *tomatl*.

tongue ▸ the tongue of a hoofed mammal as food, particularly beef, veal, lamb, or pork tongue.

top ▸ to provide with a top or topping: *baked potatoes topped with melted cheese*.

▪ to remove the top of (a vegetable or fruit) in preparation for cooking.

topping ▸ a layer of food poured or spread over a base of a different type of food to add flavor: *a cake with a marzipan topping*.

toro /'tôrō/ ▸ a pale, fatty cut of tuna used for sushi and sashimi.

-ORIGIN Japanese, 'tuna belly.'

torte ▸ a sweet cake or tart.

-ORIGIN from German *Torte*, via Italian from late Latin *torta* 'round loaf, cake.' Compare with TORTILLA.

tortelli /tôr'telē/ ▸ small pasta parcels stuffed with a cheese or vegetable mixture.

-ORIGIN Italian, plural of *tortello* 'small cake, fritter.'

tortellini /ˌtôrtl'ēnē/ ▸ small squares of pasta that are stuffed with meat or cheese and then rolled and formed into small rings.

-ORIGIN Italian, plural of *tortellino*, diminutive of *tortello* 'small cake, fritter.'

tortilla ▸ (in Mexican cooking) a thin, flat cornmeal pancake, eaten hot or cold, typically with a savory filling.

■ (in Spanish cooking) a thick omelet containing potato and other vegetables, typically served cut into wedges.

-ORIGIN Spanish, diminutive of *torta* 'cake.'

USAGE: See usage note at FLAN.

tortoni ▶ an Italian ice cream made with eggs and cream, typically served in a small cup and topped with chopped almonds or crumbled macaroons.

tostada ▶ a Mexican deep-fried corn-flour pancake topped with a seasoned mixture of beans, ground meat, and vegetables.

-ORIGIN Spanish, literally 'toasted,' past participle of *tostar.*

tostone /tō'stōnā/ ▶ a Mexican dish of fried plantains, typically served with a dip.

-ORIGIN Spanish.

tournedos /'tŏŏrnǝ͵dōz/ ▶ a small round thick cut from a fillet of beef.

-ORIGIN French, from *tourner* 'to turn' + *dos* 'back.'

tourtière /tŏŏr'tye(ǝ)r/ ▶ a kind of meat pie traditionally eaten at Christmas in Canada.

-ORIGIN French.

treacle ▶ British term for MOLASSES.

-ORIGIN Middle English (denoting an antidote against venom): from Old French *triacle,* via Latin from Greek *thēriakē* 'antidote against venom,' feminine of *thēriakos* (adjective), from *thērion* 'wild beast.'

trifle ▶ British a cold dessert of sponge cake and fruit covered with layers of custard, jelly, and cream.

trimmings ▶ informal the traditional accompaniments to something, especially a meal or special occasion: *roast turkey with all the trimmings.*

tripe ▶ the first or second stomach of a cow or other ruminant used as food.

triticale /͵triti'kālē/ ▶ a hybrid grain produced by crossing wheat and rye.

-ORIGIN modern Latin, from a blend of the genus names *Triticum* 'wheat' and *Secale* 'rye.'

trivet ▶ a small rack or plate placed under a hot serving dish to protect a table.

■ an iron tripod placed over a fire for a cooking pot or kettle to stand on.

■ an iron bracket designed to hook onto bars of a grate for a similar purpose.

–ORIGIN Middle English: apparently from Latin *tripes*, *triped-* 'three-legged,' from *tri-* 'three' + *pes*, *ped-* 'foot.'

trotter ▶ a pig's foot used as food.

truffle ▶ a strong-smelling underground fungus that resembles an irregular, rough-skinned potato, growing chiefly in broad-leaved woodland on calcareous soils. It is considered a culinary delicacy and found, especially in France, with the aid of trained dogs or pigs.

■ a soft candy made of a chocolate mixture, typically flavored with rum and covered with cocoa.

–ORIGIN probably via Dutch from obsolete French *truffle*, perhaps based on Latin *tubera*, plural of *tuber* 'hump, swelling.'

truite au bleu /ˌtrwēt ō ˈblo͞o/ ▶ a dish consisting of freshly killed trout cooked with vinegar, which turns the fish blue.

–ORIGIN French, literally 'trout in the blue.'

truss /trəs/ ▶ to tie up the wings and legs of (a chicken or other bird) before cooking.

try ▶ to melt (solid fat) to get (the oil); render: *some of the fat from fatty meat may be tried out and used.*

–ORIGIN Middle English: from Old French *trier* 'sift.'

tsimmes (also **tzimmes**) /ˈtsimis/ ▶ a Jewish stew of sweetened vegetables or vegetables and fruit, sometimes with meat.

–ORIGIN Yiddish.

tsp. ▶ abbreviation of teaspoon.

tsukemono /ˈ(t)so͞okēˈmōnō/ ▶ a Japanese side dish of pickled vegetables, usually served with rice.

–ORIGIN Japanese, from *tsukeru* 'pickle' + *mono* 'thing.'

tuile /twēl/ ▶ a thin curved cookie, typically made with almonds.

–ORIGIN French, literally 'tile.'

tuna[1] ▶ a large predatory schooling fish of the mackerel family. Species include the albacore, bluefin, and yellowfin.

■ the flesh of this fish as food, cooked fresh or eaten raw in sushi.

■ (also **tuna fish**) the flesh of this fish as food, processed and canned.

-ORIGIN from American Spanish, from Spanish *atún*.

tuna² /'t(y)o͞onə/ ▸ the edible fruit of a prickly pear cactus.

-ORIGIN via Spanish from Taino.

turban squash ▸ a winter squash with a green and orange rind, shaped somewhat like a turban.

turbot ▸ a European flatfish of inshore waters that is prized as food.

-ORIGIN Middle English: from Old French, of Scandinavian origin.

tureen ▸ a deep covered dish from which soup is served.

-ORIGIN alteration of earlier *terrine*, from French *terrine* (see **TER-RINE**), feminine of Old French *terrin* 'earthen,' based on Latin *terra* 'earth.'

turkey ▸ a large mainly domesticated game bird native to North America. It is prized as food, especially on festive occasions such as Thanksgiving and Christmas.

-ORIGIN short for *turkey cock* or *turkey hen*, originally applied to the guinea fowl (which was imported through Turkey), and then erroneously to the American bird.

Turkish coffee ▸ a rich, strong brew made by boiling finely ground coffee with water, and often sugar, in a tall, narrow pot. The frothy coffee is served in a demitasse cup and the grounds are allowed to settle before drinking.

Turkish delight ▸ a dessert made with flavored gelatin or cornstarch, often containing nuts. It is cut into squares and coated in powdered sugar.

turmeric ▸ a bright yellow aromatic powder obtained from the rhizome of a plant of the ginger family, used for flavoring and coloring in Asian cooking.

turnip ▸ a round root with white or cream flesh that is eaten as a vegetable. The leaves are also cooked and eaten.

■ a similar or related root, especially a rutabaga.

turnover ▸ a small pie made by folding a piece of pastry over on itself to enclose a sweet filling: *an apple turnover.* See word bank at **PIE**.

turtle ▸ the flesh of a sea turtle, especially the green turtle, used chiefly for soup.

-ORIGIN apparently an alteration of French *tortue* 'tortoise.'

tutti-frutti ▸ a type of ice cream containing or flavored with mixed fruits and sometimes nuts.

-ORIGIN Italian, literally 'all fruits.'

twice-baked ▸ (of bread or cookie dough) baked in a loaf and then sliced and returned to the oven to bake again until crisp.

U

udon /ˈo͞odän/ ▸ (in Japanese cooking) wheat pasta made in thick strips.

–ORIGIN Japanese.

Ugli fruit ▸ trademark a mottled green and yellow citrus fruit that is a hybrid of grapefruit and tangerine.

–ORIGIN *ugli*, alteration of **UGLY**.

umami /o͞oˈmämē/ ▸ a category of taste in food (besides sweet, sour, salty, and bitter), corresponding to the flavor of glutamates, especially monosodium glutamate.

–ORIGIN Japanese, literally 'deliciousness.'

unleavened ▸ (of bread) made without yeast or other leavening agent.

upside-down cake ▸ a cake that is baked over a layer of fruit in syrup and inverted for serving.

urn ▸ a large metal container with a tap, in which tea or coffee is made and kept hot, or water for making such drinks is boiled.

–ORIGIN late Middle English: from Latin *urna*; related to *urceus* 'pitcher.'

V

Vacherin /ˌvaSH(ə)'ran/ ▸ a type of soft French or Swiss cheese made from cow's milk.

-ORIGIN French, from earlier *vachelin*, from *vache* 'cow.'

vanilla ▸ (also **vanilla bean** or **vanilla pod**) the long podlike fruit of a tropical climbing orchid.

■ an extract obtained from cured vanilla beans or produced artificially and used to flavor ice cream and other sweet foods.

-ORIGIN from Spanish *vainilla* 'pod,' diminutive of *vaina* 'sheath, pod,' from Latin *vagina* 'sheath.'

variety meats ▸ meat consisting of the entrails and internal organs of an animal.

veal ▸ the flesh of a calf, used as food.

-ORIGIN Middle English: from Anglo-Norman French *ve(e)l*, from Latin *vitellus*, diminutive of *vitulus* 'calf.'

vegetable ▸ a plant or part of a plant used as food.

▸ of or relating to vegetables as food: *vegetable soup.*

-ORIGIN Middle English: from Old French, or from late Latin *vegetabilis* 'animating,' from Latin *vegetare* 'to enliven.'

vegetable oil ▸ an oil derived from plants, for example, OLIVE OIL and SUNFLOWER OIL.

Vegetables

acorn squash	asparagus bean	beet
agave	avocado	beet green
ancho pepper	bamboo shoot	bell pepper
artichoke	banana pepper	Bibb lettuce
arugula	banana squash	bitter gourd
ash gourd	basil	bok choy
asparagus	bean sprout	Boston lettuce

bottle gourd
brinjal
broad bean
broccoflower
broccoli
broccoli rabe
broccolini
Brussels sprout
burdock
butternut squash
cabbage
caper
carrot
cassava
cayenne pepper
celeriac
celery
chard
cherry pepper
chicory
chili pepper
Chinese cabbage
chive
cilantro
cluster bean
collard green
colocasia
corn
cos lettuce
cress
cubanelle pepper
cucumber
curry leaf
daikon
dandelion green
delicata squash
dill
drumstick
edamame
eggplant
endive
epazote
escarole
fava bean
fennel

fenugreek
fiddlehead
frisée
galangal
gherkin
ginger root
gourd
green bean
green pea
habañero pepper
haricot vert
horseradish
Hubbard squash
iceberg lettuce
jalapeno pepper
Jerusalem artichoke
jicama
kabocha squash
kale
kencur
kohlrabi
leek
lemon grass
lima bean
lotus root
mache
mangetout
marrow
mesclun
mizuna
mung bean
mushroom
mustard green
napa cabbage
nopal
okra
onion
pandan leaf
parship
parsley
parsnip
pasilla pepper
pea
pea pod
petit pois

plantain
potato
pumpkin
purslane
radicchio
radish
ramp
rhubarb
ridge gourd
romaine lettuce
runner bean
rutabaga
salsify
scallion
sea kale
Serrano pepper
shallot
shiso
show pea
snake gourd
sorrel
spaghetti squash
spinach
spring onion
sugar snap pea
summer squash
sweet potato
Swiss chard
taro
Thai chili pepper
tomatillo
turnip
wakame
wasabi
water chestnut
water chestnut
watercress
wax bean
winged bean
winter melon
yam
yard-long bean
yellow squash
zucchini

velouté /vəlōō'tā/ ▸ a rich white sauce made with chicken, veal, pork, or fish stock, thickened with cream and egg yolks.
-ORIGIN French, literally 'velvety.'

venison ▸ meat from a deer.
-ORIGIN Middle English: from Old French *veneso(u)n*, from Latin *venatio(n-)* 'hunting,' from *venari* 'to hunt.'

verjuice ▸ a sour juice obtained from crab apples, unripe grapes, or other fruit, used in cooking.
-ORIGIN Middle English: from Old French *vertjus*, from *vert* 'green' + *jus* 'juice.'

vermicelli /ˌvərmi'CHelē/ ▸ pasta made in long slender threads.
-ORIGIN Italian, plural of *vermicello*, diminutive of *verme* 'worm,' from Latin *vermis*.

veronique /ˌverə'nēk/ ▸ denoting a dish, typically of fish or chicken, prepared or garnished with grapes: *sole veronique*.
-ORIGIN from the French given name *Véronique*.

vichyssoise /ˌvēSHē'swäz/ ▸ a soup made with potatoes, leeks, and cream and typically served chilled.
-ORIGIN French (feminine), 'of *Vichy*, France.'

Vienna sausage ▸ a small frankfurter made of pork, beef, or veal.

vinaigrette ▸ salad dressing of oil, wine vinegar, herbs, and seasonings.
-ORIGIN French, diminutive of *vinaigre* 'vinegar.'

vindaloo ▸ a highly spiced hot Indian curry made with meat or fish.
-ORIGIN probably from Portuguese *vin d'alho* 'wine and garlic (sauce),' from *vinho* 'wine' + *alho* 'garlic.'

vinegar ▸ a sour-tasting liquid containing acetic acid, obtained by fermenting dilute alcoholic liquids, typically wine or cider, and used as a condiment or for pickling.
-ORIGIN Middle English: from Old French *vyn egre*, based on Latin *vinum* 'wine' + *acer* 'sour.'

virgin /'vərjin/ ▸ (of olive oil) obtained from the first pressing of olives.

viscous ▸ having a thick, sticky consistency between solid and liquid.
-ORIGIN Middle English: from Anglo-Norman French *viscous* or late Latin *viscosus*, from Latin *viscum* 'birdlime.'

vol-au-vent /ˌvôl ō ˈväN/ ▶ a small round case of puff pastry filled with a savory mixture, typically of meat or fish in a richly flavored sauce.

–ORIGIN French, literally 'flight in the wind.'

TEN FRUITS YOU HAVEN'T
TASTED
BUT SHOULD

Chocolate persimmon Beloved by Japanese connoisseurs, this type of persimmon has sweet chocolate-brown flesh with an intriguing cinnamon flavor, but if not properly pollinated, some are mouth-numbingly astringent—the commercial kiss of death.

Greengage This class of European plums has small, round, greenish fruit with incredibly rich, sweet, tender flesh. It's very delicate when ripe, but in Europe it's much appreciated and grown commercially. Formerly cultivated in the United States, it could and should be grown here again.

Mangosteen /ˈmaNGgəˌstēn/ The queen of tropical fruits, with a thick reddish purple rind encasing translucent whitish segments, and a flavor that recalls cherimoyas, lychees, and peaches mingled into one soft, moist, fragrant mouthful. Because it might host agricultural pests, it's not yet available in the mainland United States.

Miracle fruit These little red beanlike berries don't look like much, but if you chew on one, for half an hour even the sourest foods taste surpassingly sweet. Good for party tricks.

Musk strawberries This most exquisitely aromatic and flavorful of all strawberries was the favorite of 18th-century aristocrats, but it's almost impossible to find today, because it's small in size and bears scantily.

Persian mulberry This delicacy, available from private gardens and at a few California farmers markets, has insanely intense sweet-tart flavor, like a blackberry gone to heaven, but it's so fragile it can't be shipped across the road without staining everything with its black juice.

Pulusan /'pələsän/ So ultratropical it can barely be grown in Hawaii, this native of Southeast Asia, a cousin of the lychee, has an oval, dark red, leathery rind, closely set with blunt spines, enclosing extraordinarily sweet, succulent, whitish flesh.

Rutab dates /'roõtäb/ Middle Easterners know that the best dates are those at this intermediate stage between fresh and dried; eating one is like biting into a soft, sugary cloud.

Tahitian pummelo /'pəmə,lō/ Most examples of pummelo, the giant ancestor of grapefruit, have thick skin and coarse, ricey pulp, but the Tahitian variety has thin skin, juicy greenish flesh, and wonderfully intense, sweet-tart, lemon-lime flavor.

White sapote /sə'pōtä/ Too soft when ripe to ship fresh, this cousin of citrus has creamy white flesh with the texture and flavor of sweet banana custard.

David Karp writes about fruit for *Gourmet* magazine and *The New York Times*.

W

wafer ▸ a very thin, light, crisp, sweet cookie or cracker, especially one of a kind eaten with ice cream.
-ORIGIN Middle English: from an Anglo-Norman French variant of Old French *gaufre* 'honeycomb,' from Middle Low German *wāfel* 'waffle.'

waffle ▸ a small crisp batter cake, baked in a waffle iron and eaten hot with butter and syrup or fruit.
-ORIGIN from Dutch *wafel*.

waffle iron ▸ a utensil or appliance, typically consisting of two shallow metal pans hinged together, used for baking waffles.

wakame /ˈwäkəˌmā/ ▸ an edible brown seaweed used, typically in dried form, in Chinese and Japanese cooking.
-ORIGIN Japanese.

Waldorf salad ▸ a salad made from apples, walnuts, celery, and mayonnaise.
-ORIGIN named after the *Waldorf*-Astoria Hotel in New York, where it was first served.

walnut ▸ the large, wrinkled, edible seed of a deciduous tree, consisting of two halves contained within a hard shell that is enclosed in a green fruit.
-ORIGIN Old English *walh-hnutu*, from a Germanic compound meaning 'foreign nut.'

wasabi /wəˈsäbē/ ▸ a Japanese plant with a thick green root that tastes like strong horseradish and is used in cooking, especially in powder or paste form as an accompaniment to raw fish.
-ORIGIN from Japanese.

wash ▸ a thin layer of egg, milk, or other liquid spread or brushed on food before baking.

water biscuit ▸ a thin, crisp unsweetened cracker made from flour and water.

water chestnut ▸ the tuber of a tropical plant that is widely used in Asian cooking, its white flesh remaining crisp after cooking.

watercress ▸ a plant that grows in running water and whose pungent leaves are used in salads.

water ice ▸ sorbet.

watermelon ▸ the large melonlike fruit of a plant of the gourd family, with smooth green skin, sweet red pulp, and watery juice.

wedding cake ▸ a rich iced cake, typically in two or more tiers, served at a wedding reception.

weisswurst /'vīs,wərst; -,vərst/ ▸ whitish German sausage made chiefly of veal.

–ORIGIN German, literally 'white sausage.'

Welsh rarebit (also **Welsh rabbit**) ▸ another term for RAREBIT.

Wensleydale ▸ a light-yellow, firm-textured cow's milk cheese made in England.

western omelet ▸ an omelet containing a filling of onion, green pepper, and ham.

wheat ▸ a cereal plant that is the most important kind grown in temperate countries, the grain of which is ground to make flour for bread, pasta, pastry, etc.

■ the grain of this plant.

–ORIGIN Old English hwǣte, of Germanic origin.

wheatmeal ▸ flour made from wheat from which some of the bran and germ has been removed.

whey ▸ the watery part of milk that remains after the formation of curds.

–ORIGIN Old English hwǣg, hweg, of Germanic origin.

whip ▸ a utensil such as a whisk or an eggbeater for beating cream, eggs, or other food.

■ a dessert consisting of cream or eggs beaten into a light fluffy mass with fruit, chocolate, or other ingredients.

▸ to beat (cream, eggs, or other food) into a froth.

whipping cream ▸ fairly thick cream containing enough butterfat to make it suitable for whipping.

whisk ▸ to beat or stir (a substance, especially cream or eggs) with a light, rapid movement.

▸ a utensil for whipping eggs or cream.

–ORIGIN late Middle English: of Scandinavian origin.

whiskey (also **whisky**) ▸ a spirit distilled from malted grain, especially barley or rye.

–ORIGIN abbreviation of obsolete *whiskybae*, variant of *usquebaugh*, from Irish and Scottish Gaelic *uisge beatha* 'breath of life.'

USAGE: Is it **whiskey** or **whisky**? Note that the British and Canadian spelling is without the *e*, so that properly one would write of *Scotch whisky* or *Canadian whisky*, but *Kentucky bourbon whiskey* or *Irish whiskey*.

white ▸ (of bread) made from a light-colored, sifted, or bleached flour.

■ British (of coffee or tea) served with milk or cream.

▸ the outer part (white when cooked) that surrounds the yolk of an egg; the albumen.

■ white bread: *tuna on white.*

–ORIGIN Old English *hwīt*, of Germanic origin; related to WHEAT.

white chocolate ▸ a white candy flavored with cocoa butter.

USAGE: See usage note at CHOCOLATE.

whitefish ▸ a mainly freshwater fish of the salmon family, widely used as food.

white flour ▸ fine wheat flour, typically bleached, from which most of the bran and germ have been removed.

white meat ▸ pale meat such as poultry, veal, and rabbit. Often contrasted with RED MEAT.

white pepper ▸ the husked ripe or unripe berries of the pepper plant, typically ground and used as a condiment.

white sauce ▸ a sauce of flour, melted butter, and milk or cream.

white sugar ▸ highly refined sugar in the form of granules or pressed into cubes. See SUGAR.

whiting ▸ a slender-bodied marine fish of the cod family, which lives in shallow European waters and is a commercially important food fish.

-ORIGIN Middle English: from Middle Dutch *wijting*, from *wijt* 'white.'

whole food ▸ food that has been processed or refined as little as possible and is free from additives or other artificial substances.

whole-grain ▸ made with or containing whole unprocessed grains of something: *whole-grain cereals.*

whole-wheat ▸ denoting flour or bread made from whole grains of wheat, including the husk or outer layer.
▸ whole-wheat bread or flour.

wiener ▸ a frankfurter or similar sausage.
-ORIGIN abbreviation of German *Wienerwurst* 'Vienna sausage.'

Wiener schnitzel ▸ a dish consisting of a thin slice of veal that is breaded, fried, and garnished.
-ORIGIN from German, literally 'Vienna cutlet.'

wild rice ▸ the edible grain of a tall aquatic North American grass related to rice.

wine ▸ an alcoholic drink made from fermented grape juice.
■ an alcoholic drink made from the fermented juice of specified other fruits or plants: *a glass of dandelion wine.*
-ORIGIN Old English *wīn*, of Germanic origin; based on Latin *vinum.*

wineglass ▸ a glass with a stem and foot, used for drinking wine.

wine vinegar ▸ vinegar made from red or white wine and used in salads and cooking.

wintergreen ▸ (also **oil of wintergreen**) a pungent oil, now obtained chiefly from the sweet birch or made synthetically, used medicinally and as a flavoring.
-ORIGIN the plants so named because of remaining green in winter, suggested by Dutch *wintergroen*, German *Wintergrün.*

winter melon ▸ a variety of muskmelon with a sweet, edible flesh that requires a long growing season and ripens in late autumn, making it available in many supermarkets during the winter.

winter squash ▸ a squash that has a hard rind and may be stored. Compare with SUMMER SQUASH.

wok ▸ a bowl-shaped frying pan used typically in Chinese cooking.
-ORIGIN Chinese (Cantonese dialect).

Wines and Wine Grapes

Aglianco
Albariño
Alicante Bouschet
Amarone
Amontillado
Ardeche
Arneis
Asti Spumante
Barbaresco
Barbera
Barolo
Barsac
Beaujolais
Beaujolais-Villages
Beaune
blanc de blancs
blanc de noirs
Bordeaux
Bordeaux Blanc
Bordeaux Rouge
Bourgogne Blanc
Brouilly
Brunello
brut
Bual
Burger
Burgundy
Cabernet
Cabernet Franc
Cabernet
  Sauvignon
Carignane
Carnelian
Cava
Chablis
Chambertin
Chambourcin
Champagne
Charbono
Chardonnay
Château Pétrus
Chenas
Chenin Blanc

Chianti
Chianti Classico
Chianti Ruffina
Chiroubles
Claret
Classico
Concord
Condrieu
Corvina
Côte de Brouilly
demi sec
Dolcetto
doux
Durif
Eiswein
extra dry
extra sec
Fino
Fleurie
Flor
Flora
Folle Blanche
fortified
Frascati
French Colombard
Frontignac
Fumé Blanc
Gamay
Garnacha
Gattinara
Gewürztraminer
Ghemme
Grand Cru
Graves
Grenache
Grignolino
Haut-Medoc
Hermitage
Heuriger
ice wine
Johannisberg Riesling
Johannisberger
Juliènas

Kabinett
Labrusca
Lambrusco
Liebfraumilch
Madiera
Málaga
Malbec
Malmsey
Malvasia
Malvasia Blanca
Malvoisie
Manzanilla
Margaux
Marichal Foch
Marsanne
Mataro
Medoc
Melon
Meritage
Merlot
Meursault
Monastrell
Montepulciano
Montilla
Montrachet
Morgon
Moscato
Moselle
Moulin-à-Vent
Mourvedre
Mousseux
Muscadel
Muscadelle
Muscadet
Muscadine
Muscat
Muscatel
Nebbiolo
Negra Mole
Negro Amaro
Niersteiner
non-vintage
off-dry

Oloroso	Roussanne	table wine
Orvieto	Ruby Port	Taurasi
Palomino	Saint-Amour	Tavel
Pauillac	Saint-Émilion	Tawny Port
Pedro Ximénez	Saint-EstÈphe	Tempranillo
Petite Syrah	sake	Toscana
Petite Verdot	Sancerre	Traminer
Piesporter	Sangiovese	Trebbiano
Pinot	Sauternes	Trockenbeerenauslese
Pinot Bianco	Sauvgnon Blanc	Valpolicella
Pinot Blanc	Sauvignon	Vendange
Pinot Grigio	Scheurebe	Verdelho
Pinot Gris	sec	Verdicchio
Pinot Noir	sekt	Vermouth
Pinotage	Sémillon	Vernaccia
Pomerol	semisweet	vin de pays
Port	Sercial	vin de table
Pouilly-Fumé	Sherry	vin ordinaire
Premier Cru	Shiraz	vinho verde
Prosecco	Soave	vino
Régnié	Solera	Vino Nobile
Retsina	Souzao	vintage
Rhenish	Spatlese	Vintage Port
Riesling	Spumante	Viognier
Rioja	Sylvaner	Vouvray
Riserva	Symphony	White Zinfandel
Rosé	Syrah	Zinfandel

wonton ▶ (in Chinese cooking) a small round dumpling or roll with a savory filling, usually eaten boiled in soup.

–ORIGIN from Chinese (Cantonese dialect) *wān t'ān*.

Worcestershire sauce /ˈwo͝ostər,SHi(ə)r/ ▶ a pungent sauce containing soy sauce and vinegar, first made in Worcester, England.

wurst ▶ German or Austrian sausage.

–ORIGIN from German *Wurst*.

Y

yakitori /ˌyäkiˈtôrē/ ▸ a Japanese dish of chicken pieces grilled on a skewer.

–ORIGIN Japanese, from *yaki* 'grilling, toasting' + *tori* 'bird.'

yam ▸ the edible starchy tuber of a climbing plant, widely distributed in tropical and subtropical countries.

■ a sweet potato.

–ORIGIN from Portuguese *inhame* or obsolete Spanish *iñame*, probably of West African origin.

USAGE: See usage note at **SWEET POTATO.**

yeast ▸ a microscopic fungus consisting of cells that are capable of converting sugar into alcohol and carbon dioxide.

■ a grayish-yellow preparation of this obtained chiefly from fermented beer, used as a fermenting agent, to raise bread dough, and as a food supplement.

–ORIGIN Old English, of Germanic origin.

yerba maté /ˈye(ə)rbə mäˈtā/ ▸ see **MATÉ.**

yogurt ▸ a semisolid sourish food prepared from milk fermented by added bacteria, often sweetened and flavored.

–ORIGIN from Turkish *yoğurt.*

Yorkshire pudding ▸ a side dish made of unsweetened egg batter baked in beef drippings until it is puffy, crisp, and golden, typically eaten with roast beef.

yule log ▸ a log-shaped chocolate cake eaten at Christmas.

Z

---

zabaglione /ˌzäbəlˈyōnē/ ▸ an Italian dessert made of whipped and heated egg yolks, sugar, and Marsala wine, served hot or cold.
‒ORIGIN Italian.

zakuska /zəˈko͞oskə/ ▸ a substantial Russian hors d'oeuvre item such as caviar sandwiches or vegetables with sour cream dip, all served with vodka.
‒ORIGIN Russian.

zarzuela /zärˈzwälə/ ▸ a Spanish dish of various kinds of seafood cooked in a rich sauce.
‒ORIGIN Spanish, apparently from a place name.

zest /zest/ ▸ the outer colored part of the peel of citrus fruit, used as flavoring.
‒ORIGIN from French *zeste* 'orange or lemon peel.'

zester ▸ a kitchen utensil for removing fine shreds of zest from citrus fruit.

ziti ▸ pasta in the form of tubes resembling large macaroni.
‒ORIGIN Italian.

zucchini ▸ a green variety of smooth-skinned summer squash.
‒ORIGIN Italian, plural of *zucchino*, diminutive of *zucca* 'gourd.'

zuppa inglese /ˈzo͞opə iNGˈglāzē/ ▸ a rich Italian dessert resembling a trifle.
‒ORIGIN Italian, literally 'English soup.'

zwieback ▸ a rusk or cracker made by baking a small loaf and then cutting and toasting slices until they are dry and crisp.
‒ORIGIN German, literally 'twice-bake.'

MORE FOOD
FOR THOUGHT

COOKING WEIGHTS AND MEASURES

Dry Measures

Measure	Abbr.	Standard	Metric
pinch		1/8 tsp.	
gram		1/3 oz.	
ounce	oz.	1/16 lb.	28.35 g
peck		2 gal.; ¼ bushel	
pound	lb.	16 oz.	453.6 g
kilogram	k	2.2 lb.	

Fluid Measures

Measure	Abbr.	Standard	Metric
drop		$^1/_{76}$ tsp.	
dash		8 drops $^1/_5$ tsp.	1 ml
teaspoon	t.; tsp.	60 drops; $^1/_3$ tbs.	5 ml
dessert spoon		2 tsp.	10 ml
tablespoon	T.; tbs.	½ fl. oz.; $^1/_{16}$ c.; 3 tsp.	15 ml
fluid ounce	fl. oz.	2 tbs.	30 ml
jigger		1½ fl. oz.; 2 tbs.	44 ml
3 teaspoons		½ fl. oz.; 1 tbs.	15 ml
4 tablespoons		2 fl. oz.; ¼ c.	45 ml
5 tablespoons		2½ fl. oz.; $^1/_3$ c.	75 ml
8 tablespoons		4 fl. oz.; ½ c.	90 ml
12 tablespoons		6 fl. oz.; ¾ c.	135 ml
gill		4 fl. oz.	118 ml
cup	c.	8 fl. oz.; 16 tbs.	237 ml
pint	pt.	16 fl. oz.; 2 c.	473 ml
fifth		25.6 fl. oz.	757 ml
quart	qt.	32 fl. oz.; 2 pt.	946 ml or .95 1
gallon	gal.	128 fl. oz.; 4 qt.	3.8 1

Temperature

boiling (water)	212° F.; 100° C
freezing (water)	32° F.; 0° C

Volumes of Standard Cans

number 2	2½ c.
number 2½	3½ c.
number 3	5¼ c.
number 10	13 c.

Oven Temperatures

slow	250-350° F.
moderate	350-400° F.
hot	400-450° F.

Candy Stages

Thread	230-234° F.
Soft ball	234-240° F.
Hard ball	250-266° F.
Soft crack	270-290° F.
Hard crack	300-310° F.

Equivalents

1 stick butter	½ c.
2 c. butter	1 lb.
8-10 egg whites	1 c.
12-14 egg yolks	1 c.
4 slices bread	1 c. crumbs
28 saltine crackers	1 c. crumbs
14 square graham crackers	1 c. crumbs
2 c. granulated sugar	1 lb.
3½ to 4 c. confectioners's sugar	1 lb.
2½ c. packed brown sugar	1 lb.
1 c. heavy cream	2 c. whipped cream
1 c. flour	½ lb.
4 c. flour	1 lb.
1 to 1¼ c. uncooked pasta	2 c. cooked
7 oz. uncooked spaghetti	4 c. cooked

FOOD FADS TIMELINE

———————

A century ago someone, much like yourself, started his day seated at a kitchen table, much like yours, perusing a morning paper, much like the one that may have started your day. The big difference? The meal. While you may have lapped up fat-free yogurt with a café latte and Sweet'N Low chaser, our fictitious centenarian, depending where he lived, filled his plate with porridge, flapjacks, mutton or a heart-stopping amount of home-cured bacon.

How did we go from gruel to Starbucks in ten decades?

1900s

*In the early years of the last century, menus were meat-filled. New York City's haute restaurants offered elk, caribou, bear, moose, and even elephant to intrepid diners. Modest eating establishments in the Midwest served mountains of the same (minus the elephant), albeit with less fanfare and a considerably lower price tag.

*A particular favorite along the eastern seaboard was Oysters Rockefeller—baked oysters topped with savory shredded greens. Although not a 20th-century dish by definition (it was invented in 1899 by Jules Alciatore of Antoine's Restaurant in New Orleans), it reached its zenith in the early 1900s. Because of its rich ingredients, Alciatore chose John D. Rockefeller, one of the wealthiest men in the nation, as its namesake. Alciatore also (deliberately?) shrouded his creation in mystery—an early and successful marketing coup. He emphatically insisted that the finely minced greens were **not** spinach, as was commonly assumed.

*By 1909, America had an aching sweet tooth, with the average person consuming 65 pounds of sugar annually. The culprits: chocolate brownies, apple pie, devil's food cake and baked Alaska. Sweetened tea and coffee (and its newly invented decaf cousin) also contributed to our ancestors' passion for sugar.

1920s

*The unwelcome appearance of Prohibition did little to curtail the drinking habits of the masses. The Noble Experiment, as it was called, actually encouraged us to drink more, which is why it was in part repealed in 1933. In fact, the majority of the drinks we know today were concocted during Prohibition. To soak up some of the harsh bathtub gin, proprietors began offering finger foods. Delights such as Shrimp Patties, Oyster Cocktails and Mushrooms Stuffed With Pimientos filled makeshift bars. Customers brought the idea into their homes, and the cocktail party was born.

*Until recently, salads were considered "effeminate and French" by most Americans. But, on July 4, 1924, in Tijuana, Mexico, Caesar's Place was packed with Hollywood folk who had headed south for the holiday to evade the restriction of Prohibition. By the end of the busy night, the kitchen was nearly empty except for a few ingredients—romaine lettuce, Romano cheese, bread, olive oil, and some eggs. With these, proprietor Caesar Cardini whipped up the famous Caesar Salad. Food columnist and cookbook author Arthur Schwartz wrote in a 1995 article for the *New York Daily News* that Cardini believed "give the show people a little show and they'll never realize it's only a salad."

1930s

*In the '30s, during the Depression, menus were radically pared down. Protein, which is always the most expensive part of the meal, had to be reduced. Popular dishes of the period were inexpensive, one-pot meals such as macaroni and cheese, chili, oxtail soup, casseroles of all sorts and—to maintain the illusion of the abundance of beef—meat loaf, stretched to its limit with filler. City dwellers, on the other hand, were surviving on cheap meals of hot dogs and hamburgers at automats such as Horn & Hardart's. Bread and soup lines snaked around the block.

*A sign that the Depression was loosening its grip was witnessed in 1936 when Irma Rombauer, a housewife from St. Louis, published *The Joy of Cooking*. Filled with practical information written in Rombauer's accessible style, *Joy* regaled its readers with recipes for nearly everything, including longed-for meat. Though detractors criticized the book's blanding of the American palate with its use of tasteless white sauces, reliance on vegetable shortening, and insistence on overcooked vegetables, it sold out generation after generation to become one of the most beloved cookbooks of the century.

*In 1937, Hormel pitched in by developing arguably the most indestructible of all comestibles: Spam. Because its shelf life clocks in at more than seven years, few American kitchens (and later World War II military troops) were without it. Almost from Spam's inception, cults—er—fan clubs were formed to honor and praise this mighty loaf.

1940s

*Many American homes sent not only their husbands and sons, but also their household help to the war effort. Before the war there was a servant or two in many homes—now suddenly they were off to help the war effort. Standing patriotically side by side in factories across the country were hostesses and their former maids or cooks.

*Also because of the war effort, every family had to ration its food. The government restricted each American to 28 ounces of meat per week (overkill by today's standards), plus limited the amounts of sugar, butter, milk, cheese, eggs, and coffee permitted. As a result sales of convenience and prepared foods increased. This is also when margarine came in as a replacement for butter.

1950s

*Introduced in 1953 by Swanson, 98-cent TV dinners were the ultimate time- and energy-saver of the modern kitchen. A flick of the wrist turned back foil revealing turkey and stuffing floating in gelatinous gravy, whipped sweet potatoes, and peas. About a half hour in the oven, and dinner was done. With nary a dish to wash.

*Another favorite from the prepackaged '50s was California Dip. Nothing more than a mixture of Lipton Recipe Secrets Onion Soup Mix and sour cream, the dip was the first thing to disappear at parties. According to Lipton brass, over 220,000 envelopes of mix are now used daily—most of which end up as dip, not soup.

*Tuna noodle casserole, sloppy joes, frozen fish sticks, Grasshopper Pie, and drinks filled with neon-colored umbrellas conspired to make the '50s the epitome of culinary kitsch.

1960s

*Julia Child (a charming, six-foot woman with a voice reminiscent of a throttled goose) was without a doubt the quintessential dish of the 1960s. From her TV show *The French Chef* (and her landmark cookbook, *Mastering the Art of French Cooking*) came many classic dishes. Julia made good on Herbert Hoover's promise of "a chicken in every pot" with her wildly popular recipe for *coq au vin*. A simple chicken dish made with mushrooms, onions, bacon and red wine, *coq au vin* was copied in millions of kitchens around the country. The dish was so well-loved that Julia included it in many of her subsequent cook-books.

*The late '60s brought granola-crunching, Birkenstock-wearing kind of folk who eschewed anything prepackaged and began making their own foods such as fresh bread, peanut butter, and hummus. Regular items on the counter-culture menu were vegetarian chili, guacamole, gazpacho, zucchini bread, lemon bars, carrot cake, and, of course, granola.

1970s

*One of the most popular dishes of the day was the very classic, very British *Beef Wellington*—a fillet of beef tenderloin coated with pâté de foie gras and a duxelles of mushrooms that are then all wrapped in a puff pastry crust. Some believe that *Wellington's* popularity had more to do with America's competitive spirit than with any deep passion for British cuisine.

*The '70s gave rise to another icon who began her own revolution to rival Julia's. From her famous Berkeley, California, restaurant, Chez Panisse, Alice Waters reintroduced the notion of cooking with natural, seasonal ingredients—an almost forgotten concept because of the prepackaged-food boom. Her mantra: fresh food, simply prepared. To remain faithful to her ideology, she scoured organic farms for fresh, interesting salad greens and vegetables. Through sheer will Waters marginalized iceberg lettuce to make way for arugula, mesclun and chicory. Her passion and respect for food attracted a coterie of young chefs who, under her tutelage, would bring her California Cuisine to the rest of the country—a refreshing counterpoint to the excess of the next decade.

1980s

Nouvelle Cuisine, as it was coined in the late '70s in France, was the hottest thing in the U.S. in the '80s. Diners now paid astronomically more to eat significantly less, and loved it. It was a sign of status to wait a half hour for a table, eat a pigeon's portion of food, and then be the first to foist a platinum credit card on the waiter, loudly declaiming to the table, "This one's on me!"

*At home we collected all types of gourmet foods and gadgets. Cabinets overflowed with $65 bottles of virgin olive oil and 50-year-old balsamic vinegars. Countertops were cleared to make way for the new stand mixer and the food processor. And drawers fairly bulged with the newest culinary gizmos, the result of reverent pilgrimages to the Mecca of cooking, Williams-Sonoma.

*On the dessert front, chocoholics swooned when faced with decadent flourless chocolate cakes, truffles and chocolate crème brûlée. Desserts also grew skyward as pastry chefs, taking cues from architecture, built towers of sweetness that rose from the plate. Diners often wondered whether to use a fork or a sledgehammer to eat.

1990s

*Manufacturers found ways to make everything reduced fat, low fat, or fat-free—even fat. What foodie can forget where he was when he heard that Olestra, the new nonfat fat, was on its way to market? But try as we might, most of us didn't lose weight. We fooled ourselves into believing that because we were eating low-fat foods we could guiltlessly binge.

*Inspired by the availability of foreign foods, chefs began combining cuisines in a trend known as *fusion cooking*. Coconut broth and tortellini were paired with basil and steamed littleneck clams, and the results were dazzling. In an attempt to highlight these unions, anything distracting was removed so all that was left were unadulterated flavors. It was a return to simplicity, promoted by Waters two decades earlier.

*With the World Wide Web we now had instant access to millions of recipes from around the globe. Want to make *filet mignon with* *mustard port sauce and red onion confit?* (Our tastes had once again turned toward the luxurious, owing to a booming end-of-the-century economy.) Double-click Epicurious.com and dinner's nearly ready. Confused about which cookbook to buy? Consult Amazon.com. There you'll find plenty of reviews from the newest breed of critics—savvy consumers. If it's encouragement you need, stop by one of the thousands of online newsgroups for a chat.

What's next? What will a person sitting in your kitchen 100 years from now, reading this—electronically for sure—be eating?

David Leite's Web site, Leite's Culinaria (*www.leitesculinaria. com*, from which this was adapted) was named the Best Writer's Web Site for 2002 by Writer's Digest. He is a contributor to the *Encyclopedia of American Food and Drink,* forthcoming from Oxford in 2004.

FAD DIETS TIMELINE

1087—The first recorded liquid diet is attempted by William the Conqueror, who took to his bed and consumed nothing but alcohol. 860 years later, similar plans appear in *The Drinking Man's Diet* and *Martinis and Whipped Cream*.

late 1600s—A milk diet, created by author Dr. George Cheyne, is purported to render the dieter "lank, fleet, and nimble."

1811—A vinegar diet, popularized by Romantic poet Lord Byron, recommends soaking everything one consumes in vinegar, which is believed to burn fat. The plan notably resurfaced in the late 1990s with *Lose Weight with Apple Vinegar*.

1830s—Rev. Sylvester Graham preaches against the sin of gluttony, prescribing a spartan diet of coarse flatbread (known as the graham cracker), vegetables, and water, which he believed would eradicate both lust and indigestion.

1850s—Natural Hygiene, the first food-combining diet, is introduced. This popular plan, which purported to maintain a balanced pH in the body through the separation of fruits and starches, is introduced by Dr. William Hay in 1911. Combining later appears in the bestselling books *Fit for Life* (1985) and *Eat to Win* (1988), and Judy Mazel's 1981 Beverly Hills diet, which prescribed heavy consumption of fruits to aid digestion.

1860s—Low-carb dieting is introduced by English undertaker William Banting in the first bestselling diet book, *Letter on Corpulence*. "Banting" involved eating dry toast, lean meat, vegetables, and soft-boiled eggs. A regimen of hot water and minced meat patties is introduced by Dr. James Salisbury (of Salisbury steak fame).

1890s—Horace Fletcher, the "Great Masticator," publishes a popular diet book claiming significant weight loss can be achieved by chewing all food till liquid. Fletcherism was supported by John Harvey Kellogg, a healthy-living guru and the inventor of granola and cereal flakes, and practiced in his Battle Creek Sanatorium, where patients ate to the tune of a slow-chewing song.

1893—The first weight-loss pill, in the form of thyroid extract, came on the market, followed in the 1920s by laxative pills, and in the 1930s by metabolic enhancers, made from ingredients more commonly used in explosives and insecticides.

1918—Calorie counting begins with Dr. Lulu Peters's *Diet and Health with a Key to the Calories.*

1920s—The emergence of the "flapper" style—the flat-chested, hipless ideal—leads to several radical weight-loss plans including the Grapefruit and Hollywood diets, which called for 800 daily calories of black coffee and "fat-burning" grapefruits. Juice fasts also become popular.

1920s—Another Jazz Age diet, perhaps the least appetizing in history, involves swallowing a tapeworm pill to introduce a parasite into one's intestine. The tapeworm consumes the food of its host, leaving them ever-hungry but stick-thin.

1932—Dr. Stoll's Diet Aid powdered meal substitute is sold in beauty salons. The following decades produce similar weight-loss powders and liquids, including the 1938 Harrop skim milk-and-bananas plan; Mead Johnson's 1950s Metrecal; Carnation Slender in the 1960s; the Astronaut plan and the dangerous Last Chance diet in the 1970s; and Slim-Fast and the banned Cambridge diet in the 1980s.

1937—Amphetamines for weight loss were introduced. They continued to be prescribed till the 1970s, but lost favor due to side effects including heart palpitations, addiction, seizures, paranoid psychosis, and sudden death.

1951—Gayelord Hauser, perhaps the first dietician to the stars, recommends a diet of whole grains, vegetables, brewer's yeast, yogurt, and blackstrap molasses in *Look Younger, Live Longer.*

1961—High-protein, high-fat, halitosis-inducing diets return, beginning with Herman Taller's *Calories Don't Count* and Dr. Irwin Stillman's *The Doctor's Quick Weight Loss Plan.* These are followed by Dr. Robert Atkins's famed *Diet Revolution* and Herman Tarnower's Scarsdale diet in the 1970s.

1979—Low-fat weight-loss plans become popular with Nathan Pritikin's program, which excludes meat and processed foods and severely reduces fat consumption.

1979—Phenylpropanolamine, a popular appetite suppressant, became available over the counter, marketed as Dexatrim and Accutrim. Rebound effects of PPA included high blood pressure, hallucinations, heart and kidney damage and, ironically, hyperphagia.

1980s—The Breatharian plan, which attempts to liberate disciples from the "drudgery of food and drink" through "the breathing of air for food." Several followers die from dehydration.

1990—Non-prescription "fat-blockers," such as chitosan, a shellfish derivative, are introduced and quickly denounced by experts.

1992—Just in time for the carb backlash, Dr. Atkins publishes the second edition of his low-carb, high-fat bible, followed by *The Carbohydrate Addict's Diet* in 1993; Barry Sears's 1995 *The Zone*; and *Sugar Busters! Protein Power* in 1998. These diets remain wildly popular.

1993—Fat reduction reaches new levels in Dean Ornish's *Eat More, Weigh Less*.

1994—Fen-phen, comprised of fenfluramine and phentermine, was widely prescribed for weight loss. The combination pill was withdrawn from the market in 1997 after reports of one-third of users having contracted valvular heart disease.

1995—The cabbage soup plan emerges, promising significant weight loss in a week. Excessive flatulence is the main reason given by those who abandon these plans.

1996— Peter D'Adamo's *Eat Right for Your Type*, a diet book that dictates which foods to eat according to blood type, is published. The plan is considered absurd by experts amazed that it ever gained a following.

2003—Dr. Arthur Agatston's *The South Beach Diet*, a hybrid low-fat, high-carb/low-carb, high-protein plan gains a huge following.

Marina Padakis

WEB SITES

———————

Long before there was a World Wide Web, the Iinternet was already a major gathering place for food information. Listservs, usenet, telnet, gopher sites, and bulletin boards were filled with recipes, and dozens of databases of food information were available by subscription. The Web has become the dominant form of Internet publishing, and thousands upon thousands of websites are dedicated to food—and not just recipe and commercial sites, either.

This small, and by no means comprehensive, appendix deals only with American food, but with an even narrower focus. Most of these sites are at least partially historical in nature, although some manage to convey their historical information in a casual, if not altogether hysterical, fashion.

The Web is, however, a very fluid and changeable place—and many of the sites listed may already have moved or morphed into something else by the time this book goes to press. There is little that can be done to avoid that, —but sometimes a little judicious searching, through whatever search engine is most effective at the time, can discover the new location of these peripatetic sites:

Alternative-Hawaii: Ethnic Food Glossary
http://www.alternative-hawaii.com/gloss.htm#c

American Brewery History Page
http://www.beerhistory.com/

American Culinary Foundation (ACF)
www.acfchefs.org/

American Diner Museum
http://www.dinermuseum.org/links.html

An American Feast
http://www.lib.udel.edu/ud/spec/exhibits/american.html

The Appetite Network (restaurant database)
http://www.appetitenet.com

Apple of Your Pie (antique apples, history, varieties, orchards, pies, and baking)
http://www.appleofyourpie.com/index.html

Back of the Box Recipes
http://backofthebox.com/

The Boston Cooking-School Cook Book (text of Fannie Farmer's 1918 edition)
http://www.bartleby.com/87/

The Boston Cooking-School Magazine: The First Seven Volumes, 1896–1902
http://students.washington.edu/bparris/bcsm.html

A Bowl of Red News (chili)
http://www.abowlofred.com/news.shtml

Candy USA
http://www.candyusa.org/

A Chocolate Timeline
http://www.cuisinenet.com/digest/ingred/chocolate/timeline.shtml

Cookbook Collectors' Exchange
http://ccexonline.com

A Cookbook Lover's Guide
http://www.friktech.com/cai/cai.htm

Cookery Collection
http://www.lib.msu.edu//coll/main/spec_col/cookery/

Creole and Cajun Recipe Pages
http://www.gumbopages.com/recipe-page.html

Crisco: A Short History of America's Shortening
http://www.epicurus.com/food/crisco.html

The Culinary Collection
http://www.tulane.edu/~wc/text/culinary.html

Culinary History: A Research Guide
http://www.nypl.org/research/chss/grd/resguides/culryla.html

Diner City
http://www.dinercity.com/

Epicurious
http://www.epicurious.com

Family Indigestion, The Illustrated Folio of Food (dishes from
the 1950's, 1960's, and 1970's)
http://www.drokk.com/familyindigestion/index.html

FAQ of the Internet BBQ List
http://www.eaglequest.com/~bbq/faq/toc.html

Farmer's Market Online
http://www.farmersmarketonline.com

Feeding America: The Historic American Cookbook Project
http://digital.lib.msu.edu/cookbooks/

Final Meal Requests (273 last requests from death row)
http://www.tdcj.state.tx.us/stat/finalmeals.htm

Flavors of the South
http://myweb.cableone.net/howle/

Food and Culture
http://www.utexas.edu/courses/stross/bibliographies/foodbib.htm

Food and Drug Administration (FDA) Center for Food Safety
and Applied Nutrition
http://www.foodsafety.gov/list.html

Food and Nutrition Information Center (FNIC)
http://www.nal.usda.gov/fnic/

Food and Nutrition Publications
http://extension.usu.edu/publica/foodpubs.htm

Food History News
http://foodhistorynews.com/

Food History Yellow Pages
http://foodhistorynews.com/linkmain.html

Food in History
http://vi.uh.edu/pages/lprtomat/fdhmpg~1.htm

The Food Museum
http://www.foodmuseum.com/

Food Network
http://www.foodtv.com/

The Food Reference Website
http://www.foodreference.com/

Food Review
http://www.ers.usda.gov/publications/foodreview/archives/

Food Timeline
http://www.gti.net/mocolib1/kid/food.html

History Notes
http://www.gti.net/mocolib1/kid/foodfaq3.html

Foodnavigator (food technology and science)
http://www.foodnavigator.com/

Foodstuff
http://goodstuff.prodigy.com/Mailing_Lists/foodstuff.html

The Fruit Pages
http://www.thefruitpages.com/

Gallery of Regrettable Food (food advertisements from the
1950s and 1960s)
http://www.lileks.com/institute/gallery/

Garlicana
http://www.garlicfestival.com/

The Great Pop vs. Soda Controversy
http://www.ugcs.caltech.edu/~almccon/pop_soda/

A Guide to Pillsbury Cookbooks and Premiums 1869–1969
http://www.friktech.com/pills/pills1.htm

Historic Texas Recipes
http://car.utsa.edu/historicrecipes.htm

Historical Culinary and Brewing Documents Online
http://www.thousandeggs.com/cookbooks.html

Historical Facts (Jewish cookery)
http://www.pbs.org/mpt/jewishcooking/history.html

History and Legends of Favorite Foods
http://www.whatscookingamerica.net/History/HistoryIndex.htm

The History of Rations
http://www.qmfound.com/history_of_rations.htm

The History of the American Barbecue
http://www.oscaruk.fsnet.co.uk/main_page_history.html

International Chili Society
http://www.chilicookoff.com/

The International Federation of Competitive Eaters (IFOCE)
http://www.ifoce.com

It's Spam
http://www.SPAM.com/

Jell-O Museum Web Site
http://www.jellomuseum.com

Key Ingredients-Smithsonian Institution
www.museumsonmainstreet.org
   also
http://www.MOMA/KI.asp

Leite's Culinaria
http://www.leitesculinaria.com

Maryland Blue Crab
http://skipjack.net/le_shore/crab/crab.html

Moonpie.com
http://moonpie.com/

The Moxie Collectors Page
http://www.xensei.com/users/iraseski/

Newspaper Food Columns Online
http://www.recipelink.com/newspapers.html

Not by Bread Alone
http://rmc.library.cornell.edu/food/default.htm

NYFood Museum
http://www.nyfoodmuseum.org

Old Cook Books
http://www.wmol.com/whalive/cook.htm

Open Air Markets on the Web—North America and U.S.A.
http://www.openair.org/opair/namusa.html

Overrated and Underrated: Food Fads
*http://www.americanheritage.com/AMHER/2002/05/over-
under9.shtml*

Pioneer Cookin'
http://www.texfiles.com/pioneercooking/index.htm

Po' Boys Rich in Taste and History
http://www.freep.com/fun/food/qpoor14.htm

Produce Guide
http://www.1webblvd.com/coosemans/guide.htm

Professional Cooking Schools
*http://www.sallys-place.com/food/chefs-corner/
schools_pro_usa.htm*

Professional Food Organizations
http://www.sallys-place.com/food/chefs-corner/organizations.htm

RoadFood
http://www.roadfood.com/

Savory Fare (eighteenth-century American foods)
http://www.monmouth.com/~cssmith/savory.html

A Short History of Spice Trading
http://www.spiceadvice.com/history/history.html

Soulfood Searching
http://www.uwf.edu/tprewitt/sofood/soulfood.htm

Sourdough FAQs
http://www.nyx.net/~dgreenw/sourdoughfaqs.html

Southern Foodways Alliance (SFA)
http://www.southernfoodways.com/

Southwest Foodie
http://SWfoodie.com/

Special Collections in the Library of Congress: Joseph and
   Elizabeth Robins Pennell Collection
http://lcweb.loc.gov/spcoll/183.html

Taste of Wisconsin: Food and Culture in the Heartland
http://www.globaldialog.com/~tallen/

Texas Cooking Online
http://www.texascooking.com/

The Toaster Museum
http://www.toaster.org/

Traditional Food, Health, and Nutrition (Native- American
   food and foodways)
http://www.kstrom.net/isk/food/foodmenu.html

Twentieth Century Timeline Edibles and Quaffables
http://www.geocities.com/Athens/Rhodes/4190/timeline.htm

University of Florida, Institute of Food and Agricultural
   Science
http://gnv.ifas.ufl.edu

USDA Food Composition Data
http://www.nal.usda.gov/fnic/foodcomp/Data/

The Vidalia Onion Story
http://www.vidaliaga.com/history.htm

Gary Allen is the author of *The Resource Guide for Food Writers*
(Routledge, 1999.)